GOD
Listens
to Our
Children

Kids' Prayers for
Every Day of the
Liturgical Year

GOD
Listens to Our Children
Kids' Prayers for Every Day of the Liturgical Year

Kelley Renz

Our Sunday Visitor Publishing Division
Our Sunday Visitor, Inc.
Huntington, Indiana 46750

Nihil Obstat
Rev. Michael Heintz
Censor Librorum

Imprimatur
✠ John M. D'Arcy
Bishop of Fort Wayne-South Bend
December 8, 2005

The *nihil obstat* and *imprimatur* are declarations that a work is free from doctrinal or moral error. It is not implied that those who have granted the *nihil obstat* and *imprimatur* agree with the contents, opinions, or statements expressed.

To Almighty God,
You have gifted, shaped, forged, purged, protected,
blessed, guided, and called me . . .
O the power of Your call . . .
and all in the name of Love,
Who You are.

To Tom,
Benjamin, Kirsten, Alexander,
Becky, Trina,
my most special gifts.

Introduction

I walked into a Catholic school right at the beginning of the day. The principal was reading a prayer over the intercom.

> O Glorious St. Joseph, chosen by God to be the foster-father of Jesus, the chaste spouse of Mary ever Virgin, and head of the Holy Family, be the heavenly patron and defender of the Church founded by Jesus . . .

I moved over to a corner of the hallway and put my head down, drawing up my hands in a gesture of prayer, praying along with the words of the principal. Before the prayer's end, however, I was asking myself what the kids were gaining from this ancient prayer, its words so rich in the history of our Church and in the history of prayer itself. I asked myself whether they knew what the word "chaste" meant. I worried that this honor to St. Joseph may be going right over their heads.

I remember praying as a kid. The only time I really prayed the formal prayers was in formal times: Mass on Sundays and Holy Days, rosary time, meal time, and upon hearing of the death of another person. Other than that, I prayed my own made-up prayers — "Dear Jesus, bring my dad home safely." Or, "Dear God, I love You a lot and I want to give my life to You," or even "Dear God, fix my mom's car for us because she's gonna get in trouble with Dad."

Do kids today know how to do that?

Do kids today know that God is interested in their day-to-day life?

Do kids today take time to sit with God and think about things together, aware of His presence with them, pondering life events together?

Do kids today know that they can do this with God?

Then I went to the school Mass that same morning, all these thoughts still tumbling over one another in my head, and I heard the first Scripture reading: "For neither is there any god besides you who have the care of all, that you need show you have not unjustly condemned" (Wisdom 12:13). Oh, no, I thought, sometimes the words of Scripture are going to soar above their heads as well! This is really no big deal, though, because the words of Scripture fly well above my head, too. But, if this happens over and over, a kid may just turn it off altogether.

So, then and there, I committed myself to a book that would do two things:

1. Take the Scripture readings for daily Mass (as well as Sunday Mass) and write prayers for kids that would teach them a bit about those Scripture readings. Just what does "an eye for an eye" really

mean? Why is Jesus so mad at some of the Pharisees? What does Isaiah mean that I am not firm if my faith isn't firm?

2. Use life events, stages, worries, joys, and concerns of kids themselves and weave these into prayers, using the Scripture readings as a backdrop.

After a good year and a half, many nights up late, many mornings up early, many joyful words exchanged with God, and many frustrated words exchanged with God, here it is.

May principals use these to read over the intercom.

May parents give this book to their children to use day by day, mark up, and make their own.

May families read them together and discuss what issues come up following and during their prayer.

May teachers choose a topic applicable to their classes for that day, thumb to that prayer, and share it briefly with their kids or use it to spark a great discussion about God and with God, the Center of our lives.

Last of all, may all our children pick up over time the beauty, the riches, the history, and the impact of our formal Catholic prayers, finding in them, too, comfort, challenge, and intimacy with Our Lord.

Note:

The prayers are arranged according to the liturgical calendar. Each day also has a topic based on the readings and/or responsorial for that day. You can either follow the calendar day-by-day or use the index of topics to find a specific intention for which you wish to pray. For example, if bad things, bugs, or choices are on your mind, you can look up prayers about just those things in the index.

Prayers for the Immaculate Conception, the Assumption, and All Saints Day are placed at the end of the book.

Advent

First Sunday in Advent
God's Vision

Cycle A: Isaiah 2:1-5; Romans 13:11-14; Matthew 24:37-44
R: Let us go rejoicing to the house of the Lord.

Dear Lord, help us to realize that to walk in the "light of the Lord" means that we can see things as You see them. Share Your vision with us during Advent. Help us not only to see the world as You do, but to see the world as it *can* be. May our words and our actions please You. May we bring peace to our own small part of the world.

Cycle B: Isaiah 63:16b-17, 19b; 64:2-7; 1 Corinthians 1:3-9; Mark 13:33-37
R: Lord, make us turn to you; let us see your face and we shall be saved.

Dear Lord, Isaiah asked that the heavens be torn open so that You would come down. You did tear open the heavens and come down — Jesus did come, and He is still with us. Help us to recognize You, Lord. Help us to see You working in the world. You told us to be watchful. Train our eyes to look hard for You.

Cycle C: Jeremiah 33:14-16; 1 Thessalonians 3:12-4:2; Luke 21:25-28, 34-36
R: To you, O Lord, I lift my soul.

Lord Jesus, Jeremiah reminded the people that You would fulfill Your promise. You came into the world to fulfill it. Work in me, Jesus. Fulfill Your promise in me, too. Make me like You — strong, caring, determined, and wise. Let me always know just how much You love me. I will show You, Lord, how much I love You, too.

➤ *Catechism of the Catholic Church* 719

First Monday in Advent
Gratitude

Cycles B and C: Isaiah 2:1-5; Matthew 8:5-11

Cycle A: Isaiah 4:2-6: Matthew 8:5-11
R: Let us go rejoicing to the house of the Lord.

Dear Lord, today's responsorial psalm tells us to come rejoicing to Your house. Do I rejoice when I come to Mass? What would it be like without You? What if I had no one to turn to when I was afraid or upset? What if all these wars and fights had no hope of ending? Thank You, Lord, for loving us. Thank You for caring about us and showing us how to live. Help me to rejoice in You.

➤ *Catechism of the Catholic Church* 2781

First Tuesday in Advent
Growth

Isaiah 11:1-10; Luke 10:21-24
R: Justice shall flourish in his time, and fullness of peace for ever.

Dear Lord, Isaiah talks about a shoot sprouting from a stump. That means there is new growth, something is now growing in a place where it didn't seem possible, like those weeds that grow in the middle of a concrete sidewalk. You can make things grow anywhere, Lord. Make Your life grow in me; make Your life grow in the kids that are mean; make Your life grow everywhere!

➤ *Catechism of the Catholic Church* 1049

First Wednesday in Advent
Discipleship

Isaiah 25:6-10a; Matthew 15:29-37
R: I shall live in the house of the Lord all the days of my life.

Dear God, we are called to live in Your house all the days of our lives. We can't all move into church, so what exactly does that mean? Living in Your house means to walk in Your ways, do what You do, be who You are calling us to be. Today, Lord, help me to live in Your house.

➤ *Catechism of the Catholic Church* 1533

First Thursday in Advent
Faithfulness

Isaiah 26:1-6; Matthew 7:21, 24-27
R: Blessed is he who comes in the name of the Lord.

Dear Lord, we are made by You. When we act like You, we have peace; we find strength and grace and You are near. But when we choose to act badly, we lose our peace and we walk far from You. Help me to make decisions today that keep me near You. I want to be near You.

➤ *Catechism of the Catholic Church* 1064

First Friday in Advent
Gloom

Isaiah 29:17-24; Matthew 9:27-31
R: The Lord is my light and my salvation.

Dear Lord, it's hard to see through gloom and darkness. Isaiah talks a lot about darkness, the darkness of sin. We know this darkness too. When we are mean, when we have an "attitude," when we are selfish, everything is dark. We can't see You, then, Lord. And we close our hearts and refuse to change. Help us to open up to You, Jesus. You are worth opening up to. Help us to whisper an "I'm sorry" and keep on trying, for love of You, Lord.

➤ *Catechism of the Catholic Church* 1431-1432

First Saturday in Advent
Listening

Isaiah 30:19-21, 23-26; Matthew 9:35 - 10:1, 5a, 6-8
R: Blessed are all who wait for the Lord.

Dear Lord, the prophet Isaiah said that we will hear a voice that tells us, "This is the way; walk in it." We know that this voice is our conscience, the part of our mind where You teach us and speak to us. Help us learn to listen, Lord. Help us to hear Your words.

➤ *Catechism of the Catholic Church* 1777

Second Sunday in Advent
Prepare!

Cycle A: Isaiah 11:1-10; Romans 15:4-9; Matthew 3:1-12
R: Justice shall flourish in his time, and fullness of peace forever.

My Lord, John the Baptist came shouting, "Prepare the way of the Lord." He was telling people that what they were doing for God wasn't enough; something new was expected; something new was coming. The people probably started to watch, to expect. Help me to watch for You, Lord. Help me to look for You all the time.

Cycle B: Isaiah 40:1-5, 9-11; 2 Peter 3:8-14; Mark 1:1-8
R: Lord, let us see your kindness and grant us your salvation.

Dear Jesus, the prophet Isaiah talked about comfort, giving comfort to the people of God. They needed comfort. They had been overtaken by a foreign army. Many of them were made slaves. There are many in our world, Lord, who need comfort. I offer all my work today for them, Lord. I won't complain. I'll even do something really nice for someone, just for those people who are hurting. Be with them, Lord.

Cycle C: Baruch 5:1-9; Philippians 1:4-6, 8-11; Luke 3:1-6
R: The Lord has done great things for us; we are filled with joy.

Dear Lord, the prophet Baruch told people to put on the splendor of glory from God. Only people who expect a lot from God could do this. Do I expect a lot from You, Lord? Do I expect You to bring peace to the world? Do I expect You to use me to bring good things to the world? If I do, I should be walking in the splendor of Your glory, too.

➤ *Catechism of the Catholic Church* 2090

Second Monday in Advent
The Way

Isaiah 35:1-10; Luke 5:17-26
R: Our God will come to save us!

Dear God, there is a way to get to You, a holy way. When the disciples couldn't get the paralyzed man through the doorway, they opened up a hole in the roof. They found a way. I'll find a way to You, Lord. I promise to find You. I promise to let You find me.

➤ *Catechism of the Catholic Church* 1696; Matthew 7:13

Second Tuesday in Advent
Power

Isaiah 40:1-11; Matthew 18:12-14
R: The Lord our God comes with power.

Dear Lord, the responsorial psalm in today's Mass is "The Lord our God comes with power." My idea of power is not like Your idea, Lord. Your idea of power comes from love; my idea of power comes from force. Help me to understand power through love, Lord. I am most powerful when I am powered by love.

➤ *Catechism of the Catholic Church* 272

Second Wednesday in Advent
Alone

Isaiah 40:25-31; Matthew 11:28-30
R: O bless the Lord, my soul!

Dear Lord, sometimes no one is there for me. My parents can be busy; my friends can be ignoring me. But You, Lord, You never get tired of me. You are with me all the time, accepting me even when I am frustrated and angry. I thank You, Lord, for always being there for me.

➤ *Catechism of the Catholic Church* 214

Second Thursday in Advent
Kindness

Isaiah 41:13-20; Matthew 11:11-15
R: The Lord is gracious and merciful; slow to anger, and of great kindness.

Dear Lord, the Bible tells me that You are slow to anger and of great kindness. You don't have to be kind, Lord. As often as we mess up things here on this earth, I would think You'd lose Your temper with us. But You don't. You are patient with us. You are kind. May I be kind, too, Lord, and slow to anger. Make me like You.

➤ *Catechism of the Catholic Church* 1

Second Friday in Advent
Courage

Isaiah 48:17-19, Matthew 11:16-19
R: Those who follow you, Lord, will have the light of life.

Dear Lord, You teach us what is good. I can listen to You every now and then, or I can turn toward You in prayer and tell You I'm ready, I'm willing, I'm wanting to come really close to You — all the time. Show me the path, Lord. Give me courage. Challenge me. Draw me close to You!

➤ *Catechism of the Catholic Church* 945

Second Saturday in Advent
Seeing God

Sirach 48:1-4, 9-11; Matthew 17:9a, 10-13
R: Lord, make us turn to you; let us see your face and we shall be saved.

Dear Lord, the people of long ago believed that if they saw the face of God, it would be so awesome that their bodies couldn't stand it and they would die. So, they were afraid to see Your face. When You came, Jesus, You showed us the very face of God. Not only do we not die, but we see the way to eternal life. Help me to see Your face, Your way.

➤ *Catechism of the Catholic Church* 1720

Third Sunday in Advent
Speaking to God

Cycle A: Isaiah 35:1-6,10; James 5:7-10; Matthew 17:2-11
R: Lord, come and save us.

St. James tells us to make our hearts firm. Dear Lord, to make my heart firm means to never take my eyes off of You; it means to always do what You would do and not be ashamed to let others know that You are the center of my life. Make my heart firm, Lord, firm in You.

Cycle B: Isaiah 61:1-2, 10-11; 1 Thessalonians 5:16-24; John 1:6-8, 19-28
R: My soul rejoices in my God.

Dear Jesus, St. John the Baptist tells us to "make straight the way of the Lord." A straight way is an easy way. We should make it easy for You to come to us. Jesus, I know I make it hard for You to speak to me sometimes when I don't take time to pray, when I get angry and refuse to listen, when I don't try to pay attention during Mass. Help me this Advent, Lord, to make Your way straight! Help me to make it easy for You to talk to me!

Cycle C: Zephaniah 3:14-18; Philippians 4:4-7; Luke 3:10-18
R: Cry out with joy and gladness: for among you is the great and holy One of Israel.

Dear God, St. Paul tells us that our kindness should be known to all. People should know we are Christians by how kind we are. It takes courage to be kind all the time, Lord. I need Your help to do this. Kindness means sharing my time and my things. Kindness means not calling names and not talking behind others' backs. Kindness means pointing out what is good in others. Lord, help me to be kind.

➤ *Catechism of the Catholic Church* 1816

For December 17-24, see pages 19-21.

Third Monday in Advent
Self-Offering

Numbers 24:2-7, 15-17a; Matthew 21:23-27
R: Teach me your ways, O Lord.

Dear Lord, when people who did not like You demanded things from You, You did not give them what they wanted. Some of the Pharisees questioned You. Because they had no faith in You, You knew that Your answers would do no good. May I always come to You, Lord, with faith and with love for You so that I will be answered. Those Pharisees were not willing to give themselves to You. I am willing, Lord. I give myself to You.

➤ *Catechism of the Catholic Church* 548

Third Tuesday in Advent
Simplicity

Zephaniah 3:1-2, 9-13; Matthew 21:28-32
R: The Lord hears the cry of the poor.

Dear Lord, the responsorial psalm for today's Mass is, "The Lord hears the cry of the poor." We know we must help the poor. We can pray for them. We can give to them. We should always be mindful of them. Help us know, Lord, that sometimes we are poor, too. When we feel that no one loves us, when we are sick, when we have been hurt by another, when we are guilty of sin, we are the poor. If we cry to You, You will hear us, too. It is guaranteed.

➤ *Catechism of the Catholic Church* 544

Third Wednesday in Advent
Need for God

Isaiah 45:6c-8, 18, 21c-25; Luke 7:18b-23
R: Let the clouds rain down the Just One, and the earth bring forth a Savior.

Dear Lord, during Advent we remember that the world really needed You before You came as a man. Bigger nations were bullying smaller nations. People were sinning a lot, and they didn't know how to turn to You. Look at us now, Lord. Still, so many others are bullying weaker people. Nations are fighting one another. People are sinning a lot. We still need You, Lord. May more and more people live the way You showed us, Jesus. Show me how to help You come to those who don't know You.

➤ *Catechism of the Catholic Church* 358

Third Thursday in Advent
Expectations

Isaiah 54:1-10; Luke 7:24-30
R: I will praise you, Lord, for you have rescued me.

Dear Jesus, lots of people went out to see John the Baptist preach and baptize. One day You asked the people, "What did you go out to see?" You wanted to know what they expected to see. When I come to Mass, You may ask me what I am coming to see. Are my expectations high? Do I plan on being bored? Am I expecting to see You? Remind me, Lord, that my expectations can never be too high, for You are God!

➤ *Catechism of the Catholic Church 2090*

Third Friday in Advent
Obedience

Isaiah 56:1-3a, 6-8; John 5:33-36
R: O God, let all the nations praise you!

Dear God, the prophet Isaiah kept telling the people of Israel and us that we should obey; we should do what is right. This is so important because when we're doing wrong things, we can't see You or hear You as well. May I do good things so I can see You better and better.

➤ *Catechism of the Catholic Church 2098*

Third Saturday in Advent

For December 17-24, see pages 19-21.

Fourth Sunday in Advent
God's Ways

Cycle A: Isaiah 7:10-14; Romans 1:1-7; Matthew 1:18-24
R: Let the Lord enter; he is the king of glory.

Dear Lord, we are getting close to the celebration of Your birth. Isaiah writes that You shall be called "Immanuel." That name means "God with us." When You became human, You were with us. And You still are with us, Jesus. Everything we experience, You experienced too: You were cold; You were hungry; You were lonely; You were afraid; You worried about friends; You were anxious about Your studies. You were a lot like me, Jesus. Make me a lot like You.

Cycle B: 2 Samuel 7:1-5, 8b-12, 14a-16; Romans 16:25-27; Luke 1:26-38
R: Forever I will sing the goodness of the Lord.

Dear Jesus, today's responsorial psalm for Mass is "Forever I will sing the goodness of the Lord." That's a challenge, Jesus. I don't feel like singing about Your goodness when things aren't going my way. But, that's the challenge of faith, Lord. Either I believe in You and Your way of life, or I don't. When times are bad, Lord, give me the strength to stand up for You, to answer Your call, to say I love You.

Cycle C: Micah 5:1-4a; Hebrews 10:5-10; Luke 1:39-45
R: Lord, make us turn to you; let us see your face and we shall be saved.

Dear Jesus, Micah was a great prophet. He reminds us that You don't do things the way the world does. The world likes the big, the bold, the rich, the powerful. You, Lord, like the poor, the small, the weak. Jesus, You were from a town that people looked down on, so they didn't expect You to be anything great. Help me to see things the way You do, Lord, and not the way the world does. Help me not to like people just because they are big or rich or powerful. Help me to see deeper than that.

➤ *Catechism of the Catholic Church* 272

December 17
Peace

Genesis 49:2, 8-10; Matthew 1:1-17
R: Justice shall flourish in his time, and fullness of peace forever.

Dear God, the responsorial psalm at today's Mass is one we hear a lot: "Justice shall flourish in his time, and fullness of peace forever." We don't have peace, Lord. There are wars in many places. Lots of people argue, too. Only in heaven will there be perfect peace, but we are to work for peace here on earth so that, little by little, we can turn earth into heaven. Help me to work for peace, Lord. Show me how.

➤ *Catechism of the Catholic Church* 2330; Matthew 5:9

December 18
Trust

Jeremiah 23:5-8; Matthew 1:18-25
R: Justice shall flourish in his time, and fullness of peace for ever.

Dear Lord, today's gospel reading tells about Joseph's role in the birth of Jesus. He obeyed the message You gave to him in a dream, and his entire life was changed from that moment on. May I trust You, Lord, as Joseph did. May I obey You, Lord, as Joseph did. May I nurture the life of Jesus in myself and others, as Joseph did.

➤ *Catechism of the Catholic Church* 2828

December 19
Trust

Judges 13:2-7, 24-25a; Luke 1:5-25
R: My mouth shall be filled with your praise, and I will sing your glory!

Dear Jesus, Zechariah questioned the angel who told him that he would have a son who would be John the Baptist. Because of his question, Zechariah couldn't talk until John was born. Mary questioned the angel who told her about Jesus' birth, but she didn't lose her ability to speak. Zechariah's question was full of doubt; he laughed at the angel's message, thinking it too good to be true. Mary did not doubt; she was simply asking what she should do to make the angel's message come true. Help me to be like Mary, Lord, and trust in Your Word.

➤ *Catechism of the Catholic Church* 215

December 20
Glory

Isaiah 7:10-14; Luke 1:26-38
R: Let the Lord enter; he is the king of glory.

Dear Lord, today's responsorial psalm at Mass is a command: "Let the Lord enter; he is the king of glory." Where will I allow You to enter, Lord? I cannot make the world allow You to enter. I cannot make another person allow You to enter. But, I can allow You to enter me. Come into me, Lord. Enter into my heart. Let me experience Your glory. May others follow my example; then, one by one, Your glory can fill the world!

➤ *Catechism of the Catholic Church* 663

December 21
Self-Offering

Songs 2:8-14 or Zephaniah 3:14-18a; Luke 1:39-45
R: Exult, you just, in the Lord! Sing to him a new song.

Dear Lord, there are lots of important messages in the Psalms. "Exult, you just, in the Lord! Sing to him a new song." What new song am I to sing to You, Lord? If the way I live is like a song to You, how can I make it new for You? Can I be nice to someone new today? Can I do something without being asked? Can I spend more time in prayer? One or all of these will be my "new song" to You!

➤ *Catechism of the Catholic Church* 2711

December 22
Determination

1 Samuel 1:24-28; Luke 1:46-56
R: My heart exults in the Lord my Savior.

Dear Lord, the psalms tell us to "exult in the Lord." To exult means to rejoice greatly. How do I feel when I am rejoicing? I feel happy, joyful, strong. I am not afraid or worried or bored. Help me to exult in You, Lord. If I exult in You, I can take on anything!

➤ *Catechism of the Catholic Church* 736; Galatians 5:25

December 23
Jesus Is Coming

Malachi 3:1-4, 23-24; Luke 1:57-66
R: Lift up your heads and see; your redemption is near at hand.

Dear Lord, your prophet Malachi asked who could endure the day of Your coming. When You came as a baby, only those with faith could see Your greatness, only those with faith fell to their knees at the ways of God. Give me faith-filled eyes, Jesus, so I can see how You work in our world. Give me faith-filled eyes, Lord, so I can see You when You come again!

➤ *Catechism of the Catholic Church* 671

December 24
God's Kingdom

2 Samuel 7:1-5, 8b-12, 14a, 16; Luke 1:67-79
R: Forever I will sing the goodness of the Lord.

Dear Jesus, the prophet Samuel wrote about an heir of David who would make the kingdom firm. The kingdom of heaven is firm, Jesus. What about Your kingdom here on earth? How can I help to make it firm? Through my joy, my love, and my dedication to you, Jesus, I can help make Your kingdom on earth firm.

➤ *Catechism of the Catholic Church* 715

Christmas Season

December 25: Nativity of the Lord (Christmas)
Jesus Christ

Vigil: Isaiah 62:1-5; Acts 13:17, 22-25; Matthew 1:1-25 or 18-25
R: Forever I will sing the goodness of the Lord.

Dear Jesus, the older I get, the more I see the need for You in our world. I see that the joy I have in this day, the thought of You as a baby, the gift-giving, and family togetherness, is becoming, too, a deep joy in the knowledge that You are in control of this world, and that one day all these wars, all this hatred, will be transformed. You are our King.

Midnight: Isaiah 9:1-6; Titus 2:11-14; Luke 2:1-14
R: Today is born our savior, Christ the Lord.

Dear Jesus, Isaiah writes about the people who walked in darkness. So many people live in darkness, Lord. Poverty is darkness. Violence is darkness. The lack of freedom is darkness. Power can be darkness. And riches can bring about a darkness. Be our Light, Lord. Shine on all darkness. Thank You for coming. Thank You for being our Light.

Dawn: Isaiah 62:11-12; Titus 3:4-7; Luke 2:15-20
R: A light will shine on us this day; the Lord is born for us.

Happy birthday, Jesus. May all I do this day make it happy for You. I pray for all who cannot enjoy this day: I pray for those who do not know You, who do not love You. I pray for those who are hurting in any way. May they, too, very soon be able to celebrate this day of Your birth.

Daytime: Isaiah 52:7-10; Hebrews 1:1-6; John 1:1-18 or 1:1-5, 9-14
R: All the ends of the earth have seen the saving power of God.

Dear Jesus, even at the beginning in John's gospel we know that things are not going to go well between You and the world as you enter it as a man, for John writes: "But the world did not know him." Your will was done, however, and You saved me and everyone else. Let me be about making You known by the way I live, the way I speak, the things I do, and the path in life You lead me to choose. Thank You, Lord Jesus, for coming to earth as a man. I'm glad you did.

➤ *Catechism of the Catholic Church* 563

December 26
Challenge

Acts 6:8-10, 7:54-59; Matthew 10:17-22
R: In your hands, O Lord, I commend my spirit.

Dear Lord, just one day after Christmas, we celebrate St. Stephen as the first martyr following Your resurrection. St. Stephen was so filled with Your life and Your message that he was willing to die for it. Life as a Christian, Jesus, is a challenge. Our world still in so many ways doesn't want to accept You. Let me always rise to the challenge of being a Christian, Lord, with the help of Your grace.

➤ *Catechism of the Catholic Church* 2015

December 27
Love

1 John 1:1-5; John 20:1a, 2-8
R: Rejoice in the Lord, you just!

Dear Lord, You gifted St. John with a very dear love for You. John was a poet who thought a great deal about Your words and actions and what they meant. John's gospel is not easy to understand because John wants us to think hard about what Your message to us is. Touch my heart, Jesus, as You touched the heart of St. John. Gift me with a great love for You. Help me to think about Your words and actions and not miss their meaning!

➤ *Catechism of the Catholic Church* 2086

December 28
Evil

1 John 1:5-2:2; Matthew 2:13-18
R: Our soul has been rescued like a bird from the fowler's snare.

Dear Lord, I don't like this feast day of the Holy Innocents. King Herod wanted to kill You, so he ordered the deaths of all boys aged two and younger. How cruel! But, it is good that we remember this day because it reminds us that You know about the evils in our world. You know, You care, and You give us the grace to rise above the evils and change evil into good. Show me how to use Your grace, Lord.

➤ *Catechism of the Catholic Church* 421

December 29
Honesty

1 John 2:3-11; Luke 2:22-35
R: Let the heavens be glad and the earth rejoice!

Dear Jesus, St. John calls those people who say they love You but do not keep Your commandments liars. Help me to love You, Jesus, by showing You my love as I am kind to others, eager to help with chores, willing to share, and never forgetting to pray.

➤ *Catechism of the Catholic Church* 2470

December 30
Prayer

1 John 2:12-17; Luke 2:36-40
R: Let the heavens be glad and the earth rejoice!

Dear Jesus, when Mary and Joseph took you to the Temple to present You to the Father, the prophetess Anna was there. She was so close to the Father in prayer that she knew You were the Messiah, the answer to Israel's prayers. She gave thanks and praise. Jesus, draw me this close to You. Like Anna, may I see Your presence in my world.

➤ *Catechism of the Catholic Church* 2668

December 31
Jesus Christ

1 John 2:18-21; John 1:1-18
R: Let the heavens be glad and the earth rejoice!

Dear Lord, we see You as a baby in Bethlehem. Just in case we think of You too much as human, the gospel of John reminds us that You are the Word that has existed always. Yes, you came to us as a baby, but You are also God. It is important for us to know that You are both human and divine.

➤ *Catechism of the Catholic Church* 460

The Holy Family of Jesus, Mary, and Joseph
Family

Cycle A: Sirach 3:2-7, 12-14; Colossians 3:12-21 or 12-17; Matthew 2:13-15, 19-23
R: Blessed are those who fear the Lord and walk in his ways.

Dear Jesus, St. Paul's letter to the Colossians tells us how we must behave toward one another: We must have heartfelt compassion, kindness, humility, gentleness, and patience. Mary and Joseph practiced these virtues with one another. May we practice these virtues in our families, too, Lord. Please give our families grace.

Cycle B: Genesis 15:1-6; 21:1-3; Hebrews 11:8, 11-12, 17-19; Luke 2:22, 39-40
R: The Lord remembers his covenant forever.

Dear Lord, Abraham put his faith in You; Joseph and Mary put their faith in You. Help me, especially when I am afraid or angry, to put my faith in You. You deserve my trust and my belief. You call me to be your son/daughter. Help me to be as worthy as I can be of that calling.

Cycle C: 1 Samuel 1:20-22, 24-28; 1 John 3:1-2, 21-24; Luke 2:41-52
R: Blessed are they who dwell in your house, O Lord.

Dear Jesus, I bet You got into trouble for worrying Mary and Joseph when You stayed behind in Jerusalem. They were so glad to find You, and You told them they should have known You would be in the Temple. You were beginning to understand just who You were. Mary and Joseph were beginning to understand as well. May all families, Lord Jesus, support one another as they grow together.

➤ *Catechism of the Catholic Church* 2205

SECOND WEEK IN CHRISTMAS

January 1: Mary, Mother of God
Mary

Numbers 6:22-27; Galatians 4:4-7; Luke 2:16-21
R: May God bless us in his mercy.

Dear Lord, the book of Numbers tells us that You let Your face shine upon some people. What does this mean? You let Your face shine upon Mary. You blessed her more than You blessed any other human. Mary got to be the Mother of Jesus. May I look to Mary to know how to please You, Lord, that Your face may shine upon me, too.

➤ *Catechism of the Catholic Church* 492

Second Sunday after Christmas
Light

Sirach 24:1-2, 8-12; Ephesians 1:3-6, 15-18; John 1:1-18 or 1:1-5, 9-14
R: The Word of God became man and lived among us.

Dear Lord, you are called Light often in the Bible. Just as light helps us to see in darkness, You help us to see what is right and what is wrong. You help us to understand what it means to be a Christian. Thank You for coming, Jesus. Thank You for being our light, back in the times of the Bible and now.

➤ *Catechism of the Catholic Church* 529

January 2 (if before Epiphany)
Awe

1 John 2:22-28; John 1:19-28
R: All the ends of the earth have seen the saving power of God.

Dear Lord, John the Baptist knew who You were; he said he wasn't worthy to untie Your sandal strap. May I not take You for granted, Jesus. I think of You every day; I hear about You every day. I know You are God. Renew within me a sense of awe, a deep respect for Your presence.

➤ *Catechism of the Catholic Church* 1845

January 3 (if before Epiphany)
Purity

1 John 2:29 - 3:6; John 1:29-34
R: All the ends of the earth have seen the saving power of God.

Dear Jesus, St. John tells Christians to keep themselves pure. I can keep myself pure by avoiding sin, honoring my body, and reminding myself always that You should be the center of my attention. May Your grace, Lord Jesus, keep me pure.

➤ *Catechism of the Catholic Church* 2519

January 4 (if before Epiphany)
Discipleship

1 John 3:7-10; John 1:35-42
R: All the ends of the earth have seen the saving power of God.

Dear Jesus, when two people who wanted to be disciples came to You, You asked them what they were looking for. If they were just curious about the miracles, wanted to be popular with the crowds, or just thought it would be fun for a few weeks, You couldn't have them as disciples. Your disciples need to be with You for love, for the adventure of being near God Himself, and for life. Make me a disciple, Lord.

➤ *Catechism of the Catholic Church* 788

January 5 (if before Epiphany)
Joy

1 John 3:11-21; John 1:43-51
R: Let all the earth cry out to God with joy.

Dear Jesus, in today's Mass the responsorial psalm is "Let all the earth cry out to God with joy." Just how happy and overjoyed would I have to be to "cry out with joy"? Yet this is what it is like when I am filled with You. Let me experience this, Lord, and let me work hard to make sure everybody can experience it, too.

➤ *Catechism of the Catholic Church* 1829

January 6 (if before Epiphany)
Beginnings

1 John 5:5-13; Mark 1:7-11 or Luke 3:23-38 or 3:23, 31-34, 36, 38
R: Praise the Lord, Jerusalem.

Lord Jesus, this is the start of a new year. We are reading from the beginning in the gospels at Mass. How is my faith, Lord? How can it be new? What do You have in store for me? How will You touch me this year? Lead me, Lord Jesus. Help me to know what I should want from You and help me to know what You want from me.

➤ *Catechism of the Catholic Church* 2611

January 7 (if before Epiphany)
Listening

1 John 5:14-21; John 2:1-11
R: The Lord takes delight in his people.

Dear Jesus, Mary told the servants standing in front of You, "Do whatever He tells you." She had complete trust in You. Mary tells me, too, Lord Jesus, to do whatever You tell me. Help me to know what You are telling me, Jesus. Show me how to hear You.

➤ *Catechism of the Catholic Church* 2697

EPIPHANY

Epiphany
Wonder

Isaiah 60:1-6; Ephesians 3:2-3a, 5-6; Mark 2:1-12
R: Lord, every nation on earth will adore you.

Lord Jesus, the three wise men recognized You as a king. Little by little You revealed that You were not only a king, but You are God Himself. You who made all of creation became a little baby and lived like I do, because You love me so much. Gift me, Lord, with wonder and awe of Your love for me.

➤ *Catechism of the Catholic Church* 480

Monday after Epiphany (or January 7)
Freedom

1 John 3:22-4:6; Matthew 4:4:12-17, 23-25
R: I will give you all the nations for an inheritance.

Dear Jesus, St. John talks about the people who belong to the world. I know he means the people who give themselves to bad things in the world and ignore You. Help me to always keep my heart with You, even while I'm enjoying my music, my television, and my freedom.

➤ *Catechism of the Catholic Church* 1731

Tuesday after Epiphany (or January 8)
Power

1 John 4:7-10; Mark 6:34-44
R: Lord, every nation on earth will adore you.

Lord, it's easy to think of love and peace when we see You as a baby. But often our world is broken into with news of violence around us and in other countries, so we're not really surprised to hear that soon after Your birth, Herod was out to kill You. You beat Herod, however. You beat every enemy, even death. You did this, Lord Jesus, through the power of love. So, we take up Your power. "Let us love one another."

➤ *Catechism of the Catholic Church* 269

Wednesday after Epiphany (or January 9)
Adoration

1 John 4:11-18; Mark 6:45-52
R: Lord, every nation on earth will adore you.

Dear Jesus, in today's Mass the responsorial psalm is "Lord, every nation on earth will adore you." The word "adore" means to worship as God. I know You are God. You came down to earth as a man, but You never stopped being God. I like knowing that You are God, Jesus.

➤ *Catechism of the Catholic Church* 422

Thursday after Epiphany (or January 10)
Adoration

1 John 4:19-5:4; Luke 4:14-22
R: Lord, every nation on earth will adore you.

Lord Jesus, in today's Mass the responsorial psalm is "Lord, every nation on earth will adore you." The word "adore" means to love deeply. I am to love You with the kind of love that I give to no other person or thing. This type of love is a gift from You. Give me this kind of love, Jesus.

➤ *Catechism of the Catholic Church* 2096

Friday after Epiphany (or January 11)
Peace

1 John 5:5-13; Luke 5:12-16
R: Praise the Lord, Jerusalem.

Dear Jesus, in today's Mass the responsorial psalm is "Praise the Lord, Jerusalem." Why is Jerusalem so important to You? It was the first city set up just for You. Everyone inside that city loved You. But now, Lord, Jerusalem is full of violence and fear as different people fight over it. Show us how to make peace, Lord Jesus, by trusting in You.

➤ *Catechism of the Catholic Church* 2305; Ephesians 2:14; Matthew 5:9

Saturday after Epiphany (or January 12)
Jesus Christ

1 John 5:14-21; John 3:22-30
R: The Lord takes delight in his people.

Dear Lord, when St. John the Baptist saw You, he said, "He must increase and I must decrease." He meant that people had to stop looking to him and start following You. St. John knew that if he focused entirely on You, he would have great joy. If I focus entirely on You, I will have great joy, too. Help me to know how to do this, Jesus, to pray to You, to trust You, to make You the center of my life.

➤ *Catechism of the Catholic Church* 2133

Baptism of the Lord
Trust

Cycle A: Isaiah 42:1-4, 6-7; Acts 10:34-38; Matthew 3:13-17
R: The Lord will bless his people with peace.

My Lord Jesus, You allowed St. John the Baptist to baptize You even though You are God and didn't need to be baptized. This confused John, but he trusted You and did what You told him to do. You ask me to do things I don't understand, Jesus. Sometimes I don't understand why You ask me to come to church. Sometimes I don't understand why You tell me to be kind to those who are not kind to me. Help me to trust You, Jesus, and do what You ask of me. Help me to show You that I love You.

Cycle B: Isaiah 55:1-11; 1 John 5:1-9; Mark 1:7-11
R: You will draw water joyfully from the springs of salvation.

Dear Lord Jesus, after You were baptized, the gospel says that the heavens were torn open and the Spirit came down on You like a dove. I would have liked to have seen that, Lord. Now that the heavens are torn open, the door to heaven is always open. You will never shut the door. I can always come in. You can always hear my prayers. I can always talk to You and listen to You.

Cycle C: Isaiah 40:1-5, 9-11; Titus 2:11-14, 3:4-7; Luke 3:15-16, 21-22
R: O bless the Lord, my soul!

My God, when John the Baptist talked about Jesus, he said that Jesus would baptize with the Holy Spirit and with fire. The closer I come to Jesus, the more the Spirit comes into my heart. The Spirit makes my heart "burn" with love for Jesus. I want to do things that please Jesus. I want to become the person Jesus calls me to be. This happens to me in a special way with the Sacrament of Confirmation. Thank you, God, for this baptism of fire.

➤ *Catechism of the Catholic Church* 2614

Ordinary Time

First Monday in Ordinary Time
Church

Year 1: Hebrews 1:1-6; Mark 1:14-20
R: Let all the angels worship him.

Dear Jesus, after You died and rose again, the early Church had to figure out just who You were and what Your coming to us meant. You taught these early Church people that You are the Son of God — You weren't just a prophet; You weren't just an angel. What was hard for them to learn is easy for me because it has been taught for so long. Thank You, Jesus, for the faith of those who came before me. Thank You for the Catholic Church.

Year 2: 1 Samuel 1:1-8; Mark 1:14-20
R: To you, Lord, I will offer a sacrifice of praise.

Dear Jesus, as a Catholic, I hear the word "sacrifice" all the time. A sacrifice is something we offer to You. Today's responsorial psalm in Mass says, "To you, Lord, I will offer a sacrifice of praise." I praise You, Jesus, for the sacrifice You made, the sacrifice of Your very life for us. Help me to offer sacrifices to You — praise, kind deeds for others, not complaining, being joyful — all for love of You.

➤ *Catechism of the Catholic Church* 2045

First Tuesday in Ordinary Time
Expectation

Year 1: Hebrews 2:5-12; Mark 1:21-28
R: You have given your Son rule over the works of your hands.

Dear Jesus, when You spoke, people listened. There are some people who talk and talk, but they don't really mean what they say. Your every word was and is full of truth, full of meaning for each person who chooses to listen. Help me, Lord Jesus, to hear You, to read Your word in the Bible, to learn how to listen. Give me the gift of expecting Your words to touch me deeply.

Year 2: 1 Samuel 1:9-20; Mark 1:21-28
R: My heart exults in the Lord, my Savior.

Dear God, great things happen when we team up with You. Hannah couldn't have children, but through her prayers to You, she was blessed with Samuel. You told us to come after You. Give me the courage to come after You, Jesus, and the desire to know just what great things we can end up doing!

➤ *Catechism of the Catholic Church* 489

First Wednesday in Ordinary Time
Jesus Christ

Year 1: Hebrews 2:14-18; Mark 1:29-39
R: The Lord remembers his covenant forever.

Dear Jesus, we can never say to You, "You don't know what's it's like!" because You do. You became like us. You suffered. You laughed. You were sick. You had toothaches. You lost a parent. You had friend troubles. You had trouble learning what You were being taught. You know what it's like to be 7, or 11, or 14. I can bring my cares to You. You not only care about them and me, but You remember how it was!

Year 2: 1 Samuel 3:1-10, 19-20; Mark 1:29-39
R: Here I am, Lord; I come to do your will.

Lord Jesus Christ, Samuel said to You, "Speak, Lord, your servant is listening." But I don't hear Your voice like I hear others talk to me. My heart is still learning how to listen to You. But, I don't have to wait until my heart is ready to hear; You have said plenty that You want me to know about in the Bible. Those words are for me. Give me the desire, Lord, to read the Bible everyday, to discover Your message to me written there.

➤ *Catechism of the Catholic Church* 458

First Thursday in Ordinary Time
Forgiveness

Year 1: Hebrews 3:7-14; Mark 1:40-45
R: If today you hear his voice, harden not your hearts.

Lord Jesus, I can harden my heart. I can shut my heart down so that I can't hear You, my parents, my friends, my teachers, or anyone else. I can do this by being mad. I can do this because I'm hurt. I can do this because I want to do things my own way! Get through to me when I'm like this, Lord. Unclench my fists. Help me to let go, forgive myself and others, and be open. It's not fun to walk around with a hard heart.

Year 2: 1 Samuel 4:1-11; Mark 1:40-45
R: Redeem us, Lord, because of your mercy.

Jesus, you healed a man and told him not to tell anyone. But he did. He told people, and the word spread around. So, everyone in that area knew what You did. They all wanted to see You; and they all wanted something from You. You couldn't just walk around in that place and enjoy Yourself or have a bit of peace. But You still gave, and healed, and blessed, and taught. Help me, Lord, to be giving, too, especially when I am tired and when I'd rather go off by myself.

➤ *Catechism of the Catholic Church* 520

First Friday in Ordinary Time
Temptation

Year 1: Hebrews 4:1-5, 11; Mark 2:1-12
R: Do not forget the works of the Lord.

Dear Lord, the Bible tells me to be on my guard. That means I am always to make certain that I'm ready for temptation. If I'm tempted to cheat, I'm ready to commit myself to You and turn away from another's work. If I'm tempted to lie, I'm ready to commit myself to You and be honest. If I'm tempted to talk badly about someone, I'm ready to commit myself to You and be understanding instead. Temptation will always come. Help me, Jesus, to be ready and be faithful.

Year 2: 1 Samuel 8:4-7, 10-22a; Mark 2:1-12
R: For ever I will sing the goodness of the Lord.

Lord Jesus, You got mad when they started whispering that You couldn't forgive sins. Here You were giving a man peace of mind, freeing him from the burden of his sins, and they were getting mad because You were doing something only God can do. You gave certain men the gift of freeing us from our sins. You forgive us through these priests. Thank you, Lord, for the gift of Reconciliation. Give my heart the desire to receive this gift and this grace.

➤ *Catechism of the Catholic Church* 1421

First Saturday in Ordinary Time
Courage

Year 1: Hebrews 4:12-16; Mark 2:13-17
R: Your words, Lord, are spirit and life.

Lord Jesus, You made friends with people no one else wanted to be around. You saw the good in them, and being around You brought out this goodness. May I seek out those no one else wants to be around. May I be kind. May I never add to their loneliness and pain. May I never make them sad. And may I never stand by while someone else picks on them. May I be the person You call me to be.

Year 2: 1 Samuel 9:1-4, 7-19, 10:1; Mark 2:13-17
R: Lord, in your strength the king is glad.

Lord Jesus, Your way isn't often the popular way. It would have been easy for You to do what the leaders wanted You to do and say only what they wanted You to say. But You didn't. You knew that people were not loving God enough. You knew that the leaders weren't teaching the right things. You knew that people were being cast out and hurt. When You spoke, You pointed out all these things. You showed us how to love. Give me courage, Lord, to follow Your example and love like You did.

➤ *Catechism of the Catholic Church* 1303

Second Sunday in Ordinary Time
Vocation

Cycle A: Isaiah 49:3, 5-6; 1 Corinthians 1:1-3; John 1:29-34
R: Here I am, Lord; I come to do your will.

Dear Lord, the prophet Isaiah had a pretty tough job. You were telling him what to say to Your people. Sometimes the message wasn't good. This had to be hard on Isaiah. But, Isaiah kept doing it. He didn't turn You down. He didn't run away. What was it about being close to You, Lord, that kept Isaiah going? You gave him strength, yes, but what else? Why was being close to You so important to this man? Give me the desire to find out, Lord. Draw me close to You.

Cycle B: 1 Samuel 3:3b-10, 19; 1 Corinthians 6:13c-15a, 17-20; John 1:35-42
R: Here I am, Lord, I come to do your will.

Dear Jesus, You are forever saying, "Come." No matter how close we come to You, You want us to come even closer. Show me the way, Jesus. I want to be very close to You. I want to know You like no one else has ever known You. Show me how. Teach me, Lord. I want to answer Your call.

Cycle C: Isaiah 62:1-5; 1 Corinthians 12:4-11; John 2:1-11
R: Proclaim his marvelous deeds to all the nations.

Dear God, I've had such good news before that I couldn't wait to blurt it out to my friends and family. That's how people get when they are around You, Lord. It's like the feelings of love and joy are just going to burst out of them. Show me what this is like, Lord. Grant me the desire to know the joy that comes from being around You.

➤ *Catechism of the Catholic Church 27*

Second Monday in Ordinary Time
Seeing God

Year 1: Hebrews 5:1-10; Mark 2:18-22
R: You are a priest forever, in the line of Melchisedek.

My Lord Jesus, back when the words of the Bible were being written, its messages were new to the people who read them and heard them. People talk so much about You, Lord, that it sometimes gets old to me and boring. Open my heart and my ears, dear Son of God, so that I may hear these words in a new way for me. Make my heart burn for You and for Your message for me and for my world.

Year 2: 1 Samuel 15:16-23; Mark 2:18-22
R: To the upright I will show the saving power of God.

Dear God, the responsorial psalm in today's Mass is "To the upright I will show the saving power of God." Why only to the upright? Why only to the people who are trying to be good? Help me to know that it is easier for me to see You and understand Your words, God, when I am trying to be good. Doing bad things makes it harder for me to see You. Help me to want to see You, Lord. Help me to be good.

➤ *Catechism of the Catholic Church* 2519

Second Tuesday in Ordinary Time
Faith

Year 1: Hebrews 6:10-20; Mark 2:23-28
R: The Lord will remember his covenant for ever.

Dear Lord, the letter to the Hebrews in the New Testament calls our faith an anchor. An anchor keeps a boat from drifting off. Make my faith like an anchor, Lord. May my faith be strong enough to keep me close to You. The currents of today — people not believing in You, people thinking they can do what they want whenever they want, people wanting to buy everything they see — these currents are powerful and they tend to make me drift away from You. Make my faith an anchor, Lord. Keep me close.

Year 2: 1 Samuel 16:1-13; Mark 2:23-28
R: I have found David, my servant.

Lord Jesus, You made Sundays for us. You made one day a week for me and You. You didn't make one hour for us, or five minutes; You made one day. That's how important You think our relationship is, that You and I should have 24 hours of time just to be together and get to know one another. You are the Almighty God, and You want to spend time with me. Here I am, Lord. I'm here.

➤ *Catechism of the Catholic Church* 1167

Second Wednesday in Ordinary Time
Sundays

Year 1: Hebrews 7:1-3, 15-17; Mark 3:1-6
R: You are a priest for ever; in the line of Melchisedek.

Dear Lord, You got in trouble when You healed a man on the Sabbath because healing was considered work and You weren't supposed to work on the Sabbath. This made You mad because You knew that to heal another was the best thing a person can do on the Sabbath. You told the leaders that they were not understanding the Sabbath rest. Our Sabbath — Sunday — is meant for doing the will of God: feeding the poor, serving others, focusing on God. It is a day when we are to look at You and get others to look at You, too.

Year 2: 1 Samuel 17:32-33, 37, 40-51; Mark 3:1-6
R: Blessed be the Lord, my Rock!

Dear Lord, we have lots of rules. Rules in school, rules at home, rules for driving, rules even for playing. Our Church, too, has rules, and one of them is to make sure that Sunday is holy. This is a very good rule, Lord. Help me to see how important it is to set aside a whole day just for You. May I think about You a lot on Sundays. May this be the day when I always ask You what You want me to do. Am I becoming the person You want me to be? Am I helping to make this world the way You want it?

➤ *Catechism of the Catholic Church* 2173

Second Thursday in Ordinary Time
Trust

Year 1: Hebrews 7:25 - 8:6; Mark 3:7-12
R: Here am I, Lord; I come to do your will.

Dear Lord, no one is beyond saving. Your love has the power to make even terrorists change their minds and work for peace. You never give up on anyone; help me not to give up on anyone either. It is easier to give up on some people — those in prison, those with deadly illnesses, those in faraway countries suffering from poverty and starvation. May I pray for them, Lord, lift all these up to You and know that You will touch them and change them.

Year 2: 1 Samuel 18:6-9; 19:1-7; Mark 3:7-12
R: In God I trust; I shall not fear.

Dear Lord, why do I need to trust You? I can trust You to give me the things I need most: the strength to make it through difficult times; the hope to always know that Your good will win over the bad I see; the wisdom to know the difference between what will bring good into my life and what will bring bad; the courage to make the right decisions. I can trust You, Lord, to help me with all these things. Thank You, and remind me to ask You for these things.

➤ *Catechism of the Catholic Church* 214

Second Friday in Ordinary Time
Church

Year 1: Hebrews 8:6-13; Mark 3:13-19
R: Kindness and truth shall meet.

Dear Lord, there were lots of disciples around You when You named the Twelve. You wanted twelve of them to be closest to You and know exactly what You were teaching. These were the ones who were in charge of making sure Your message lasted even after You ascended to heaven. We call these special twelve "apostles." When one of them died, another was appointed. We have apostles even today; they are called bishops. Thank You, Lord Jesus, for giving us apostles so Your teaching is still clear to us.

Year 2: 1 Samuel 24:3-21; Mark 3:13-19
R: Have mercy on me, God, have mercy.

Lord Jesus, when You named the twelve who would be Your apostles, our Church began. You taught them; they taught those around them; and others teach us today. I, too, am in charge of our Church. I am responsible for making the Church strong and attractive to others. Make me a good example of the Catholic Church.

➤ *Catechism of the Catholic Church* 949

Second Saturday in Ordinary Time
Belief

Year 1: Hebrews 9:2-3; 11:14; Mark 3:20-21
R: God mounts his throne to shouts of joy; a blare of trumpets for the Lord.

Dear Jesus, after You started preaching, You went home to Nazareth. Members of Your family said You were out of Your mind. It was too hard for them to believe that someone they had grown up with would now be healing people and casting out demons. Why couldn't they believe in You, Jesus? Forgive me for the times I don't believe in You. When I am hopeless about my school work, about my family problems, or about my friends, I am not believing in You and Your love for me to make things better. May I believe in You, Lord.

Year 2: 2 Samuel 1:1-4, 11-12, 19, 23-27; Mark 3:20-21
R: Let us see your face, Lord, and we shall be saved.

Dear Jesus, it probably hurt Your feelings when Your family in Nazareth said You were out of Your mind. They came to get You and make You stop preaching. They were embarrassed by You. You and Mary must have been very hurt by their reactions to You. May I never hurt You, Jesus. May I believe in You and always show pride for my faith in You. Following You is hard sometimes, Jesus. Give me courage.

➤ *Catechism of the Catholic Church* 162

Third Sunday in Ordinary Time
Bible

Cycle A: Isaiah 8:23-9:3; 1 Corinthians 1:10-13, 17; Matthew 4:12-23 or 4:12-17
R: The Lord is my light and my salvation.

Dear Lord Jesus, when You came, You said You were the Light. You said Your words would give us new light to see by. Your words are in the Bible. Show me how important the Bible is, Jesus. Give me the desire to have a Bible, to keep one in my room, to open it every day and read just a little. I want to see and understand with this new light, Your light.

Cycle B: Jonah 3:1-5, 10; 1 Corinthians 7:29-31; Mark 1:14-20
R: Teach me your ways, O Lord.

My Jesus, when You came, You said the kingdom of God is here. Never before had God been so open with us. By coming among us, You showed us what God is like in ways we never knew before. And the words You spoke are in the Bible. Give me the desire, Lord Jesus, to read the Bible, especially the gospels of Matthew, Mark, Luke, and John. In the gospels, I can read Your descriptions of God. I can learn about the kingdom.

Cycle C: Nehemiah 8:2-4a, 5-6, 8-10; 1 Corinthians 12:12-30 or 12:12-14, 27; Luke 1:1-4; 4:14-21
R: Your words, Lord, are Spirit and life.

Dear Jesus, Luke's gospel tells how You went to the synagogue to pray. You did this regularly. Even though You were still God when You walked around here on earth, You still worshipped the Father. You did this because You knew that human beings need God as much as they need food or air or water. Luke's gospel tells us this. Give me the desire, Lord, to find out what else the gospel of Luke tells me about You. And may I attend Mass on Sundays, in imitation of You.

➤ *Catechism of the Catholic Church* 81

Third Monday in Ordinary Time
Mercy

Year 1: Hebrews 9:15, 24-28; Mark 3:22-30
R: Sing to the Lord a new song, for he has done marvelous deeds.

Dear Lord, it's fun to be known by someone famous. If I walked into school with the Pope and he had his arm around me, that would be really neat. What the Bible says is that You will appear before God for me. You, the Son of Almighty God, will go before God the Father with me. You will stand there with me and tell the Father all the good things I've done. Help me to do lots of good things, Jesus.

Year 2: 2 Samuel 5:1-7, 10; Mark 3:22-30
R: My faithfulness and my mercy shall be with him.

Lord Jesus, King David, the Bible says, grew in strength because You were with him. I can grow in strength, too, if I stay near You. I can be strong enough to do good things when I'm tempted to do bad things. I can be strong enough to see between right and wrong. I can be strong enough to obey my parents when I'd rather not. Every time I do what You want me to do, dear Lord, I grow stronger. Thank You for Your grace.

➤ Hebrews 9:24; *Catechism of the Catholic Church* 519

Third Tuesday in Ordinary Time
God's Family

Year 1: Hebrews 10:1-10; Mark 3:31-35
R: Here am I, Lord; I come to do your will.

Dear Lord, You said that anyone who does the Father's will is Your mother, brother, sister. I am not only Your friend but part of Your family. Help me, Lord, to act like I am part of Your family, to be joyful, to be patient with others, to be considerate, to be kind. Thank You for this honor, Lord. May You be proud of me as a family member.

Year 2: 2 Samuel 6:12b-15, 17-19; Mark 3:31-35
R: Who is this king of glory? It is the Lord!

Dear Lord, I belong to You. I need to think about that. That is awesome. I think of the miracles You performed, the people You healed, the dead You raised, the people You forgave. I think of the Cross You carried, the death You died, the tomb You walked out of, and I am very proud to belong to You. I praise You, O Son of God!

➤ *Catechism of the Catholic Church* 2233

Candlemas: The Presentation of the Lord (February 2)
Listening

Malachi 3:1-4; Hebrews 2:14-18; Luke 2:22-40 or 2:22-32
R: Who is this king of glory? It is the Lord.

Lord Jesus, when Mary and Joseph presented You in the Temple, several people were there who knew who You were. Simeon and Anna knew that You were the child who would grow into a king and offer salvation to people. Simeon and Anna knew this because they knew how to listen to the Holy Spirit. Help me, dear Lord, to listen to Your Spirit so that I may see You more clearly, love You more dearly, and follow You more nearly.

➤ *Catechism of the Catholic Church 529*

Third Wednesday in Ordinary Time
Growth

Year 1: Hebrews 10:11-18; Mark 4:1-20
R: You are a priest for ever, in the line of Melchisedek.

Dear Lord, you talk about a farmer sowing seed. Some of it falls onto the path where it can't grow at all. Some of it falls into rocky ground and it grows, but it doesn't have good roots so it dies. Some of it falls into good ground where it grows good roots and becomes strong. I need to be like the good ground, Jesus, so that when Your word comes into me, it will grow strong roots. Make me good ground, Lord.

Year 2: 2 Samuel 7:4-17; Mark 4:1-20
R: For ever I will maintain my love for my servant.

Dear Jesus, sometimes I'm like the rocky ground when I hear Your message. When a seed tries to grow in rocky ground, the sun scorches it because it doesn't have good roots. When I hear Your word, sometimes I let anger, worry, or temptation get in the way, and Your word dies inside of me. I'm glad I can change, Lord. I can try again to be good ground for Your word. Help me, Lord, to try again.

➤ *Catechism of the Catholic Church 543*

Third Thursday in Ordinary Time
Faith

Year 1: Hebrews 10:19-25; Mark 4:21-25
R: Lord, this is the people that longs to see your face.

Dear Jesus, it doesn't sound fair when You say to the one who has, more will be given and to the one who has little, what little he has will be taken away. That sounds like the rich will get richer and the poor will have what little money they have taken away. But, You're not talking about money, Lord, are You? You are talking about faith. If I have just a little faith, I will lose it easily, as soon as some big temptation comes along. But, if I have lots of faith, I'll resist temptations, and my faith will grow even more!

Year 2: 2 Samuel 7:18-19, 24-29; Mark 4:21-25
R: The Lord God will give him the throne of David, his father.

Lord Jesus, You said lots of things to make us think hard. Your words were not easy to understand back when You walked around on earth, and they are not so easy to understand now either. You did this on purpose. If You were easy, we might forget about You too easily. You challenge us to think, to wonder, to question, to search. Challenge me, Lord. Help me to think about You a lot and to search for You even more.

➤ *Catechism of the Catholic Church* 162

Third Friday in Ordinary Time
Kingdom of Heaven

Year 1: Hebrews 10:32-39; Mark 4:26-34
R: The salvation of the just comes from the Lord.

Dear Lord, a mustard seed is so tiny, I can barely see it in the palm of my hand. But, if I plant it, that little thing grows into a big bush! I've seen lots of seeds, Lord. It is amazing, really, that they break open and grow to much bigger things. That's how the kingdom You talked about is. Your kingdom started when You came, and each good act I do is like a seed. I may think it's a small thing, but You take it and make it grow big. Help me, Lord, to do lots of good things and plant many seeds for You.

Year 2: 2 Samuel 11:1-4a, 5-10a, 13-17; Mark 4:26-34
R: Be merciful, O Lord, for we have sinned.

Dear Jesus, there's a lot of bad in the world. I see and hear bad news on the television. I know there are wars in the world. I know people are hurting. Help me remember what happened with King David. He sinned by having another man killed. You took that bad thing and made good come out of it. Take all this bad, Lord, and make good come out of it. Show me how to help You do this. May Your kingdom come!

➤ *Catechism of the Catholic Church* 541

Third Saturday in Ordinary Time
Storms

Year 1: Hebrews 11:1-2, 8-19; Mark 4:35-41
R: Blessed be the Lord the God of Israel; he has come to his people.

Dear Jesus, I can imagine what it must have been like on that boat when the storm was raging. The boat was bobbing up and down, water splashing in, wind howling, and it was dark. If I were one of the disciples, I would have been afraid. I would have been mad at You, maybe, because You were sleeping! The disciples woke You up and told You that you were all going to die. But You were calm. You stood and commanded the sea to be quiet. And the storm calmed. What must have the disciples thought of You then?! Help me remember this when I have storms in my life. You give me an example of remaining calm, trusting in You to see me through.

Year 2: 2 Samuel 12:1-7a, 10-17; Mark 4:35-41
R: Create a clean heart in me, O God.

Lord Jesus, I have lots of storms in my life. Real storms that I am sometimes afraid of. And other storms like arguments, breakups, and sicknesses. You showed the disciples what to do in the middle of storms. You remained calm. You stood and commanded the storm to go away. And it did. In my storms of life, I need to remain calm, call on You, and trust You to calm things. Give me a heart that trusts in You, Jesus.

➤ *Catechism of the Catholic Church* 305

Fourth Sunday in Ordinary Time
Searching

Cycle A: Zephaniah 2:3; 3:12-13; 1 Corinthians 1:26-31; Matthew 5:1-12a
R: Blessed are the poor in spirit; the kingdom of heaven is theirs!

Dear Lord, You tell me to seek You. Why do I need to seek You if You are already here? I need to seek You because I don't think of You enough. I forget sometimes to pray. I forget to act like You want me to act. And sometimes I don't understand Your ways. All these are good reasons for me to seek You. When I seek You, I am thinking about You; I am praying to You; I am wondering about You. Doing this brings me closer to You. Bring me close, Lord.

Cycle B: Deuteronomy 18:15-20; 1 Corinthians 7:32-35; Mark 1:21-28
R: If today you hear his voice, harden not your hearts.

Lord Jesus, St. Paul tells the people of Corinth to focus on You and be free of all worries. When I worry about things, I am not focusing on You, am I? I am focusing on my worry. St. Paul knew that worry can take our attention from You. If I trust in You, Jesus, I can let go of my worries, be happy, and be a good example to others. Show me how to focus on You, Lord.

Cycle C: Jeremiah 1:4-5, 17-19; 1 Corinthians 12:31 - 13:13 or 13:4-13; Luke 4:21-30
R: I will sing of your salvation.

Dear Jesus, St. Paul tells us what love is: love is patient, kind. Love doesn't find fault. You showed us what love is, Lord: Love is giving Your life for others. You ask me to love. Help my heart to listen to You, Lord. May I not be like the people of Your hometown who rejected You. They couldn't see who You were; they didn't believe Your words. Open my heart, Lord. Show me how to love.

➤ *Catechism of the Catholic Church* 31

Fourth Monday in Ordinary Time
Weakness

Year 1: Hebrews 11:32-40; Mark 5:1-20
R: Let your hearts take comfort, all who hope in the Lord.

Lord Jesus, sometimes I feel really weak. When I hear about a lot of bad things happening, it feels like I lose my strength. I feel afraid, small, and vulnerable. When a lot of people around me start making fun of someone else and I know I should be strong and tell them to stop, I get afraid and realize how weak I can be. Help me to know, Jesus, that if I admit to You my weakness, You somehow make me strong. Your strength comes into me and can take away my fear and guide me to do what is right. Teach me how to look to You when I am weak.

Year 2: 2 Samuel 15:13-14, 30; 16:5-13; Mark 5:1-20
R: Lord, rise up and save me.

Dear Jesus, the responsorial psalm in today's Mass is "Lord, rise up and save me." I want to shout these words at times. When I lose a friend, when I can't understand my work, when I'm not getting along with my parents, when I'm hurt or mad or lost, I want to say to You, "Lord, rise up and save me." Lots of people in the gospels cried out to You, Jesus. You didn't turn Your back on any of them. The sick man, the blind man, the woman who'd lost a son, the man possessed . . . You heard them all. You will hear me, too. Lord, rise up and save me!

➤ *Catechism of the Catholic Church 272*

Fourth Tuesday in Ordinary Time
Longing for God

Year 1: Hebrews 12:1-4, Mark 5:21-43
R: They will praise you, Lord, who long for you.

Lord Jesus, You are surrounded by people, touching You from all sides. One woman, knowing she will be healed if she can only touch You, touches You as You go by. Immediately You swing around and ask, "Who touched me?" You knew her touch was different. She believed in You; she longed for Your power to heal her. You knew her touch and her faith were unique, unlike so many others who just wanted to be around You because You were popular or because it was what everyone else was doing. This woman loved You, and You knew it. Know me, Lord. Gift me with such a desire for You. Let me know that touching You will not only heal me but will change my entire life.

Year 2: 2 Samuel 18:9-10, 14b, 24-25a, 30 - 19:3; Mark 5:21-43
R: Listen, Lord, and answer me.

My Lord, let my faith in You be different. There were thousands of people who surrounded You every day. You knew a lot of them wouldn't remember You a day after You left their cities. But, there were others who You knew were deeply touched by You, Your words, Your presence. Make me one of these, Lord. May You matter a lot to me. May I expect a lot from You. May You expect a lot from me.

➤ *Catechism of the Catholic Church 2557*

Fourth Wednesday in Ordinary Time
Fearing God

Year 1: Hebrews 12:4-7, 11-15; Mark 6:1-6
R: The Lord's kindness is everlasting to those who fear him.

Dear Lord, the responsorial psalm for today's Mass is "The Lord's kindness is everlasting to those who fear him." Jesus, You don't want me to fear You like I fear the dark or a spooky movie. You want me to fear You like I fear the Grand Canyon, or the ocean, or anything that makes my eyes grow wide and my mouth say, "Wow!" This kind of fear commands my full attention. May I give You my full attention, Lord.

Year 2: 2 Samuel 24:2, 9-17; Mark 6:1-6
R: Lord, forgive the wrong I have done.

Lord Jesus, if I "take offense" at someone, it means that I am angry with him or her. When You went to Your hometown, the Bible says that they "took offense" at You. You were preaching and healing. Those who had open hearts were touched by You. But most of them had closed hearts. This must have hurt Your feelings, Jesus. May I never take offense at You. May I always have an open heart when I hear Your word.

➤ *Catechism of the Catholic Church* 1831

Fourth Thursday in Ordinary Time
Friendship

Year 1: Hebrews 12:18-19, 21-24; Mark 6:7-13
R: O God, we ponder your mercy within your temple.

Dear Lord, when You sent Your disciples out to other towns to practice preaching about You, You sent them in pairs. You know that we need one another. We need friends who support us and who believe what we believe. Gift me with good friends, Lord, friends who help me do what is right. May my friendship be a gift to those I spend time with, too. Give me courage, Lord, to be a friend to those who are alone.

Year 2: 1 Kings 2:1-4, 10-12; Mark 6:7-13
R: Lord, you are exalted over all.

Lord Jesus, You sent out your disciples two by two. Together, these couples went to other towns and preached and healed. I wonder how they felt when, by invoking Your name, they actually healed a person. At the end of each day, they must have sat up late talking about the miracles they saw one another perform. Give me a friend, Lord, that I can feel comfortable talking with about You. May I also be someone that others can talk to about God. Give my friends and me the gift of awe and wonder about You, Lord.

➤ *Catechism of the Catholic Church* 1879

Fourth Friday in Ordinary Time
Sin

Year 1: Hebrews 13:1-8; Mark 6:14-29
R: The Lord is my light and my salvation.

Lord Jesus, King Herod knew he should listen to John the Baptist and change his life, but he didn't. Instead, he had John killed. This is how ugly sin can be. Sin can blind us. We can end up doing awful things if we keep on sinning. Sin separates us from You, Lord. Let me take sin seriously. I want to be near You all the time. Lord Jesus, give me Your strength.

Year 2: Sirach 47:2-11; Mark 6:14-29
R: Blessed be God my salvation!

Dear Lord, Mark's gospel says that King Herod liked to hear John the Baptist preach. Herod knew deep down that John was holy. John was telling Herod to change his life and stop doing so many bad things. But sin made Herod weak. There are lots of people, Lord, who know they should change their lives and turn to You, but sin makes them weak, too. I pray for them today, Lord. Through my prayers and my sacrifices today, Lord, help one person turn to You.

➤ *Catechism of the Catholic Church* 1850

Fourth Saturday in Ordinary Time
Need for God

Year 1: Hebrews 13:15-17, 20-21; Mark 6:30-34
R: The Lord is my shepherd; there is nothing I shall want.

Lord Jesus, You and Your disciples had worked all day — preaching, listening, calming arguments, answering questions. You pulled Your disciples away for some rest. But just as You were about to sit down, all of you saw hundreds and hundreds of people on their way to You. Instead of being angry and complaining, Lord, the Bible says that Your "heart was moved with pity." You felt sorry for all those people. They needed God, and they knew You were their answer. Be our answer, Lord. So many people need You so badly. May all those who are mean to others see and feel their need for You.

Year 2: 1 Kings 3:4-13; Mark 6:30-34
R: Lord, teach me your statutes.

Lord Jesus, You and Your disciples had worked all day — preaching, listening, calming arguments, answering questions. You pulled your disciples away for some rest. But just as You were about to sit down, all of you saw hundreds and hundreds of people on their way to You. Instead of being angry and complaining, Lord, the Bible says that your "heart was moved with pity." You felt sorry for all those people. Help me to respond to others' needs like You did, Jesus. May I be patient, even when I am tired. May I continue to give to others, just like You did.

➤ *Catechism of the Catholic Church* 2443

Fifth Sunday in Ordinary Time
Vocation

Cycle A: Isaiah 58:7-10; 1 Corinthians 2:1-5; Matthew 5:13-16
R: The just man is a light in darkness to the upright.

Dear Lord, You tell me to let my light shine. My light is my joy, my trust in You, my love for You, my hope for You. If I am to let my light shine, then I can't be afraid of things, or worried about things — not if I really trust that You will be with me in all things. If I am to let my light shine, then I have to keep my eyes fixed on You, so that I end up doing in my life what You created me to do. Let my light shine, Jesus.

Cycle B: Job 7:1-4, 6-7; 1 Corinthians 9:16-19, 22-23; Mark 1:29-39
R: Praise the Lord, who heals the brokenhearted.

My Lord, everyone seemed to have their own ideas about You and what they wanted You to do. I know how that feels. My parents or teachers or friends think I should do certain things with my life. I just don't know for sure. I know I need to check with You. You know what You have called me to do. Help me to see myself as You see me, Lord. You knew what You were about. Help me know what I'm about.

Cycle C: Isaiah 6:1-2a, 3-8; 1 Corinthians 15:1-11 or 3-8, 11; Luke 5:1-11
R: In the sight of the angels I will sing your praises, Lord.

Dear Jesus, when you called Peter to not only follow You but to be the leader, it probably made some people scratch their heads. Peter was loud. Sometimes he did things without thinking. He was bossy. And, he really didn't seem to be the "religious" kind. Call me, Lord. Help me to see like You did. You see what I can become. Show me, too.

➤ *Catechism of the Catholic Church* 2030

Fifth Monday in Ordinary Time
God-Centered

Year 1: Genesis 1:1-19; Mark 6:53-56
R: May the Lord be glad in his works.

Dear Lord, people wanted to be where You were. They knew You were special; the words You spoke, the things You did, touched them because they knew You were the truth. There are lots of things in the world for me to think about, to see, to do, to spend my time with. No matter what I do or think, Jesus, let me always come back to You. You are the truth. You are what life is about.

Year 2: 1 Kings 8:1-7, 9-13; Mark 6:53-56
R: Lord, go up to the place of your rest!

The responsorial psalm from today's Mass is, "Lord, go up to the place of your rest!" Lord, You still have to fight to be on the throne of our lives. So many of us make war, fight and kill one another, hate one another. Your ways, Jesus, should be our ways by now. But no, we still sin; we still are mean; we still are selfish. Use me, Lord Jesus. Help me to know what to do to put You in the center of people's lives so that they stop being mean and selfish and hateful. That way You can rest.

➤ *Catechism of the Catholic Church* 2825

Fifth Tuesday in Ordinary Time
Loving God

Year 1: Genesis 1:20 - 2:4a; Mark 7:1-13
R: O Lord, our God, how wonderful your name in all the earth!

Dear Jesus, You got really mad at some of the leaders of the Jewish people who made up so many rules people had a hard time following them. You came to show us that one thing is necessary: loving You. It is simple, but it is hard, too. If I love You, I am kind, not mean. I am accepting, not rejecting or judgmental. I am patient, not running over others to get what I want. If I love You, Lord, I do my absolute best in what I am called to do at this time: I learn, I study, I serve, I play. All for You, and all how You would want me to. Let me love You, Lord.

Year 2: 1 Kings 8:22-23, 27-30; Mark 7:1-13
R: How lovely is your dwelling place, Lord, mighty God!

Lord Jesus, You got really mad at some of the leaders of the Jewish people because they were making up all kinds of excuses to not be true lovers of God. Help me not to make excuses, Lord. If I say Mass is boring so that's why I don't participate, let me realize that is just an excuse and try harder. If I couldn't get my homework done because I was tired, let me realize that is just an excuse and push myself a bit harder to get my studies done. If I say being nice to that person will get me made fun of, let me realize that is just an excuse. Give me courage to reach out anyway. No more excuses, Lord.

➤ *Catechism of the Catholic Church* 2086

Fifth Wednesday in Ordinary Time
Excuses

Year 1: Genesis 2:4b-9, 15-17; Mark 7:14-23
R: O bless the Lord, my soul!

Lord Jesus, some people look for excuses when they do something bad. If they are mean to someone, they say that person caused them to be mean. You teach us differently. You teach us to look at our own hearts. If we are mean, it's because there is something wrong in our hearts and in our thoughts. We must always try to make our thoughts and hearts kind and considerate, compassionate and patient. It is not easy all the time; but we are called to be just like You.

Year 2: 1 Kings 10:1-10; Mark 7:14-23
R: The mouth of the just murmurs wisdom.

Dear Jesus, when You were a man here on earth, people thought that things they ate or things they touched made their hearts and souls dirty. If they ate a piece of pork, they thought it was a sin and made them dirty on the inside. Before I laugh about that, Lord, help me to realize that we can do the same thing. If we see a person with really poor and dirty clothes on, we think that person is dumb, or scary, or not worth talking to. We still let what's on the outside make us judge what's on the inside of a person. Help me to know people by what they say and do, not by what they wear or eat or look like.

➤ *Catechism of the Catholic Church* 1432

Fifth Thursday in Ordinary Time
Prejudice

Year 1: Genesis 2:18-25; Mark 7:24-30
R: Blessed are those who fear the Lord.

Dear Lord, St. Mark tells us about a woman who made You laugh. The Jews were the chosen people, and it was common in Your day for Jews to refer to non-Jews as dogs. This non-Jewish woman asked You to heal her daughter. Acting like some of the mean Jews of Your day, You told her that it wasn't right to do such good things to "the dogs." The woman, whom You knew was not going to walk away mad or sad, responded, "Yes, but even the dogs eat the crumbs that fall from the chosen people's tables." You must have laughed. So there in that one brief conversation, You showed the mean Jews who looked down on everyone else that it was okay to accept all people and give good things to all people. May I make You laugh, Lord!

Year 2: 1 Kings 11:4-13; Mark 7:24-30
R: Remember us, O Lord, as you favor your people.

Dear Lord, everyone is part of Your kingdom. Our culture teaches us to look down on some people. We look down on people in prison. We look down on terrorists and violent people. We can even look down on the poor or people of other races, religions, or countries. You, Lord, have the power to save everyone. Maybe our acceptance of everyone will help them to not commit crime or be violent. Maybe our acceptance of everyone will lead to our being so concerned for others that poverty and prejudice will go away, for good.

➤ *Catechism of the Catholic Church* 1825

Fifth Friday in Ordinary Time
Miracles

Year 1: Genesis 3:1-8; Mark 7:31-37
R: Blessed are those whose sins are forgiven.

Dear Lord, no one was able to cure the deaf or the mute. In Your day, it was believed that only God could cure these people. So, the miracles you performed were done for more reason than just healing this or that person. You were showing the people around You that You were God Himself. They had to have been overcome with awe at the thought that God was among them. God is among me and my family and my church community. May I have the gift of awe at this fact. Gift me with awe, O Lord!

Year 2: 1 Kings 11:29-32; 12:19; Mark 7:31-37
R: I am the Lord, your God; hear my voice.

Lord Jesus, when You performed miracles, You wanted people to begin wondering about You and Your message. You wanted them to begin questioning who You were and where You were from. You wanted people to know that You were God coming to visit them. I need to know this because You didn't heal everyone around You back then, and You don't heal everyone who is sick now. Sometimes that makes me mad, especially if a sick person is one I love. Some times, You ask those who have become sick to cope with the illness and trust that You will give them strength. This is hard, Lord. Help me to trust in You, too.

➤ *Catechism of the Catholic Church* 548

Fifth Saturday in Ordinary Time
Faith

Year 1: Genesis 3:9-24; Mark 8:1-10
R: In every age, O Lord, you have been our refuge.

Lord Jesus, when You fed four thousand people, You didn't want them to be amazed at the miracle. You didn't want them to follow You so You would do it again and they could witness it. You wanted them to "get it." You wanted them to begin to question just who You were. You wanted them to know that God was with them, among them, feeding them. How many of them got caught up in the miracle and missed that message? May I "get it," Jesus. May I realize just how awesome it is that Almighty God is with me.

Year 2: 1 Kings 12:26-32; 13:33-34; Mark 8:1-10
R: Remember us, O Lord, as you favor your people.

Lord Christ, You fed the Israelites in the desert as Moses led them. They were filled with bread from heaven for years. In Mark's gospel, You have four thousand people in front of You, and You ask Your disciples to feed them. Your disciples knew well that Moses and the Israelites were fed many years before. But, the disciples still didn't realize You were God, and they asked You how they could possibly feed all these people in the desert. I bet they looked back on this time after You had risen from the dead and laughed at their unbelief. The disciples grew in their faith. Help me to grow in my faith in You, too, Jesus.

➤ *Catechism of the Catholic Church* 1335

Sixth Sunday in Ordinary Time
Choice

Cycle A: Sirach 15:15-20; 1 Corinthians 2:6-10; Matthew 5:17-37 or 5:20-22a, 27-28, 33-34a, 37
R: Blessed are those who follow the law of the Lord.

In the book of Sirach, we read that we all have a choice between life or death, between good or evil. It seems as if this choice is a "no-brainer." Of course, we will pick life; we will pick the good. But it isn't always that easy. Sometimes, dear Lord, it is easier to go ahead and hit someone, or hurt someone's feelings, or be angry. Sometimes, Jesus, it is easier to cheat, lie, eat too much, or get into things that I shouldn't. Sometimes, Lord, the evil looks very good. Give me eyes like Yours, Jesus. Help me to see. Help me to choose the good. Help me to choose life.

Cycle B: Leviticus 13:1-2, 44-46; 1 Corinthians 10:31 - 11:1; Mark 1:40-45
R: I turn to you, Lord, in time of trouble, and you fill me with the joy of salvation.

People who had leprosy in Your day, Lord Jesus, had to live apart from everyone else, and when they came into town to get things they needed, they had to yell, "Unclean! Unclean!" so that people would know they had this contagious disease and would steer clear of them. I bet some people made sport of them, thereby hurting them even more. Many probably used their contagion as an excuse to not even glance their way, talk to them, or show concern in any way. Don't let me use excuses to not be nice to someone, Lord. May I never act like someone isn't even there. May I acknowledge them with a smile, a word or two. It might just be the one act that makes their day!

Cycle C: Jeremiah 17:5-8; 1 Corinthians 15:12, 16-20; Luke 6:17, 20-26
R: Blessed are they who hope in the Lord.

Lord, You blessed the poor and cursed the rich. That scares me, Lord, because compared to many people in the world, I am rich. Teach me what You mean, Lord. May I never become so connected to the things that I have that I put You second. May I never love my stuff more than I love another person. May I take time to care for people more than I take time to enjoy all the things I have. People before things, Lord. Teach me this.

➤ *Catechism of the Catholic Church* 1733

Sixth Monday in Ordinary Time
Signs

Year 1: Genesis 4:1-15, 25; Mark 8:11-13
R: Offer to God a sacrifice of praise!

Lord, Mark's gospel records a moment when You were upset with the people who were following You just to see the miracles. They wanted proof before they would believe in You. They kept asking for "a sign" that they should follow You. And it was never enough. They never would just commit to belief in You, so You told them "no sign would be given." You were healing; You were forgiving. Soon You would die and rise from the dead. Yet, You knew that not even that would be good enough for people like that. You know that it takes faith to believe, not signs and wonders. Give me the strength and the love to give my heart to You, Lord, and not demand anything from You before doing so.

Year 2: James 1:1-11; Mark 8:11-13
R: Be kind to me, Lord, and I shall live.

Lord Jesus, St. James tells us that our faith will be tested. Sometimes it will not be easy to follow You. A lot of people ask for signs from You that everything is okay in these difficult times. That is okay to do. But if I say I will walk away from You unless I get a sign, then I become like the people in today's gospel. They wanted more and more signs, and You knew, Jesus, that it would never be enough for people like this. Let the signs I ask for be like my asking for a hug from You, not like a threat that I will leave if I don't receive.

➤ *Catechism of the Catholic Church* 157

Sixth Tuesday in Ordinary Time
Friendships

Year 1: Genesis 6:5-8; 7:1-5, 10; Mark 8:14-21
R: The Lord will bless his people with peace.

Dear Jesus, You said a lot of things that Your disciples did not understand. You told them to beware of the leaven of the Pharisees. They didn't understand that You meant the example of the Pharisees. Some of them said good things but did bad things. I need to watch out whom I hang around with and listen to. If their messages or examples are not good, I need to find others to hang around, others who are good both in word and in action. Give me this courage, Lord. Help me to make good choices.

Year 2: James 1:12-18; Mark 8:14-21
R: Blessed the man you instruct, O Lord.

Dear Lord, if I hang around people who speak badly of others or who do mean things, it will affect how I act and how I think. You told Your disciples to watch out who they hung out with and listened to. If You wanted them to make sure they had friendships with good people, I know You want me to have good friendships, too. Give me the wisdom to choose my friends well.

➤ *Catechism of the Catholic Church* 1939

Sixth Wednesday in Ordinary Time
Giving Up

Year 1: Genesis 8:6-13, 20-22; Mark 8:22-26
R: To you, Lord, I will offer a sacrifice of praise.

Dear Jesus, even You had to try again. You took the blind man out of the city to heal him. At first his eyesight came back blurry, so You tried again. Maybe it was his lack of faith. Maybe it just took two tries. Don't let me give up too easily, Lord. When I am trying to do something good and I at first fail or encounter difficulty, remind me to ask You for strength to keep trying.

Year 2: James 1:19-27; Mark 8:22-26
R: Who shall live on your holy mountain, O Lord?

Dear Lord, if I am to become more and more a Christian, then I need to act like one. Christians don't give up when things get hard or confusing. May I never give up on You, Lord. May I study hard for love of You. May I choose good friends for love of You. May I honor my parents and elders for love of You. May I do all like You did, Jesus — with all my heart.

➤ *Catechism of the Catholic Church* 841

Sixth Thursday in Ordinary Time
Jesus Christ

Year 1: Genesis 9:1-13; Mark 8:27-33
R: From heaven the Lord looks down on the earth.

Dear Jesus, You asked Your disciples a strange question. You wanted to know who they thought You were. You wanted them to make up their own minds. Were You who You said You were, the Son of God? What did they really believe about You? Jesus, You ask that question of me, too. Who are You to me? May I always have the faith to answer, "You are my Lord and my God."

Year 2: James 2:1-9; Mark 8:27-33
R: The Lord hears the cry of the poor.

Lord Jesus, there are special people around me who seem to know a lot about You. Help me to listen to them like the disciples must have listened to Peter after he said he believed You were the Son of God. You gave Peter special knowledge of You, too. Give me a listening heart, Jesus. Give me a thirst to know You more and more.

➤ *Catechism of the Catholic Church* 1391

Sixth Friday in Ordinary Time
God-Centered

Year 1: Genesis 11:1-9; Mark 8:34 - 9:1
R: I will praise your name for ever, Lord.

Lord Jesus, why do You say that I must deny myself? What does that mean? I am afraid that it means I must give up all the things that I like. But, when You were here on earth, You enjoyed a lot of things. You were, however, totally centered on God the Father. You didn't care about Yourself as much as You cared about Your Father. I need to be like that. I need to care more about You and the Father than I care about myself. I need to be God-centered and not self-centered. Help me to understand what this means.

Year 2: James 2:14-24, 26; Mark 8:34 - 9:1
R: Blessed the man who greatly delights in the Lord's commands.

Dear Jesus, when I hear the words in the Bible about denying myself, I don't like it. I think it means that I can't do what I want or enjoy what I like. Let me take the risk of denying myself— giving up something just once for someone else — and see what my experience is. May I be intrigued to do it again and again — just to see if this joy Christians talk about is truly what I find. "Blessed the [person] who greatly delights in the Lord's commands."

➤ *Catechism of the Catholic Church* 2544

Sixth Saturday in Ordinary Time
Jesus Is God

Year 1: Hebrews 11:1-7; Mark 9:2-13
R: I will praise your name for ever, Lord.

Dear Lord, Your disciples were going to need a big boost before You suffered and died. You took the three leaders, the ones everyone seemed to trust and follow well, and You were transfigured in front of them. When You were arrested and killed, these three had this vision of You to lean back on to help them believe in Your resurrection. You are God. Peter, James, and John had to have been in awe of You. Give me, too, this gift of awe, Lord.

Year 2: James 3:1-10; Mark 9:2-13
R: You will protect us, Lord.

Lord Jesus, sometimes when I think of You here on earth with us, being born as a baby, living and dying, I can forget You are God. I can sometimes think of You as a friend too much — You are not just a friend, Lord. You are God. I don't fall on my knees to my friends, Jesus. But I do kneel down to You. I want to kneel down, because I do think Your ways are better than my ways; that's why I kneel. I kneel to Your ways. Remind me, Lord, that You are God. You do know better than I.

➤ *Catechism of the Catholic Church* 424

Seventh Sunday in Ordinary Time
Perfection

Cycle A: Leviticus 19:1-2, 17-18; 1 Corinthians 3:16-23; Matthew 5:38-48
R: The Lord is kind and merciful.

Lord Jesus, You said that we should be perfect. Many people figure we can't be perfect, so they ignore what You said. What did You mean, Lord, if You know we can't be perfect? The people of Your day had their problems. They hated the Romans; they hated the Samaritans; they hated tax-collectors. They believed in an "eye for an eye." There wasn't much mercy. You introduced what was to them a totally new way: loving your enemies, doing good to those you once hated. Even though Your words about loving your enemies are not new to me, I still need to be more perfect than I am right now. I can never be totally perfect, but I can be better. I can do good to those I don't like. I can stop tormenting those who are not "in." I can pray for those everyone else makes fun of. I can pray for those who make fun of me. Let me see like You do, Jesus, and help me to love like You do, too.

Cycle B: Isaiah 43:18-19, 21-22, 24b-25; 2 Corinthians 1:18-22; Mark 2:1-12
R: Lord, heal my soul, for I have sinned against you.

Dear Lord, You told a man who couldn't walk to rise up, pick up the mat that he was lying on, and go home. Maybe that man thought it was easier to stay the way he was. People threw money or food at him. He stayed alive. Maybe he didn't like being healed. Sometimes I act like that, too. Maybe I don't want to be healed of my prejudices against some people. Maybe I don't want to be healed of my mean ways of thinking about some people. Maybe I don't want to be healed of my lazy ways of studying or my less than nice way of talking to my parents. It's easier to hate, to be mean, to be lazy, and to talk back. Let me know, Lord, what it's like to stop myself from making that mean remark. Let me know what it's like to do my work right away and even check it. Let me know what it's like to answer my parents in a respectful and joyful way. I just might feel power. I just might feel peace. And those are nice feelings. Give me power, Lord!

Cycle C: 1 Samuel 26:2, 7-9, 12-13, 22-23; 1 Corinthians 15:45-49; Luke 6:27-38
R: The Lord is kind and merciful.

Dear Jesus, St. Paul told the people who lived in Corinth that they bore "the image of the heavenly one." They were Christians, so they represented You. They were Your image here on earth, just as I am Your image now. If I am Your image, Lord, I need lots of grace to represent You well. Don't let me forget that, Jesus — I am Your image. Pull me closer to You, Lord, so that my actions, my words, my very thoughts will make You proud of me.

> *Catechism of the Catholic Church* 1811

Seventh Monday in Ordinary Time
Belief

Year 1: Sirach 1:1-10; Mark 9:14-29
R: The Lord is king; he is robed in majesty.

Dear Jesus, how strong is my belief in You? How easily would I turn my back on You? A man in the gospel asked You to heal his son. Before You did, You asked him whether he believed You could do this. He gave a great answer. He said, "I do believe, help my unbelief!" He knew that he didn't believe perfectly. Neither do I, Lord. I may go through difficult times when my belief is tested. May I ask You every day, Lord, to strengthen my belief in You. I do believe, Lord, but help me believe more and more!

Year 2: James 3:13-18; Mark 9:14-29
R: The precepts of the Lord give joy to the heart.

Lord Jesus, St. James tells us that wisdom from above is pure, gentle, peaceable, full of mercy. I know that the more I believe in You, the more pure, the more gentle, the more peaceable, the more merciful I will be. I need purity to control what I allow my eyes and ears to see and hear. I need gentleness so people aren't afraid to come to me. I need peace because the world has too much war. I need mercy so that I forgive others. All these things are signs that I belong to You; they are signs that I believe in You. Strengthen my belief, my Lord!

> *Catechism of the Catholic Church* 943

Seventh Tuesday in Ordinary Time
Prayer

Year 1: Sirach 2:1-11; Mark 9:30-37
R: Commit your life to the Lord, and he will help you.

Lord Jesus, You were telling the apostles that You were going to be rejected and betrayed in Jerusalem the final time You went there with them. You had to have been upset when You told them this because You knew You were going to die soon. Were they paying attention to You? No, they were arguing about which of them was the best! I know how You felt then, Lord Jesus. I get upset over some things and when I try to tell someone about it, that person just doesn't listen. It hurts my feelings. Your apostles hurt Your feelings, too. Help me to pay attention to You, Lord. Your words are important. Your message to me is important. Help me always to hear what You have to say.

Year 2: James 4:1-10; Mark 9:30-37
R: Throw your cares on the Lord, and he will support you.

Lord Jesus, look at the mess the world is in. There are wars everywhere. People are killing one another. I can try to ignore all of this, but that just makes me afraid. I can bring all this mess to You in prayer; that makes me feel powerful. When I ask You to do something about a bad situation, it does make me feel powerful. I feel Your power, Your ability to control things. And then I know that whatever happens, You have me and those I love — and even those making all the violence — right in the palm of Your hand. Help me remember to pray.

➤ *Catechism of the Catholic Church* 2633

Seventh Wednesday in Ordinary Time
Peace

Year 1: Sirach 4:11-19; Mark 9:38-40
R: O Lord, great peace have they that love your law.

Dear Lord, You say that we have peace if we love Your law. But all I see in the world is mostly war and hatred. Help me to understand that You speak of peace of mind and peace of heart. The more I love You, the more will my mind and my heart remain at peace regardless of what is happening around me. As more and more people come to love You, Lord, only then will we see peace not only in ourselves but in our world also.

Year 2: James 4:13-17; Mark 9:38-40
R: Blessed are the poor in spirit; the kingdom of heaven is theirs.

Dear Jesus, You speak of the kingdom of heaven. In that kingdom there will be peace. Help me to remember that You also said the kingdom is now. The kingdom of heaven begins here on earth, and with every good thing that I do, I help to bring about the kingdom You promised. Every little bit of good that I do is like adding a brick to the wall of the kingdom. Challenge me, Lord, to add many, many bricks!

➤ *Catechism of the Catholic Church* 2308

Seventh Thursday in Ordinary Time
Conversion

Year 1: Sirach 5:1-8, Mark 9:41-50
R: Blessed are they who hope in the Lord.

Dear Jesus, it sounds funny when You tell us to cut our hands off rather than miss out on seeing heaven. I know what you mean though. If we fall into a pattern of sinning, we'd better do radical things to get out of sinning so we don't lose heaven. We must do battle with the parts of ourselves that cause us to sin: the mean part, the selfish part, the jealous part, the lazy part. Help me to win the battle and become who You expect me to become!

Year 2: James 5:1-6; Mark 9:41-50
R: Blessed are the poor in spirit; the Kingdom of heaven is theirs!

Dear Jesus, You were very harsh with leaders. Leaders are gifted by You with great talents. With these gifts come great responsibility, too. Leaders have the responsibility to make sure that how they are leading is how You would lead. Leaders must be mindful of the poor. Leaders must always give a good example because people are watching them all the time. If I am to be a leader, Lord, help me to develop a habit of praying always so I learn to lean on You as I lead. I pray now for the leaders of my family, my classes, my school, my city, my state, my church, my country. All these need You, Lord. I lift them up to You.

➤ *Catechism of the Catholic Church* 545

Seventh Friday in Ordinary Time
Friendship

Year 1: Sirach 6:5-17; Mark 10:1-12
R: Guide me, Lord, in the way of your commands.

Dear Jesus, it says in the Bible that a faithful friend is beyond price. So You, Jesus, value the friendships that we have. You want us to have good friends. You want us to be good friends. Good friends help to teach us what You are like. Therefore, Lord, help me to be a good friend. Help me to be the gift that You give to another.

Year 2: James 5:9-12; Mark 10:1-12
R: The Lord is kind and merciful.

Dear Jesus, St. James tells us not to complain about one another. That's hard. People get in my way, take my time, want me to do things I don't want to do. And I do want to complain about this. So why does St. James tell me not to? Complaining makes me impatient. Complaining hurts another's feelings. Complaining makes me miss out on my vocation now: My vocation now is to be there for others. Help me to remember this, Lord, when I'm tempted to complain.

➤ *Catechism of the Catholic Church* 1023

Seventh Saturday in Ordinary Time
Heaven

Year 1: Sirach 17:1-15; Mark 10:13-16
R: The Lord's kindness is everlasting to those who fear him.

Lord Jesus, small children are focused on the adults in their world, especially their mothers and fathers. Their security comes from the adults who care for and love them, and so it is natural that they should be so focused on them. You said we need to accept the kingdom of heaven like a small child. We need to be very focused on helping You bring about heaven here on earth. I join with You, Jesus. I will work with You to bring about Your kingdom.

Year 2: James 5:13-20; Mark 10:13-16
R: Let my prayer come like incense before you.

Dear Jesus, the apostles thought You didn't want to be bothered with children because Your mission was so important. Show us that You don't think like we think. Nothing is more important than a child. All of us are Your children. All of us are important to You. Help me, Lord, to make those around me feel accepted and important. May I, too, Jesus, know that I am important to You.

➤ *Catechism of the Catholic Church* 2802

EIGHTH WEEK IN ORDINARY TIME

Eighth Sunday in Ordinary Time
Trust

Cycle A: Isaiah 49:14-15; 1 Corinthians 4:1-5; Matthew 6:24-34
R: Rest in God alone, my soul.

Lord Jesus, You tell us to trust in You in today's Gospel. If we put You first, if we put making Your kingdom come here on earth by caring for Your people and loving You as best we can, You promised to take care of us, to make sure we are loved and fed and protected. Teach me Your ways, Jesus. May I trust You!

Cycle B: Hosea 2:16b, 17b, 21-22; 2 Corinthians 3:1-6; Mark 2:18-22
R: The Lord is kind and merciful.

Dear God, You promised that I could know You. The prophet Hosea tells me this. He writes that You will lead me into the desert and speak to my heart and I will know You. My desert, Lord, is any hard time I go through. During hard times, I really look to You and concentrate on You, because I can trust that You will help me through. Speak to my heart, Lord; I want to know You.

Cycle C: Sirach 27:4-7; 1 Corinthians 15:54-58; Luke 6:39-45
R: Lord, it is good to give thanks to you.

Jesus, You said, "From the fullness of the heart the mouth speaks." This means that if You are in my heart, others will know it by the way I speak. I will speak with kindness and patience. When I am mean, Lord, I need to ask You to come into my heart. I trust that You will come to me.

➤ *Catechism of the Catholic Church* 2828

Eighth Monday in Ordinary Time
Selfishness

Year 1: Sirach 17:20-24; Mark 10:17-27
R: Let the just exult and rejoice in the Lord.

The prophet Sirach tells us to hate intensely what God does not like. I know what You do not like, Lord Jesus. You do not like when I am mean. You do not like when I am selfish. You do not like when I am greedy. Help me to hate sin and do everything I can to make my heart big, like Your heart. I need Your grace, Jesus, to help me to do this. Amen.

Year 2: 1 Peter 1:3-9; Mark 10:17-27
R: The Lord will remember his covenant for ever.

Sometimes, Lord, it seems like I'll never be able to stay away from being mean and selfish. People make me mad. People expect me to do things I don't want to do. I react with mean words and even refuse to do things they ask of me. But St. Peter in today's readings tells me about this living hope. With hope that is always living, I can trust that one day I will be able to not react in a mean way. Help me to believe in myself, like You believe in me, Lord.

➤ *Catechism of the Catholic Church* 1818

Eighth Tuesday in Ordinary Time
Knowledge of God

Year 1: Sirach 35:1-12; Mark 10:28-31
R: To the upright I will show the saving power of God.

Dear Lord, today's responsorial psalm, "To the upright I will show the saving power of God," tells me an important truth. As long as I am upright, as long as I am trying my best to be a good person, I will be able to see Your saving power. I will be able to see You work in our world. I will be able to recognize how You work through me and through others. I want to see You, Lord!

Year 2: 1 Peter 1:10-16; Mark 10:28-31
R: The Lord has made known his salvation.

Lord Jesus, today's responsorial psalm, "The Lord has made known his salvation," tells me that I am able to know You. When You came into our world as a man, You showed us just what God is like. Help me to study Your word, Lord, in the Bible, so that I can know You more and more.

➤ *Catechism of the Catholic Church* 851

Eighth Wednesday in Ordinary Time
Service

Year 1: Sirach 36:1, 4-5a, 10-17; Mark 10:32-45
R: Show us, O Lord, the light of your kindness.

Lord Jesus, in today's gospel we get a good look at the way of life You call us to. You said that You came to serve. If You served, then how can we complain about serving others? No, we should seek to serve others — to feed the poor, clothe the naked, visit the imprisoned, comfort those who mourn. Teach me Your ways, Jesus.

Year 2: 1 Peter 1:18-25; Mark 10:32-45
R: Praise the Lord, Jerusalem.

Dear Lord, James and John wanted You to promise them that they would be at Your right and left in the kingdom of Heaven. This was important to them. They wanted to be special to You. You told them they would have to live as You lived, standing up for what is right, teaching, loving others. I want to be special to You, too, Lord. Help me to follow Your example.

➤ *Catechism of the Catholic Church* 1733

Eighth Thursday in Ordinary Time
Understand

Year 1: Sirach 42:15-25; Mark 10:46-52
R: By the word of the Lord the heavens were made.

Lord Jesus, Bartimaeus was blind. He told You he wanted to see, and You gave him his sight. Sometimes I am blind, Lord Jesus: I don't understand my studies; I don't understand other people. Remind me that I can come to You as Bartimaeus did and ask You to help me see, help me understand. Thank you, Lord Jesus, for caring when I don't understand.

Year 2: 1 Peter 2:2-5, 9-12; Mark 10:46-52
R: Come with joy into the presence of the Lord.

Dear Lord, there is a lot of prejudice in the world. We are tempted to think other people are wrong when we don't understand them. We are blind when we are prejudiced. We are not seeing like You see. Challenge us, Lord, to grow away from prejudice. Help us to see others like You see them.

➤ *Catechism of the Catholic Church* 2303

Eighth Friday in Ordinary Time
Giving

Year 1: Sirach 44:1, 9-13; Mark 11:11-26
R: The Lord takes delight in his people.

Lord Jesus, it sounds funny now to read how You cursed the fig tree for having no fruit. You were hungry when You went over to it, looking for figs. You came to it needy, and it did not fill Your need. When others come to us needy — needing kindness, understanding, help — may we be ready with the fruit of our willingness to share, to help, to be kind. May our lives be fruitful!

Year 2: 1 Peter 4:7-13; Mark 11:11-26
R: The Lord comes to judge the earth.

Dear Jesus, it scares me a bit that you cursed the fig tree and it withered up. You were showing Your disciples that if we do not give fruit now — meaning if we do not practice being nice, being compassionate, being unselfish, being helpful now — we probably won't later in our lives either. Help me to start being fruitful now, Lord. Teach me how.

➤ *Catechism of the Catholic Church* 2013

Eighth Saturday in Ordinary Time
Joy

Year 1: Sirach 51:12cd-20; Mark 11:27-33
R: The precepts of the Lord give joy to the heart.

Lord, the responsorial psalm in today's Mass, "The precepts of the Lord give joy to the heart," teaches me an important lesson. Precepts are ways; so, the ways of the Lord give joy to the heart. This teaches me that if I follow Your way, I will be joyful. Following You and doing Your will causes joy. Help me to experience this joy, Lord. May I really want this joy.

Year 2: Jude 17:20b-25; Mark 11:27-33
R: My soul is thirsting for you, O Lord my God.

Lord Jesus, the leaders who were against You didn't believe in John the Baptist either. So You knew that they were not going to believe in You. They had closed their hearts. Open my heart, Lord. Open it wide for You. May You never see any sign in me of not believing in You. I want the joy of belonging to You. I believe in the joy that comes from following You!

➤ *Catechism of the Catholic Church* 2500

Ninth Sunday in Ordinary Time
Choice

Cycle A: Deuteronomy 11:18, 26-28, 32; Romans 3:21-25, 28; Matthew 7:21-27
R: Lord, be my rock of safety.

Lord Jesus, we either follow Your ways and find blessing in life, or we ignore Your ways and find great unhappiness. You made us, so You know us. You know how we work. The path You teach is what will fulfill us and bring us joy. I choose You, Lord. I choose Your ways. Teach me all that this choice means, Lord. Give me wisdom that I may choose You all the time.

Cycle B: Deuteronomy 5:12-15; 2 Corinthians 4:6-11; Mark 2:23 - 3:6 or 2:23-28
R: Sing with joy to God our help.

Lord Jesus, the people who were against You seemed very mean. Even though You cured a man and restored him to health, making him very happy, the people against You got mad about it! They chose to hate You instead of accept You. May I choose to love You, Lord, and show You my love by my actions, my words, and my prayers.

Cycle C: 1 Kings 8:41-43; Galatians 1:1-2, 6-10; Luke 7:1-10
R: Go out to all the world and tell the good news.

Lord Jesus, many people come to me. They either walk away with You or without You. If I am kind, they walk away with You. If I am mean, they walk away without You. Help me to choose to give You to others by being nice, by being accepting, by not judging, by not talking about others in a mean way. May I, time after time, choose to share You with others.

➤ *Catechism of the Catholic Church* 1732

Ninth Monday in Ordinary Time
Taking Care

Year 1: Tobit 1:3; 2:1a-8; Mark 12:1-12
R: Blessed the man who fears the Lord.

Dear Jesus, the parable that You tell in today's gospel — about the vineyard that You created and made so nice — is about our Earth. You created it and gave it to us to care for. How well are we caring for it, Lord? How well am I caring for it? Open my eyes, Lord, to know how to treat Your Earth properly. May I teach others to do the same.

Year 2: 2 Peter 1:2-7; Mark 12:1-12
R: In you, my God, I place my trust.

Dear Lord, the master of the vineyard sent servants to speak to the caretakers of the vineyard, and the caretakers killed the servants. So the master sent his son thinking the caretakers would respect his son, but they killed the son, too. Jesus, you told this parable because You knew many of the leaders wanted to kill You. They were caretakers, but they did not take care of anyone except themselves. When we are selfish like that, we can end up doing awful things. Help me be a good caretaker, Lord. Help me to take care of those around me, take care of Earth, and take care of my faith.

➤ *Catechism of the Catholic Church* 2402

Ninth Tuesday in Ordinary Time
God–Centered

Year 1: Tobit 2:9-14; Mark 12:13-17
R: The heart of the just one is firm, trusting in the Lord.

Dear Jesus, I like the gospel story where the leaders were trying to get You in trouble, so they asked You if it was right to pay taxes to Caesar, the Roman leader who was mean to the Jews. You knew they were trying to get You in trouble, so You asked them to show You the coin used to pay taxes. The coin had Caesar's head on it, so You said give it to Caesar, it has his picture on it. But then You became very serious and said to them firmly, "But give to God what is God's." I belong to God. May I give myself to You, Lord, everyday to use as You wish.

Year 2: 2 Peter 3:12-15a, 17-18; Mark 12:13-17
R: In every age, O Lord, you have been our refuge.

Lord Jesus, St. Peter told us to grow in grace and knowledge of You. May I take time every day, Lord, to think about You and my relationship with You. May I take time to pray, to sit in Your presence to see what You have to tell me. Show me, Lord, how to grow in grace and knowledge of You. You are the center of all things. May I make You a part of everything I do.

➤ *Catechism of the Catholic Church* 1889

Ninth Wednesday in Ordinary Time
Wisdom

Year 1: Tobit 3:1-11a, 16-17a; Mark 12:18-27
R: To you, O Lord, I lift up my soul.

My Lord, the Pharisees and Sadducees were asking You questions, trying to get You to say something against the Law so that they could have You arrested. They weren't allowing Your answers to change their minds or their hearts; they were dead set against You. Help me, Lord, when my heart is hard, when I am stubborn, when I refuse to listen. Give me an open and loving heart.

Year 2: 2 Timothy 1:1-3, 6-12; Mark 12:18-27
R: To you, O Lord, I lift up my eyes.

Dear Jesus, Your answers to all the questions of the leaders who were trying to trip You up had to have made them mad. They wanted You to say something against the Law so that they could arrest You. But You kept challenging them with Your answers. I wish I could have seen some of those exchanges, Lord. I would have been glad to stand beside You as You answered them and put them in their place. I stand beside You now, Jesus. Help me to know what is good and what is bad so well that I can put what is bad in its place, in Your name, Jesus.

➤ *Catechism of the Catholic Church* 546

Ninth Thursday in Ordinary Time
Faith

Year 1: Tobit 6:10-11; 7:1bcde, 9-17; 8:4-9a; Mark 12:28-34
R: Blessed are those who fear the Lord.

Dear Jesus, so many people were around You and not many of them under-stood Your message. Their hearts were not open; their faith was not deep enough. Help me, Lord, to grow in my faith. Make my heart open to You and Your word. May I please You with my responses to people. May I make You proud with my behavior in school, at home, and with my friends.

Year 2: 2 Timothy 2:8-15; Mark 12:28-34
R: Teach me your ways, O Lord.

Dear Jesus, so many people were fighting for Your attention. I would have wanted Your attention, Lord. I would have wanted You to talk to me. I would have wanted You to be around me, to notice me. Help me to realize, Lord, that You do talk to me. You do notice me. You are around me. Help me to see. Help me to listen. Help me to respond. Amen.

➤ *Catechism of the Catholic Church* 1254

Ninth Friday in Ordinary Time
Believe!

Year 1: Tobit 11:5-17; Mark 12:35-37
R: Praise the Lord, my soul!

Dear Lord, I'll believe my friend has one hundred dollars if I see the money. I'll believe if I see. You're not like that, Jesus. You expect me to believe first. You have given me the strength, the wisdom, the faith to believe first. May I believe, Lord, because I do want to see! I want to see You! May I believe with all my heart, my mind, and my soul!

Year 2: 2 Timothy 3:10-17; Mark 12:35-37
R: O Lord, great peace have they who love your law.

Dear Lord, the responsorial psalm for today's Mass, "O Lord, great peace have they who love your law," doesn't seem like it's true. There are people who love your law who live in countries that are at war. There are kids who love You who live in violent homes. What kind of peace do they have? There's a peace that lives in our hearts, that calms us, that reminds us that You are in control, Lord. This is the peace we all can have, and it doesn't leave us when we are at war, or when there is yelling or hitting. No, Lord, Your kind of peace lives in the heart. Let me love You, Lord, and come to know this kind of peace. Amen.

➤ *Catechism of the Catholic Church* 1064

Ninth Saturday in Ordinary Time
Self-Offering

Year 1: Tobit 12:1, 5-15, 20; Mark 12:38-44
R: Blessed be God, who lives for ever.

Dear Lord, why is it that I feel hesitation when You ask for all of me? Maybe it's because I'm not sure what it means to give You all of me. Maybe it's because I think that means You are going to ask me to be a priest or a religious. Maybe it's because I think it will be boring and I won't be able to listen to my music, watch my shows, or eat pizza. Help me to see, Jesus, that You don't ask for all of me when I get older. You ask for all of me right now. Help me to respond to You, Lord, and realize that it is anything but boring!

Year 2: 2 Timothy 4:1-8; Mark 12:38-44
R: I will sing of your salvation.

Lord Jesus, You are touched when people give to You all that they have. Help me to understand what this means for me. If I am to give You all of me, what does that mean? Give me the courage and the desire to ask You what this means for me. May I tell You in prayer that I do want to give myself to You. Teach me, Lord, to listen to You. I am ready. Touch my heart.

➤ *Catechism of the Catholic Church* 2544

Lent

Ash Wednesday
Lent

Joel 2:12-18; 2 Corinthians 5:20-6:2; Matthew 6:1-6, 16-18
R: Be merciful, O Lord, for we have sinned.

Dear Jesus, sin can enter into our lives so easily. We talk back. We don't do what we're supposed to do. We're mean to one another. We allow ourselves to get bored with Mass. But now Lent is here. We give something up so that we can get stronger — so we don't talk back; we do what we're supposed to do; we're kind to one another; and we pay attention and try to get our minds and hearts around what is going on at Mass. Help me to take this time seriously, a time to make of myself a better person for love of You, Lord.

➤ *Catechism of the Catholic Church* 1430

Thursday after Ash Wednesday
Strength

Deuteronomy 30:15-20; Luke 9:22-25
R: Blessed are they who hope in the Lord.

Lord Jesus, during Lent we focus on the time You spent in the desert. You went there to be strengthened. You knew by this time in Your life that You were going to be killed. You needed strength. Lent is my time in the desert, Lord, to strengthen myself. May I pray more, give up more, and think about You more often. Bless me, Lord, during this time of Lent.

➤ *Catechism of the Catholic Church* 540

Friday after Ash Wednesday
Fasting

Isaiah 58:1-9a; Matthew 9:14-15
R: A heart contrite and humbled, O God, you will not spurn.

Dear Jesus, You don't want us to fast if we continue to sin, too. Giving up candy while we continue to talk back to parents and teachers is not the focus of Lent. Giving up talking back to parents and teachers is more what You want. You want my Lenten observance to make me a better person. You want what I give up to bring me closer to You. Teach me, Lord. May my fasting bring me closer to You.

➤ *Catechism of the Catholic Church* 1434

Saturday after Ash Wednesday
Sin

Isaiah 58:9b-14; Luke 5:27-32
R: Teach me your way, O Lord, that I may walk in your truth.

Dear Jesus, even back in Your day, people acted like they were better than others. The Pharisees didn't think You should have been hanging around tax collectors because tax collectors were considered sinners. But You had dinner with the tax collectors. They were more open to You than the Pharisees were. Help me, Lord, to resist any temptation to think myself better than someone else.

➤ *Catechism of the Catholic Church* 2839

First Sunday in Lent
Temptation

Cycle A: Genesis 2:7-9; 3:1-7; Romans 5:12-19 or 5:12, 17-19; Matthew 4:1-11
R: Be merciful, O Lord, for we have sinned.

Dear Jesus, You were in the desert for a long time. You hadn't eaten. In that weakened state, Satan came with temptation, trying hard to get You to walk away from God the Father. Even when You were weak, Jesus, You were able to resist temptation, push Satan away, and not sin. Help me, Lord, to not give in to temptation. Help me to refuse to be mean, to talk back, to lie, to hurt another in any way. Make me strong, Lord, in the face of temptation.

Cycle B: Genesis 9:8-15; 1 Peter 3:18-22; Mark 1:12-15
R: Your ways, O Lord, are love and truth, to those who keep your covenant.

Dear Jesus, the gospel says that the Spirit drove You into the desert. What did that feel like? I get urgings to do something, a thought pops into my head, to do something good or to check something out. Is that the Spirit in me? Help me, Lord, to know when the Spirit is driving me to do something. I don't want to miss the Spirit's call.

Cycle C: Deuteronomy 26:4-10; Romans 10:8-13; Luke 4:1-13
R: Be with me, Lord, when I am in trouble.

Dear Jesus, I don't like when I am asked to give something up. But I believe that You will take my offering and help another; giving something up and offering it for another is like saying an extra-strength prayer for that person. I can give up candy and offer it up for the people who die in war each day. I can give up complaining and offer it up for a kid who has cancer. You hear all prayers, Lord. You see my actions, my sacrifices, too. All these things I do during Lent deepen my ability to love and remind me that we are all Your Body, the Body of Christ, and what I do can help even those far away from me.

➤ *Catechism of the Catholic Church* 2099

First Monday in Lent
Kindness

Leviticus 19:1-2, 11-18; Matthew 25:31-46
R: Your words, Lord, are Spirit and life.

Dear Jesus, if someone I love gets hurt by another, it hurts me too. If someone I love gets praise or a gift from another, it makes me happy, too. Help me to realize that You love all those around me. When I am mean to them, it is like being mean to You. When I am nice to them, it is like being nice to You. May I have the courage and wisdom and goodness to be kind to all people, knowing that I am being kind to You.

➤ *Catechism of the Catholic Church* 2443

First Tuesday in Lent
Trust

Isaiah 55:10-11; Matthew 6:7-15
R: From all their distress God rescues the just.

Dear Lord Jesus, there are people I know who command a lot of respect. Whatever they say is paid attention to. When they say to do something, it gets done. And these people are human. What about Your word, Lord?! You are God! If I listen to and trust a human being, how much more must I believe Your word? Let me trust You, Lord. Let me trust everything You have said. On You I can depend.

➤ *Catechism of the Catholic Church* 222, 227

First Wednesday in Lent
Rejecting God

Jonah 3:1-10; Luke 11:29-32
R: A heart contrite and humbled, O God, you will not spurn.

Dear Jesus, today's responsorial psalm at Mass is "A heart contrite and humbled, O God, you will not spurn." Do you spurn anyone, Lord Jesus? I spurn, or turn away, from some people I don't like, but do You? Do You turn away from anyone? May I always know, Lord, that You do not turn from anyone; it is we who turn from You. Thank You for this, Lord. I could not live without You. May my actions and my words and my thoughts always be pleasing to You, O Lord.

➤ *Catechism of the Catholic Church* 2567

First Thursday in Lent
Trust

Esther C:12, 14-16, 23-25; Matthew 7:7-12
R: Lord, on the day I called for help, you answered me.

Dear Jesus, You don't always give me what I ask for. I know that. I also know, Lord Jesus, that You will do what is best for me. You will make sure that whatever happens to me, the very best will come from it. Even when things are hard, You make certain that I am blessed by it. Thank You, Lord Jesus. Help me to trust in You, even when it doesn't seem like You are answering me.

➤ *Catechism of the Catholic Church* 1062

First Friday in Lent
Righteousness

Ezekiel 18:21-28; Matthew 5:20-26
R: If you, O Lord, mark iniquities, who can stand?

Lord Jesus, You talked about our righteousness. You want us to think about how "right" we are with You. Are our thoughts okay with You? Are our words okay with You? Are our actions okay with You? You don't want us to just think about being good, You want us to do good things, to think good things, to say good things. Only then are we righteous.

➤ *Catechism of the Catholic Church* 1042

First Saturday in Lent
An Eye for an Eye

Deuteronomy 26:16-19; Matthew 5:43-48
R: Blessed are they who follow the law of the Lord!

Lord God, I think that if someone is mean to me, I can be mean to that person. It's just fair that way. But You say it is not right. Just because someone else is mean does not mean I should be mean. I am given a choice: I can choose to be nice; I can choose to be like You, Lord, even when someone is mean to me. Help me to be strong, to be wise, to be good, Lord Jesus. To be mean is to be weak. You offer me more strength than that.

➤ *Catechism of the Catholic Church* 1970

Second Sunday in Lent
Hardships

Cycle A: Genesis 12:1-4a; 2 Timothy 1:8b-10; Matthew 17:1-9
R: Lord, let your mercy be on us, as we place our trust in you.

Dear Lord, today's second reading from St. Paul's letter to Timothy says, "Bear your share of hardship for the gospel." This means, Lord, that following You, being a Christian, is sometimes hard to do. Sometimes being a Christian is a hardship. Give me courage, Jesus, to be a good follower of You. Help me to do good when I don't want to. Help me to tell the truth even when it's easier to lie. Help me to do what I'm told to even when I can get out of it. This makes me a good Christian. This makes You proud of me.

Cycle B: Genesis 22:1-2, 9a, 10-13, 15-18; Romans 8:31b-34; Mark 9:2-10
R: I will walk before the Lord, in the land of the living.

Dear Jesus, You took Peter, James, and John and went up a high mountain. Once there, You rose above the earth and spoke with Elijah and Moses. When Peter, James, and John saw this, they were strengthened in their belief in You. They would need this strength, Lord, because soon You would be arrested and killed. Soon, things would get very hard for You and for them. Being a disciple isn't always easy, Lord. Give me strength to be a good disciple when things are hard in my life.

Cycle C: Genesis 15:5-12, 17-18; Philippians 3:17 - 4:1 or 3:20-4:1; Luke 9:28b-36
R: The Lord is my light and my salvation.

Dear Lord, the responsorial psalm in today's Mass is "The Lord is my light and my salvation." We wouldn't need to talk about God as light if we didn't have to deal with darkness. Darkness can be a lot of things: It can be hard times; it can be misunderstanding; it can be sin; it can be pain. I have to deal with darkness sometimes, Lord. Teach me to call on You, for You are my light.

➤ *Catechism of the Catholic Church* 2427

Second Monday in Lent
God's Vision

Daniel 9:4b-10; Luke 6:36-38
R: Lord, do not deal with us according to our sins.

Dear Lord, there are some people who think You focus on the bad things that we do. I sin every day, Lord. Do You see each sin? Do you get mad at me? Help me to remember, Lord, that You love me deeply. You want to forgive me. I just have to let You forgive me by telling You I'm sorry and trying again. You don't focus on the things I do wrong. You focus on the person You call me to become.

➤ *Catechism of the Catholic Church* 220

Second Tuesday in Lent
Seeing God

Isaiah 1:10, 16-20; Matthew 23:1-12
R: To the upright I will show the saving power of God.

Dear Lord, the responsorial psalm in today's Mass teaches me something very important. It is, "To the upright I will show the saving power of God." If I am upright — that is, if I am as good as I can be — then over time, I will be able to see You. People who don't care about being good can't see You work in the world, Lord. But those who try hard to be good can recognize Your ways; they can see how You work. I want to see You, Lord. Help me to be good, so I can see You.

➤ *Catechism of the Catholic Church* 31

Second Wednesday in Lent
Disappointment

Jeremiah 18:18-20; Matthew 20:17-28
R: Save me, O Lord, in your kindness.

Lord Jesus, how did Your disciples react when You told them that You would be crucified? You came to heal, to teach love, to challenge some to become better people. You told people that You are God, and instead of welcoming You and learning everything they could about You while You were with us, some of them got together and planned to kill You! Your disciples must have been so disappointed in the way some people turned from You. But they didn't allow this disappointment to keep them from preaching about You and telling everyone they could about You. Encourage me, too, Jesus, especially when I am disappointed.

➤ *Catechism of the Catholic Church* 943

Second Thursday in Lent
The Poor

Jeremiah 17:5-10; Luke 16:19-31
R: Blessed are they who hope in the Lord.

Dear Jesus, in the gospel read at today's Mass, the beggar Lazarus dies. He laid outside the rich man's house and no one ever helped him. There are so many people like Lazarus in our society, Lord. They suffer, and so few people even try to help them. Move me, Jesus, to try my best to help the poor — the friendless, the hungry, the angry, the homeless. I may not have money to give them, but I can pray for them; I can sacrifice for them. Don't let me forget them.

➤ *Catechism of the Catholic Church* 2462

Second Friday in Lent
Faith

Genesis 37:3-4, 12-13a, 17b-28a; Matthew 21:33-43, 45-46
R: Remember the marvels the Lord has done.

In today's Mass, Lord Jesus, the responsorial psalm is "Remember the marvels the Lord has done." Remembering what You have done is important for me. I know You have helped me in my life. I need to remember these times, because when things get hard for me, it is easy to think You don't care about me. Remembering what You have done for me in the past will help me to have faith in You and in Your love for me when I am having a tough time. May I always trust You, Lord.

➤ *Catechism of the Catholic Church* 164

Second Saturday in Lent
Prodigal Son

Micah 7:14-15, 18-20; Luke 15:1-3, 11-32
R: The Lord is kind and merciful.

Do I really understand, Lord Jesus, the story of the prodigal son? I've heard it so many times. I'd love to run off with a lot of money and be on my own. I would love to not have to depend on anyone. But, just as the story tells me, that isn't reality. We are supposed to depend on others. We need others. And others need us. That is how You made us, Lord. Help me to be glad for others in my life — for my family, my friends, my classmates, my teachers. Thank You, Lord, that I am not alone.

➤ *Catechism of the Catholic Church* 166

Third Sunday in Lent
Need

Cycle A: Exodus 17:3-7; Romans 5:1-2, 5-8; John 4:5-42 or 4:5-15, 19b-26, 39a, 40-42
R: If today you hear his voice, harden not your hearts.

Dear Jesus, You led the Israelites out of Egypt. You parted the Red Sea for them to cross. When they were thirsty in the desert, they began to complain. They even wished that they could go back to slavery. They did not trust that You would satisfy their thirst. They hadn't learned yet to look to You for what they needed. Help me, Lord, to come to You when I need. You know what I need, and You will always guide me and help me.

Cycle B: Exodus 20:1-17 or 20:1-3, 7-8, 12-17; 1 Corinthians 1:22-25; John 2:13-25
R: Lord, you have the words of everlasting life.

Lord Jesus, people needed rules to live by, so You gave us the Ten Commandments. Write these rules on my heart, Lord. They mean so much more than just what the words say. Each commandment teaches me about humankind and about You. Show me how to study the commandments and learn from them. Show me how I need them to grow in faith and in love.

Cycle C: Exodus 3:1-8a, 13-15; 1 Corinthians 10:1-6, 10-12; Luke 13:1-9
R: The Lord is kind and merciful.

Dear Lord, the Israelites needed someone to save them. They cried out to You, and You heard them. You sent Moses to lead them out of slavery. You hear my cries, too, Lord. When I am tired, when I am discouraged, when I am overwhelmed, You hear my cry and come to strengthen me, to encourage me, to give me courage. Thank You, Lord Jesus, for hearing my needs.

➤ *Catechism of the Catholic Church* 2648

Third Monday in Lent
Belief

2 Kings 5:1-15ab; Luke 4:24-30
R: Athirst is my soul for the living God. When shall I go and behold the face of God?

Lord Jesus, the people in Your hometown of Nazareth did not believe in You. Even though they had heard Your words and seen Your works, they did not believe. Deepen my belief in You, Lord Jesus. Deepen my belief in Your words — You will overcome all evil in the world; You are the way to peace, to joy. You can forgive any sin. You can heal all the ways that I am blind. Turn any doubt I have, Lord, into deep faith!

➤ *Catechism of the Catholic Church* 548

Third Tuesday in Lent
Forgiveness

Daniel 3:25, 34-43; Matthew 18:21-35
R: Remember your mercies, O Lord.

Lord Jesus, You told a story about a king who forgave a great debt that was owed him by a servant. The servant, however, refused to forgive another's debt. When the king found out about this, he was very angry with the servant for not forgiving like he forgave. Lord, You are very good to me: You forgive me when I do something wrong. How often do I withhold my forgiveness? Help me to see the ways that I hold a grudge. Help me to forgive.

➤ *Catechism of the Catholic Church* 2843

Third Wednesday in Lent
Rules

Deuteronomy 4:1, 5-9; Matthew 5:17-19
R: Praise the Lord, Jerusalem.

Dear Jesus, it's hard to obey all the rules. There are rules for everything. There are laws for everything. Instead of me being critical about all the rules and all the laws, help me to see how they are needed. Without them, Lord, things would get chaotic, and people could end up being mean to one another. Your laws, Lord, the commandments, are so very important; if they are obeyed rightly, we have peace. Rules and laws that are for our own good are blessed by You, Lord. Help me to respect these rules and obey them.

➤ *Catechism of the Catholic Church* 346

Third Thursday in Lent
Close to God

Jeremiah 7:23-28; Luke 11:14-23
R: If today you hear his voice, harden not your hearts.

Dear Jesus, the book of the prophet Jeremiah is one of the saddest books in the Bible. You called Jeremiah to tell Your people that they were wandering away from You. The people would not listen to Jeremiah. They did not care whether they were close to You, Lord. There are people today, Lord, who don't seem to care whether they are close to You or not. I pray for them, Lord. May I always care about my relationship with You. Keep me close to You, Jesus. May my example make others want to be close to You, too.

➤ *Catechism of the Catholic Church* 1

Third Friday in Lent
Hearing God

Hosea 14:2-10; Mark 12:28-34
R: I am the Lord your God: hear my voice.

Dear Lord, you have said, "I am the Lord your God: hear my voice." How do I hear Your voice, Lord? You speak through other people, my parents, my teachers, even my friends. You speak through the Bible. You speak through priests and bishops. There are many ways for me to hear You, Lord. Let me listen well!

➤ *Catechism of the Catholic Church* 1101

Third Saturday in Lent
Mercy

Hosea 6:1-6; Luke 18:9-14
R: It is mercy I desire, and not sacrifice.

Dear Jesus, what do You mean by mercy? You want us to have mercy on others. You value mercy above anything else we might offer You. By mercy You mean helping others with what they need — food, education, comfort, advice, friendship, and sharing our love for You. Teach me to show mercy, Lord. Praying to You everyday and showing mercy are the best ways to love and follow You.

➤ *Catechism of the Catholic Church* 2447

Fourth Sunday in Lent
Pleasing God

Cycle A: 1 Samuel 16:1b, 6-7, 10-13a; Ephesians 5:8-14; John 9:1-41 or 9:1, 6-9, 13-17, 34-38

R: The Lord is my shepherd; there is nothing I shall want.

Dear Lord, St. Paul tells us in his letter to the Ephesians that we should "learn what is pleasing to the Lord." What pleases You, Lord Jesus? When I try my best, when I don't complain, when I believe in myself, when I trust You, when I do what is right, when I reach out to others, when I don't talk back, when I say I'm sorry, when I pray. All these things please You. May Your Holy Spirit move me to please You every day.

Cycle B: 2 Chronicles 36:14-16, 19-23; Ephesians 2:4-10; John 3:14-21

R: Let my tongue be silenced, if I ever forget you!

Dear Lord, I have heard this verse from the Bible many, many times — "For God so loved the world that He gave His only Son." Jesus, You came to teach us, to show us how to love, to be with us for a while as a human being, and to save us by Your death and resurrection. Because of this, I want to please You with all I do. Pleasing You is my way of saying Thank You.

Cycle C: Joshua 5:9a, 10-12; 2 Corinthians 5:17-21; Luke 15:1-3, 11-32

R: Taste and see the goodness of the Lord.

Lord Jesus, when You told the story of the prodigal son, You gave us a great gift. Sometimes I'm like the son that ran away. Sometimes I'm like the son that stayed with the father and then got mad and jealous by how his brother was treated when he came home. Sometimes I'm even like the father, wanting someone to come home and be good. No matter how I am each day, Lord, You love me and understand me. Touch my heart that I may love You. Touch my mind that I may understand You.

➤ *Catechism of the Catholic Church 2447*

Fourth Monday in Lent
Peace

Isaiah 65:17-21; John 4:43-54
R: I will praise you, Lord, for you have rescued me.

Dear Lord Jesus, the prophet Isaiah writes about Jerusalem being a place where there will be rejoicing and happiness. Jerusalem now is divided. Bombs and gunfire are heard there everyday. Help me to realize, Lord, that peace in Jerusalem, in other parts of the world, in my country, and even in my home cannot happen unless we all work for peace. Every kind act of mine strengthens peace in the world. Every sinful act of mine strengthens evil in the world. Help me, Jesus, to strengthen peace!

➤ *Catechism of the Catholic Church* 2305

Fourth Tuesday in Lent
Openness to God

Exodus 47:1-9, 12; John 5:1-16
R: The Lord of hosts is with us; our stronghold is the God of Jacob.

Lord Jesus, people were not supposed to work on the Sabbath. A man was suffering from a disease, and You met him on the Sabbath. You healed him. The leaders of the Jews accused You of working because You healed a man. They got mad at You. How could they not see that doing good could never break the law?! They were jealous of You. I pray, Lord, that people in the world will be open to You and receive You without judging, without fear, without jealousy.

➤ *Catechism of the Catholic Church* 1989

Fourth Wednesday in Lent
Imitating Jesus

Isaiah 49:8-15; John 5:17-30
R: The Lord is gracious and merciful.

Jesus, You knew the Father very well. Through Your prayer, actions, and words, You grew in Your knowledge of the Father. You became like the Father. I will become more and more like You if I pray to You, if I behave as You want me to, if I speak about You. I want to be like You, Jesus. May I think of You all the time.

➤ *Catechism of the Catholic Church* 510

Fourth Thursday in Lent
Complaining

Exodus 32:7-14; John 5:31-47
R: Remember us, O Lord, as you favor your people.

Dear God, You got mad at Your people in the desert after Moses led them out of Egypt. Even after the parting of the waters of the Red Sea, even after the manna that miraculously was there on the morning they were so hungry, even after You told Moses to strike the rock and water came gushing forth from it, still Your people complained and turned away from You. Help me to realize, God, when my faith grows weak and I complain about going to Church or I don't take time to pray to You, help me remember that those miracles belong to me, too. That was my family, my ancestors in the faith, who followed Moses out of Egypt, who walked on the bottom of the Red Sea as the water piled up on either side. That was my family who saw that water spring from that rock. And You, O God, who did all those things, have something to say to me. May I listen to You, God. May I listen!

➤ *Catechism of the Catholic Church* 2578

Fourth Friday in Lent
Loving God

Wisdom 2:1a, 12-22; John 7:1-2, 10, 25-30
R: The Lord is close to the brokenhearted.

Lord Jesus, about one hundred years before You came, the writer of the book of Wisdom wrote, "For if the just one be the son of God, he [God] will defend him and deliver him from the hand of his foes. With revilement and torture let us put him to the test that we may have proof of his gentleness and try his patience." The Holy Spirit inspired this writer, one hundred years before You came, to write about how You would be treated. You were tortured; You were hated and reviled. And even though the people of Your time knew the writings in the book of Wisdom, the words did not matter to them. May they matter to me, Lord Jesus. May I show You today just how much You matter to me!

➤ *Catechism of the Catholic Church* 478; Galatians 2:20

Fourth Saturday in Lent
Question

Jeremiah 11:18-20; John 7:40-53
R: O Lord, my God, in you I take refuge.

Dear Lord, in the readings for today's Mass, I learn about Jeremiah, Your prophet. He was rejected like You were. He even referred to himself as a "trusting lamb led to slaughter." We call You, Jesus, the lamb of God. Why were You and Your prophets rejected? Why do people not want to hear Your messages? I know many did hear — I can read Jeremiah's message even today in the Bible. And millions upon millions still hear You, Jesus. But, why were you and Jeremiah put through so much suffering when you first came? I have all these questions in my heart, Lord. Teach me. Help me to hear Your answers.

➤ *Catechism of the Catholic Church* 385;
2 Thessalonians 2:7; 1 Timothy 3:16

Fifth Sunday in Lent
Heart

Cycle A: Ezekiel 37:12-14; Romans 8:8-11; John 11:1-45 or 11:3-7, 17, 20-27, 33b-45
R: With the Lord there is mercy and fullness of redemption.

Dear Lord, St. Paul wrote that those who are in the flesh cannot please God. This means that if I only worry about what my physical body wants and needs, then I'm not thinking about You. I should take good care of my body. I should also take good care of my soul. May I pray each day, Lord. May I come and spend some time with You each day.

Cycle B: Jeremiah 31:31-34; Hebrews 5:7-9; John 12:20-33
R: Create a clean heart in me, O God.

Dear Lord, You told the prophet Jeremiah that one day You would write Your law on the hearts of Your people. You did this writing, Lord, with Jesus. If I come to know Jesus as best I can, then I know that Your law is written on my heart; if I try to know Jesus, then I will not only be able to tell right from wrong, but will also have the courage and strength to do right and avoid what is wrong. May Your laws and Your ways be written on my heart, Lord. May I know Jesus by heart!

Cycle C: Isaiah 43:16-21; Philippians 3:8-14; John 8:1-11
R: The Lord has done great things for us; we are filled with joy.

Lord Jesus, St. Paul told the Philippians that he had been taken possession of by You. Do You possess me, Lord? Am I Yours? Do You want me? I know You want me, Lord. Help me to know how to give myself to You. Help me to realize what an adventure life can be if I say to You, "Here I am, Lord! Send me!"

➤ *Catechism of the Catholic Church* 2563

Optional Mass for Fifth Week in Lent
Glory

2 Kings 4:18b-21, 32-37; John 11:1-45
R: Lord, when your glory appears, my joy will be full.

Dear Lord, what does Your glory look like? Psalm 17 tells us that when Your glory appears, our joy will be full. What does Your glory look like, Jesus? Do I see some of Your glory now? Do I feel Your glory when I get close to You? Will You show me some of Your glory if I ask? Some people gave up everything after they saw or felt Your glory. Share Your glory with me, Lord. Show me Your glory!

➤ *Catechism of the Catholic Church* 319

Fifth Monday in Lent
Fear

Daniel 13:1-9, 15-17, 19-30, 33-62 or 13:14c-62; John 8:12-20
R: Even though I walk in the dark valley I fear no evil; for you are at my side.

Dear God, the responsorial psalm for today's Mass is one I hear often: "Even though I walk in the dark valley I fear no evil; for you are at my side." When I am afraid, Lord, I want to call to You and have the trust in You to not be so afraid. I know this takes a lot of prayer and a lot of trust. When I am afraid, Lord, may I call on You to calm me and increase my trust.

➤ *Catechism of the Catholic Church* 1808

Fifth Tuesday in Lent
Jesus Christ

Numbers 21:4-9; John 8:21-30
R: O Lord, hear my prayer, and let my cry come to you.

Lord Jesus, You referred to Yourself as "I AM." "I AM" is the name that God gives Himself in the Old Testament. All the Jews of Your day knew this, so they knew that You were claiming to be God when You used this title. Instead of rejoicing that God had become man and visited us, they grew angry and hated You. May I never doubt You, Jesus. May I rejoice in the fact that You love us so much that You became limited like us and lived and died with us. Thank You for coming. Thank You for Your resurrection, which shows us that You can overcome anything for us, even death.

➤ *Catechism of the Catholic Church* 430

Fifth Wednesday in Lent
Protection

Daniel 3:14-20, 91-92, 95; John 8:31-42
R: Glory and praise for ever!

Dear Lord, the stories in the book of Daniel scare me. Bad people put Shadrach, Meshach, and Abednego in a furnace because they wouldn't believe that any other god existed except You. But when the fires of the furnace were started, the fire didn't burn the three men. Help me to know, Lord, that no matter what happens to me, You will guard me. You will protect my heart and my soul and never let me be separated from You.

➤ *Catechism of the Catholic Church* 2815

Fifth Thursday in Lent
Names

Genesis 17:3-9; John 8:51-59
R: The Lord remembers his covenant for ever.

Dear Lord, names are very important to You. You changed Abram's name to Abraham. You changed Simon's name to Peter. My name is precious to You because it represents me. May I respect Your name, too, Lord. May I never use Your name in anger or frustration.

➤ *Catechism of the Catholic Church* 203

Fifth Friday in Lent
Tests

Jeremiah 20:10-13; John 10:31-42
R: In my distress I called upon the Lord, and he heard my voice.

Dear Jesus, I will be tested in my life as a Christian. Others will make me angry, and I will have to control myself. Things will not go as I want them to, and I will have to try to not complain. Friends will hurt my feelings and say they are sorry, and I will have to forgive them. Help me to behave like a Christian, Lord, and do what You would want me to do.

➤ *Catechism of the Catholic Church* 272

Fifth Saturday in Lent
Lost

Ezekiel 37:21-28; John 11:45-56
R: The Lord will guard us, as a shepherd guards his flock.

Lord Jesus, a shepherd stays with the sheep and keeps them together. They are safe when they are together. If one sheep wanders away, the shepherd will leave to find it and bring it back. You are a shepherd to me, Lord. If I wander away, You will come looking for me. If I get lost, You will find me and help me. You always know where I am.

➤ *Catechism of the Catholic Church* 336

Palm Sunday
Focus

Cycle A: Isaiah 50:4-7; Philippians 2:6-11; Matthew 26:14-27 or 27:11-54
R: My God, my God, why have you abandoned me?

Lord Jesus, You had just a few days to live. You were focused on the Father and on making sure Your disciples would be okay once Your suffering began. What was going to keep them from just going back to the life they had before You called them? They knew, however, that Almighty God had touched them through You. Maybe they didn't really know You were God, but they knew God was present in You. They believed, and the grace You would give them, Your words to them in those final days, would strengthen them. May these days until Easter be special for me, too, Jesus. May I walk with You as I never have before, watching, waiting, praying, listening.

Cycle B: Isaiah 50:4-7; Philippians 2:6-11; Mark 14:1 - 15:47 or 15:1-39
R: My God, my God, why have you abandoned me?

Dear Lord, the responsorial psalm for Palm Sunday is "My God, my God, why have you abandoned me?" You spoke these words from the cross. You knew the words; they are from Psalm 22, a psalm You would have prayed often during Your life. Did You think that Your Father had abandoned You? Were You afraid? I get afraid, too, Jesus. Your Father came to You when You called. I know You will come to me when I call.

Cycle C: Isaiah 50:4-7; Philippians 2:6-11; Luke 22:14 - 23:56 or 23:1-49
R: My God, my God, why have you abandoned me?

Dear Jesus, the reading of Your Passion — the story of Your arrest, beating, and crucifixion — is long. Sometimes I don't even hear it. But I know it should touch me. I know if I gave up my life for someone, I would want that person to pay attention to me, to thank me, and to hear what I had to say. Help me to enter into the story, Jesus. Help me to give You my attention, my time, my mind during this Mass and during this week. You have something powerful to say to me. May I be listening!

➤ *Catechism of the Catholic Church* 1708

Monday in Holy Week
Choice

Isaiah 42:1-7; John 12:1-11
R: The Lord is my light and my salvation.

Dear Jesus, You made blind people see. You raised people from the dead. You took diseases away from people. All these wonderful things You did and yet some people did not care; they didn't change their lives because of You. Help me to look at my life during this Holy Week, Jesus. Have I changed my life because of You? Have I tried hard to turn away from behavior that does not please You? Do I take time to pray to You every day, many times during the day? May I choose to do what pleases You, Lord. May I choose to be around You all the time.

➤ *Catechism of the Catholic Church* 1970

Tuesday in Holy Week
Strength

Isaiah 49:1-6; John 13:21-33, 36-38
R: I will sing of your salvation.

Dear Jesus, this is Holy Week. You will die on the cross on Friday. Yet, the Church uses these words for the responsorial psalm for today's Mass: "I will sing of your salvation." Should we be in the mood for singing? Help me to see, Lord, that rejoicing, singing, praising You actually makes us stronger. And if I am strong, then I can better handle the suffering and hardships of Good Friday.

➤ *Catechism of the Catholic Church* 1090

Wednesday in Holy Week
Pay Attention

Isaiah 50:4-9a; Matthew 26:14-25
R: Lord, in your great love, answer me.

Dear God, in the first reading from today's Mass, the prophet Isaiah proclaims that You have told him how to "speak to the weary a word that will rouse them." To rouse someone means to wake them up, make them pay attention. Your words made people pay attention, Jesus. Your life, Your words, Your death, Your resurrection rouse me; they make me pay attention. May I always be roused by You!

➤ *Catechism of the Catholic Church* 1618

Chrism Mass
Bishops

Isaiah 61:1-3a, 6a, 8b-9; Revelation 1:5-8; Luke 4:16-21
R: Forever I will sing the goodness of the Lord.

Dear Lord, the Chrism Mass — the Mass during which the bishop blesses the oils that will be used for the sacraments during the rest of the year — is a special Mass. You chose apostles to carry on Your message. We believe that our bishops are apostles, too. Thank You, Lord, for our bishop. May I pray for him every day. Thank You, too, for the sacraments.

➤ *Catechism of the Catholic Church* 1594

Holy Thursday/Mass of the Lord's Supper
Priests

Exodus 12:1-8, 11-14; 1 Corinthians 11:23-26; John 13:1-5
R: Our blessing cup is a communion with the Blood of Christ.

Dear Lord Jesus, this is the Mass during which we celebrate the priesthood. This is the Mass that celebrates the Last Supper, where You gave us Yourself under the signs of bread and wine, and You commanded that we do the same. Thank You, Lord, for the great gift of the Eucharist. Thank You for calling certain people to be priests and bring Your presence to our community in a special way. Thank You for all these things. Lead me, Lord, to a special reverence for these gifts. Amen.

➤ *Catechism of the Catholic Church* 1592

Good Friday/Passion
Celebration of the Lord's Passion

Isaiah 52:13-53:12; Hebrews 4:14-16; 5:7-9; John 18:1-19:42
R: Father, into your hands I commend my spirit.

Dear Jesus, how do You want me to feel and think about Your Passion? As I grow to know and love You, the suffering You went through is hard to listen to. It even makes me mad. Sometimes I wish we wouldn't read it. Help me to realize though, Lord Jesus, that each year You will gift me with a new thought about Your suffering — why You went through it and how Your suffering mixes with all the suffering in the world and helps heal it. Help me to let You know in some way, Lord, that I appreciate what You did to save me.

➤ *Catechism of the Catholic Church* 1708

Easter Season

Easter Vigil
Our Story

Genesis 1:1 - 2:2 or 1:1, 26-31a; Genesis 22:1-18 or 22:1-2, 9, 10-13, 15-18;
Exodus 14:15 - 15:1; Isaiah 54:5-14; Isaiah 55:1-11; Baruch 3:9-15, 32 - 4:4;
Ezekiel 36:16-17a, 18-28; Romans 6:3-11; Matthew 28:1-10 **(Cycle A)**; Mark
16:1-8 **(Cycle B)**; Luke 24:1-12 **(Cycle C)**
R: Create a clean heart in me, O God.

Risen Lord, the nine readings in today's Mass show the history of our salvation. If I listen closely, I will hear how You created us, how we made dumb
choices and turned away from You, and how You loved us enough to come to
us as a man to speak to us, to be with us, to give us the Eucharist, to suffer and
die for us, and to rise from the dead. What a story, Lord! Write this story on
my heart!

➤ *Catechism of the Catholic Church* 1026

Easter Sunday
Rejoice

Acts 10:34a, 37-43; Colossians 3:1-4 or 1 Corinthians 5:6b-8; John 20:1-9 (Morning Mass); Luke 24:13-35 (Afternoon or Evening Mass)
R: This is the day the Lord has made; let us rejoice and be glad.

Risen Lord, what does it mean to rejoice? I suppose it's like the happiest I have ever been and even more than that. To rejoice means to be so happy, you laugh out loud. That's how the disciples must have felt when they saw You resurrected. They saw You killed. They knew You had died. But here You were, standing in front of them. Help me to realize what an awesome moment for them that was. Help me to realize what an awesome moment for me that is! May I rejoice in You!

➤ *Catechism of the Catholic Church* 646; 1 Corinthians 15:35-50

Easter Monday
Resurrection

Acts 2:14, 22-33; Matthew 28:8-15
R: Keep me safe, O God; you are my hope.

Risen Lord, again the chief priests who had conspired to put You to death were presented with an opportunity to believe in You. The guard who had been at the tomb went to the chief priests and told them Your body was gone. Instead of being open to Your truth that You had risen, they again closed their hearts. Your Resurrection, Lord, is presented to me every Sunday at Mass. Open my heart, Lord. Stretch my mind. Challenge me to listen to You, to watch for You every day, but especially at Sunday Mass.

➤ *Catechism of the Catholic Church* 1166

Easter Tuesday
God-Centered

Acts 2:36-41; John 20:11-18
R: The earth is full of the goodness of the Lord.

Risen Lord, in the reading from Acts in today's Mass, St. Peter tells us to save ourselves from this corrupt generation. St. Peter is telling me to guard my mind and my heart from the evil things in our society. Help me to do this, Lord. Sometimes I don't know what is evil and what is good. Help me to guard my mind and my heart and to always keep You as the center of my life.

➤ *Catechism of the Catholic Church* 1618

Easter Wednesday
Sharing Christ

Acts 3:1-10; Luke 24:13-35
R: Rejoice, O hearts that seek the Lord.

Risen Lord, St. Peter says something so important in the reading from Acts in today's Mass. A crippled man comes to him and asks for money. St. Peter tells the man, "I have neither silver nor gold, but what I do have I give you: in the name of Jesus Christ the Nazorean, rise and walk." And the crippled man walked for the first time in his life. May I be like St. Peter, Lord. May I give to others what I have. I have You. May I share You with others. Teach me how.

➤ *Catechism of the Catholic Church* 152

Easter Thursday
Kindness

Acts 3:11-26; Luke 24:35-48
R: O Lord, our God, how wonderful your name in all the earth!

Risen Lord, when You appeared to Your disciples, they were afraid they were seeing a ghost. You immediately reassured them. You didn't take pleasure in their being afraid, nor did You make fun of them. Open my heart, Jesus, that I may never make fun of someone else or act happy and laugh when another is afraid or confused. May I step forward and immediately reassure them.

➤ *Catechism of the Catholic Church* 1832

Easter Friday
Cornerstone

Acts 4:1-12; John 21:1-14
R: The stone rejected by the builders has become the cornerstone.

Risen Lord, the responsorial psalm for today's Mass is "The stone rejected by the builders has become the cornerstone." A cornerstone is the strongest stone in a building. All the building's weight can lean on it. You are the cornerstone, Jesus. I can lean on You; I can depend on You. You are powerful and strong.

➤ *Catechism of the Catholic Church* 756

Easter Saturday
Example

Acts 4:13-21; Mark 16:9-15

R: I will give thanks to you, for you have answered me.

Risen Lord, You told Your disciples, "Go into the whole world and proclaim the Gospel to every creature." What does this command mean for me, Lord? How should Your message affect the way I talk, the way I act, the way I play, the way I am with my parents, teachers, and others? People should know I am a Christian by who I am becoming. Mold me, Jesus. Make me someone You can be proud of.

➤ *Catechism of the Catholic Church* 1709

Second Sunday in Easter
Awe

Cycle A: Acts 2:42-47; 1 Peter 1:3-9; John 20:19-31
R: Give thanks to the Lord, for he is good, his love is everlasting.

Risen Lord, in today's first reading at Mass it says, "Awe came upon everyone." Attract me, Lord, to You and Your message so that I may experience this awe, this awesome feeling that goes hand in hand with following You.

Cycle B: Acts 4:32-35; 1 John 5:1-6; John 20:19-31
R: Give thanks to the Lord, for he is good, his love is everlasting.

Risen Lord, many of the first readings from Mass in the Easter season come from the book of Acts. The Church is really smart, Lord. The Church uses this book to show us that faith is seen in our acts. Our acts can make our faith stronger if they are good; and our acts can weaken our faith if they are bad. Help me to read the book of Acts, Lord, and make sure that my acts strengthen my faith.

Cycle C: Acts 5:12-16; Revelation 1:9-11a, 12-13, 17-19; John 20:19-31
R: Give thanks to the Lord, for he is good, his love is everlasting.

Risen Lord, in today's gospel reading, the disciples are hiding. The leaders in Jerusalem have killed You (they think), and now they are ready to kill anyone else who talks about You. Even though the doors are locked, You appear in the middle of the room. This is how following You is, Lord; it is full of surprises. It is hard, yes, but our eyes get to see awesome things. Help me to see, Lord, by following You very closely.

➤ *Catechism of the Catholic Church* 1299

Second Monday in Easter
Courage

Acts 4:23-31; John 3:1-8
R: Blessed are all who take refuge in the Lord.

Risen Lord, Peter and John were arrested and threatened to never speak about You again. They went back to all the disciples and prayed. The house where they were praying shook, and they were all filled with the Holy Spirit. Show me too, Lord, that You will always be with me when I act like a follower of Yours, even in the face of those who want me to do something wrong. Give me courage through Your Holy Spirit!

➤ *Catechism of the Catholic Church* 1303

Second Tuesday in Easter
Generosity

Acts 4:32-37; John 3:7b-15
R: The Lord is king; he is robed in majesty.

Risen Lord, in the beginning of the Church, people brought all their possessions and gave them to the Church to give out to all so that they could have what they needed. No one went hungry. Help me to be willing to give up things that I have so that others can have the basic things, like food and shelter and clothes. Give me a generous heart, Lord.

➤ *Catechism of the Catholic Church* 1832

Second Wednesday in Easter
Psalms

Acts 5:17-26; John 3:16-21
R: The Lord hears the cry of the poor.

Risen Lord, help me to depend on the Bible to get to know You better. The psalms tell me a lot about You. Psalm 34 says, "The angel of the Lord encamps around those who fear him, and he delivers them." I know that to fear You means to respect You and know that You are first in our lives. So if I make You first, Lord, then You will surround me with Your presence and deliver me from anything that tries to harm me. Thank You, Lord!

➤ *Catechism of the Catholic Church* 2586

Second Thursday in Easter
Justice

Acts 5:27-33; John 3:31-36
R: The Lord hears the cry of the poor.

Risen Savior, sometimes it is hard to do what is right. The apostles proclaimed Your word, as You told them to do. They were arrested and yelled at. The apostles told their captors that it was better for them to obey God than to obey human leaders who made unjust laws. There are unjust laws today, too; laws that allow the killing of babies, laws that make one class of people better than others. May I pray for those who are willing to stand up against these unjust laws, Lord. And may I stand up against them, too, when I grow older.

➤ *Catechism of the Catholic Church* 2286

Second Friday in Easter
God's House

Acts 5:34-42; John 6:1-15
R: One thing I seek: to dwell in the house of the Lord.

Risen Lord, the responsorial psalm for today's Mass is "One thing I seek: to dwell in the house of the Lord." This makes me think of heaven. I want to live in heaven. But, Lord, help me to realize that I can and should live in Your "house" all the time. Living in Your house means living the way You ask me to live. What do You ask of me, Lord? Help me to hear Your answer.

➤ *Catechism of the Catholic Church* 661

Second Saturday in Easter
Power

Acts 6:1-7; John 6:16-21
R: Lord, let your mercy be on us, as we place our trust in you.

Risen Lord, I hear the story of Your walking on the sea at other times during the year. But, hearing it right after celebrating Easter is different. I have just celebrated the power of Your resurrection. Not even dying could keep hold of You, so how could I be surprised that walking on water would be hard for You!? Remind me, Lord, of Your power when I am in need so that I can call upon You!

➤ *Catechism of the Catholic Church* 269

Third Sunday in Easter
Worship

Cycle A: Acts 2:14, 22-33; 1 Peter 1:17-21; Luke 24:13-35
R: Lord, you will show us the path of life.

Risen Lord, Peter delivers a sermon in today's first reading from the book of Acts. He tells the Jews that You are the one who the Bible said would come. You, Jesus, lived long before David the king, long before Abraham, long before Adam and Eve. You, Jesus, are God. You have lived forever, and You will live forever. This is a mystery that I cannot understand, but I believe. May I never doubt Your power.

Cycle B: Acts 3:13-15, 17-19; 1 John 2:1-5a; Luke 24:35-48
R: Lord, let your face shine on us.

Risen Lord, John tells us in his letter in the Bible that if we say we believe in You but do not act with kindness and generosity, then we are liars. We cannot truly believe in You if we do not behave as You would want us to behave. I cannot say I have a friend if I do things that my friend doesn't like. It is the same with You, Lord. Help me to act in ways that please You.

Cycle C: Acts 5:27-32, 40b-41; Revelation 5:11-14; John 21:1-19 or 21:1-14
R: I will praise you, Lord, for you have rescued me.

Risen Lord, the Bible tells us to worship You. Why is it good for us to worship You, Lord? I know You are powerful and loving. I know You made me and I do want to thank You and get to know You, but why is it good for me to worship You? Show me, Lord, that when I worship, I feel joy. When I worship, I realize that I have You to depend on. When I worship, I feel powerful because I know that I am not alone.

➤ *Catechism of the Catholic Church* 2096

Third Monday in Easter
Martyrdom

Acts 6:8-15; John 6:22-29
R: Blessed are they who follow the law of the Lord!

Risen Lord, Stephen is the first disciple we know of who is killed after Your resurrection. Stephen is killed for talking about You. I pray for those who are in danger for loving You, Lord. Guard their hearts and minds so that even if they are threatened with death, they will stay close to You and know Your peace and love.

➤ *Catechism of the Catholic Church* 2506

Third Tuesday in Easter
Witness to Christ

Acts 7:51 - 8:1a; John 6:30-35
R: Into your hands, O Lord, I commend my spirit.

Risen Lord, when Stephen was being killed, he cried out, "Behold, I see the heavens opened and the Son of Man standing at the right hand of God." Those who love you greatly receive great things from You, Lord. Help me to show You great love, Lord.

➤ *Catechism of the Catholic Church* 2473

Third Wednesday in Easter
Holy Spirit

Acts 8:1b-8; John 6:35-40
R: Let all the earth cry out to God with joy.

Risen Lord, even though the disciples and apostles knew Stephen was killed for preaching about You, they continued to preach. Your Spirit gave them courage. Your Spirit told them what to say and where to go. Your Spirit healed many people through the touch of the disciples and apostles. Give me Your Spirit, too, Lord. Fill me with courage and wisdom!

➤ *Catechism of the Catholic Church* 690

Third Thursday in Easter
Obedience

Acts 8:26-40; John 6:44-51
R: Let all the earth cry out to God with joy.

Risen Lord, Your Spirit told Philip where to go to teach people about You, and Philip went. I "hear" You tell me to do many things — obey my parents, work and study hard, be good to my body, read the Bible. May I do what You ask of me, Lord, just like Philip.

➤ *Catechism of the Catholic Church* 2340

Third Friday in Easter
St. Paul

Acts 9:1-20; John 6:52-59
R: Go out to all the world and tell the Good News.

Risen Lord, what attracted You to Saul? He was having Christians arrested. He knew that they could be killed; so, he hunted them. He hated Christians, and yet You still went to the trouble of converting or changing him. You took away his sight. You spoke to him and told him to stop hurting Your people. You changed his name to Paul, and he became one of Your strongest preachers. Paul must have known Your deep love, for not even his bad actions separated him from You. May I realize that You never give up on anyone, Lord.

➤ *Catechism of the Catholic Church* 2657; Romans 15:13

Third Saturday in Easter
Power

Acts 9:31-42; John 6:60-69
R: How shall I make a return to the Lord for all the good he has done for me?

Risen Lord, Peter was preaching about You. He came upon a Christian woman who had died. He raised her to life by calling upon You. Once again, everyone could see that You have power over life and death. Help me to realize that You have power over all things in my life, Lord. Help me to trust in Your power.

➤ *Catechism of the Catholic Church* 2725

Fourth Sunday in Easter
Heart

Cycle A: Acts 2:14a, 36-41; 1 Peter 2:20b-25; John 10:1-10
R: The Lord is my shepherd; there is nothing I shall want.

Dear Risen Lord, I can't imagine wanting something so bad that I would be willing to give up everything for it. Maybe there is a person in my life for whom I would give up everything. Help me to know You so dearly, Lord, that I will be willing to give up all I have for You. Be the center of my heart.

Cycle B: Acts 4:8-12; 1 John 3:1-2; John 10:11-18
R: The stone rejected by the builders has become the cornerstone.

Risen Lord, what do You look like? What does Your resurrected body look like? St. John's letter tells us that we will have a glorified body like Yours after You come again. How did St. John know that? Did You tell him to tell us? May I be so close to You, Lord, that I can tell people what You want them to know!

Cycle C: Acts 13:14, 43-52; Revelation 7:9, 14b-17; John 10:27-30
R: We are his people, the sheep of his flock.

Risen Savior, the words of St. John's gospel tell me that nothing can take me away from You, not even my lack of faith. When I don't feel like my faith is all that strong, remind me, Lord, that You are still holding on to me. Remind me that You always love me. Remind me how important I am to You. May I always show You how important You are to me.

➤ *Catechism of the Catholic Church* 2563

Fourth Monday in Easter
Care for All

Acts 11:1-18; John 10:1-10
R: Athirst is my soul for the living God.

Risen Lord, You do not reject anyone. St. Peter thought You meant only to save the Jews, and You had to show him in a dream You were for everyone. Help me to pray for everyone, Lord, because You care for everyone. Help me to be concerned for the people in Africa, Asia, South America. May I lift them up to You in prayer, especially those who are hurting, because You care about them. And when I pray to You for them, You help them even more because You love that I care. Give me a big heart, Lord.

➤ *Catechism of the Catholic Church* 2793

Fourth Tuesday in Easter
Holy Spirit

Acts 11:19-26; John 10:22-30
R: All you nations, praise the Lord.

Risen Lord, after St. Stephen was killed, Your people went to many other places to preach about You. When they went as far as Greece, they found others who were preaching about You already! In so few years, word about You had spread that far, without the aid of computers or telephones or even mail! The Holy Spirit drove people to spread Your message of love and compassion. May the Spirit fill me, Lord. May the Spirit drive me!

➤ *Catechism of the Catholic Church* 1108

Fourth Wednesday in Easter
Setting Apart

Acts 12:24 - 13:5a; John 12:44-50
R: O God, let all the nations praise you!

Risen Lord, in the book of Acts the Holy Spirit tells the community that Saul and Barnabas should be "set apart . . . for the work to which I have called them." What am I set apart to do, Lord? What are You calling me to do? Help me to listen to You and be willing to do all that You ask of me.

➤ *Catechism of the Catholic Church* 31

Fourth Thursday in Easter
Power

Acts 13:13-25; John 13:16-20
R: For ever I will sing the goodness of the Lord.

Risen Lord, it would make me feel really funny and awkward if I washed the feet of my friends. You washed Your disciples' feet to show them that true power comes in service to others for love of God. Teach me about this true power, Lord. It's not the power of the world. The world likes power to be loud and forceful. Your power is quiet and gentle, confident; after all, You are God. Teach me Your ways, Lord Jesus.

➤ *Catechism of the Catholic Church* 1704

Fourth Friday in Easter
Believe!

Acts 13:26-33; John 14:1-6
R: You are my Son; this day I have begotten you.

Risen Lord, to believe in something is not weak. Believing is powerful! When I truly believe in something or someone, then I act differently, I think differently. When I believe in a friendship, that changes how I act around my friend. I trust him. I share with him. I open myself to him. I believe in You, Lord Jesus. So, I trust You. I share with You. I open myself to You.

➤ *Catechism of the Catholic Church* 227

Fourth Saturday in Easter
Choice

Acts 13:44-52; John 14:7-14
R: All the ends of the earth have seen the saving power of God.

Risen Lord, as the reading from Acts shows us today, following You is choice. The older I get, the more I realize that to be good, to be kind, to do the right thing is not as easy as it used to be. To be good, to be like You, is a choice. I must choose. To be able to choose You, Lord, is a great gift. What if I didn't have You to choose? What if Your grace and strength weren't there for me to receive? Thank you, Lord, that I can choose You.

➤ *Catechism of the Catholic Church* 1033

Fifth Sunday in Easter
Example

Cycle A: Acts 6:1-7; 1 Peter 2:4-9; John 14:1-12
R: Lord, let your mercy be on us, as we place our trust in you.

Risen Lord, in today's readings to be a Christian is a very public thing. These readings were written before persecutions began. Jews joined Greeks in worship of God through Jesus. How public do I allow my worship of You to be? Am I ashamed to show my faith? Give me courage, Lord. Let me be proud to stand up for You.

Cycle B: Acts 9:26-31; 1 John 3:18-24; John 15:1-8
R: I will praise you, Lord, in the assembly of your people.

Risen Lord, Saint John writes in the second reading today that we ought to love in deed and in truth. That means that I should show love through what I do and through what I know is true. I know that You are Lord. I know that You rose from the dead in order to take my hand and show me how to live, not like the world wants me to live — wanting money and things and lots of food and ignoring the people who are hurting — but how You want me to live — aware of Christian values, aware of those who are hurting, aware of the example I give to others.

Cycle C: Acts 14:21-27; Revelation 21:1-5a; John 13:31 - 33a, 34-35
R: I will praise your name forever, my king and my God.

Risen Lord, today's responsorial psalm is "I will praise your name forever, my king and my God." Show me, Lord, that when I praise You, I am happy. To praise brings on joy. Joy makes me feel strong and capable of taking on anything. It is smart to praise You, Lord. It gives me confidence. It connects me with You. And You are God!

➤ *Catechism of the Catholic Church* 2639

Fifth Monday in Easter
Give God Credit

Acts 14:5-18; John 14:21-26
R: Not to us, O Lord, but to your name give the glory.

Risen Jesus, what does this responsorial psalm for today's Mass mean? It is "Not to us, O Lord, but to your name give the glory." Does this mean that we are to give all the credit to You for all the good that we do? Is it You and Your power within us that helps us to do good things, to do well on tests, to have courage to be kind to even the outcast kids? Is this Your power? Let me learn, Lord, to thank You for all the good that I can do. Thank You for helping me. Thank You for being within me and for caring about me.

➤ *Catechism of the Catholic Church* 224

Fifth Tuesday in Easter
Courage

Acts 14:19-28; John 14:27-31a
R: Your friends make known, O Lord, the glorious splendor of your kingdom.

Risen Lord, Paul was *stoned* for talking about You. How must that feel — to be stoned, to have people throw rocks at you as hard as they can? Yet, Paul got back up and went back into that city. I can't imagine the courage he must have had. This was courage that You gave him. Give me this kind of courage, Lord, when I am attacked by other kids who want me to act in ways that would disappoint You; by the attraction of movies and shows that I shouldn't watch; by my own lack of motivation when I should study and work. Give me courage, Lord, to stand up for what is right, like Paul did.

➤ *Catechism of the Catholic Church* 2742

Fifth Wednesday in Easter
Arguing

Acts 15:1-6; John 15:1-8
R: Let us go rejoicing to the house of the Lord.

Risen Lord, in the reading from Acts Your followers are arguing over what they should do. Things weren't clear to them all the time. Some wanted to make certain rules and others did not. Our Church is like that today, too. We argue over what should be and should not be in our Church. Be with us, Lord, as we argue. May we do what You want us to and make rules that please You. Remind me, Lord, to pray for our Church every day.

➤ *Catechism of the Catholic Church* 2623

Fifth Thursday in Easter
Example

Acts 15:7-21; John 15:9-11
R: Proclaim God's marvelous deeds to all the nations.

Risen Lord, the responsorial psalm tells me to proclaim Your marvelous deeds to all the nations. How am I supposed to do this, Lord? Do I stand up in the middle of my classmates and yell, "God is good!"? Or, do I ask You every day to be with me, to be in my mind that I may think only what is good, to be in my mouth that I may say only what is good, to be in my hands that I may do only what is good. May I speak no evil, do no evil, and think no evil, Lord. Let me proclaim You and Your ways by how I live.

➤ *Catechism of the Catholic Church* 935

Fifth Friday in Easter
Is God Boring?

Acts 15: 22-31; John 15:12-17
R: I will give you thanks among the peoples, O Lord.

Risen Lord, today's first reading shows me that Your ways are not meant to be a burden on anyone. Living according to Your way is freeing; it brings peace. It brings a deep joy. The world tries to tell me, Lord, that living Your way is boring. Help me to discover the joy of living Your way, Lord. Help me to discover what is true.

➤ *Catechism of the Catholic Church* 2500

Fifth Saturday in Easter
Holy Spirit

Acts 16:1-10; John 15:18-21
R: Let all the earth cry out to God with joy.

Risen Lord, may I listen carefully to the words of the first reading today. The apostles are traveling to city after city proclaiming You. But the Holy Spirit does not allow them to go into certain cities. How did the Spirit keep them from entering the cities? Were the apostles uneasy about going and did they know the Spirit didn't want them to go there because of this uneasiness? Teach me, Lord, to listen to the Spirit, Your Spirit, within me. May I know what Your Spirit wants me to do and not do.

➤ *Catechism of the Catholic Church* 1830

Sixth Sunday in Easter
Peace

Cycle A: Acts 8:5-8, 14-17; 1 Peter 3:15-18; John 14:15-21
R: Let all the earth cry out to God with joy.

Risen Lord, after Your resurrection, Your disciples went to many other nations proclaiming You. Only when all nations believe in You and live according to Your ways will we have peace in the world. I pray, Lord, for my country and for all other countries that we may turn to You and cry out to You to heal those who are hurting and show us how to live in peace.

Cycle B: Acts 10:25-26, 34-35, 44-48; 1 John 4:7-10; John 15:9-17
R: The Lord has revealed to the nations his saving power.

Risen Lord, You have shown us how to have peace. We must live how You taught us to live — caring for one another, being kind, sharing, doing good. May my example move others to know and love You, Lord. The more we learn to love You, the sooner we will have peace in our world.

Cycle C: Acts 15:1-2, 22-29; Revelation 21:10-14, 22-23; John 14:23-29
R: O God, let all the nations praise you!

Risen Lord, the reading from the book of Revelation assures me that we will experience peace in the world. When You come again, You will bring peace. And those who have lived as You have said will recognize You when You come. May I live like You tell me to, Lord, so that I will recognize You when You come again.

➤ *Catechism of the Catholic Church* 2820

Sixth Monday in Easter
Support

Acts 16:11-15; John 15:26 - 16:4a
R: The Lord takes delight in his people.

Risen Savior, You notice our needs. Lydia from today's first reading wanted to know all about You, and Paul needed support and a place to make his home base while he preached in that area. You brought Paul and Lydia together, and through Lydia's wealth, Paul was able to preach about You for a long time. You know what we need, Lord. You know what I need. May I trust You to give me what I need.

➤ *Catechism of the Catholic Church* 1926

Sixth Tuesday in Easter
Listening

Acts 16:22-34; John 16:5-11
R: Your right hand saves me, O Lord.

Risen Lord, why didn't Paul and Silas run when you caused the earthquake and the doors of the jail flew open? Your Spirit must have told them that the guard's heart was open enough to become a follower. So, instead of running away, Paul and Silas stayed in the jail and, by doing this, won all the guards over to following You. May I be able to hear Your Spirit as well as Paul and Silas did, Lord. Teach me to listen to You.

➤ *Catechism of the Catholic Church* 2578

Sixth Wednesday in Easter
Now

Acts 17:15, 22 - 18:1; John 16:12-15
R: Heaven and earth are full of your glory.

Risen Lord, Paul spoke to the people of Athens. Many of them doubted his words when he told them about Your resurrection. Others told Paul that they would hear him again later. I wonder how many came back to hear Paul again. I wonder if they missed the opportunity to get to know You and become Your follower. May I not put You off, Lord, for later in my life. May I follow You now.

➤ *Catechism of the Catholic Church* 2784

Sixth Thursday in Easter
Example

Acts 18:1-8; John 16:16-20
R: The Lord has revealed to the nations his saving power.

Risen Lord, when Your Spirit sent Paul to the city of Corinth to preach about You, many in the town came to believe in You. Many people stepped forward to help Paul. What about my town, Lord? Do most of the people I know believe in You? Can I tell whether or not they believe in You by how they act? Can they tell if I believe in You by the way I am?

➤ *Catechism of the Catholic Church* 2182

Sixth Friday in Easter
Hardships

Acts 18:9-18; John 16:20-23
R: God is king of all the earth.

Risen Lord, there were people in Corinth who wanted to have Paul arrested. They tried to start trouble for him. This time Paul did not end up in prison. And Paul wasn't mean to those who didn't like him. Troublemakers are every-where, Lord. Sometimes they will cause trouble for me; sometimes they won't. Give me the grace to do what is right even when someone is being mean to me, Lord.

➤ *Catechism of the Catholic Church* 1435

Sixth Saturday in Easter
King

Acts 18:23-28; John 16:23b-28
R: God is king of all the earth.

Risen Lord, this is the second day in a row that "God is king of all the earth" is the responsorial psalm. If You are king of all the earth, then that means You have control. In the end, Lord, You have control. This is why I don't have to be afraid. This is important for me to know. You are king of the earth, Lord Jesus. And, You are king of my life, too.

➤ *Catechism of the Catholic Church* 671

Ascension of the Lord
Vocation

Cycle A: Acts 1:1-11; Ephesians 1:17-23; Matthew 28:16-20
R: God mounts his throne to shouts of joy: a blare of trumpets for the Lord.

Risen Lord, Your disciples stood looking up into the sky as You disappeared into the clouds. I bet they thought to themselves, "Now what?" It was now time for them to start doing what You had taught them for three years to do: to tell others about You. That's my job, too, Lord. Show me how to tell others about You.

Cycle B: Acts 1:1-11; Ephesians 1:17-23 or Ephesians 4:1-13 or 4:1-7, 11-13; Mark 16:15-20
R: God mounts his throne to shouts of joy: a blare of trumpets for the Lord.

Risen Lord, the second reading from Ephesians teaches us that some are called to be prophets, some are called to be evangelists, some are called to be pastors and teachers, others ministers. These roles all meant specific things in Your day. Today, also, You call each of us to a certain way of following You. Help me to discover what You call me to, Lord. As You rose into the heavens, may I rise to Your call.

Cycle C: Acts 1:1-11; Ephesians 1:17-23 or Hebrews 9:24-28, 10:19-23; Luke 24:46-53
R: God mounts his throne to shouts of joy: a blare of trumpets for the Lord.

Risen Lord, I wish I could have seen You rise into the air. I wish I could have seen many of the miracles You performed: walking on the water, raising the dead, changing water into wine. Give me eyes to see the miracles You perform today, Lord. Teach me to see You. Teach me to hear You.

➤ *Catechism of the Catholic Church* 672

Seventh Sunday in Easter
Prayer

Cycle A: Acts 1:12-14; 1 Peter 4:13-16; John 17:1-11a
R: I believe that I shall see the good things of the Lord in the land of the living.

Risen Lord, after Your ascension, what did the disciples do? They gathered together to pray. They gathered together to ask You just what they needed to do first. Teach me, Lord, before I undertake any important task, to come to You in prayer and ask for Your guidance.

Cycle B: Acts 1:15-17, 20a, 20c-26; 1 John 4:11-16; John 17:11b-19
R: The Lord has set his throne in heaven.

Risen Lord, after Your ascension, the disciples gathered to pray and choose another to fill the shoes of Judas. They left this decision to You, and so they prayed for Your Spirit's guidance as to which man would replace Judas. The choice fell to Matthias. Teach me, Lord, to pray to Your Spirit before I make big decisions. Show me Your will.

Cycle C: Acts 7:55-60; Revelation 22:12-14, 16-17, 20; John 17:20-26
R: The Lord is king, the most high over all the earth.

Risen Lord, just before they threw stones at Stephen to kill him, the enemies of Stephen heard him say he was seeing Jesus in the sky, standing at the right hand of God. Stephen was faithful to You. Stephen loved You. And, at the end of his life, You were there with him as he was killed. Give me faith, Lord, that You will be with me at all times, especially when I am in trouble.

➤ *Catechism of the Catholic Church* 2616

Seventh Monday in Easter
Holy Spirit

Acts 19:1-8; John 16:29-33
R: Sing to God, O kingdoms of the earth.

Risen Lord, You told Your disciples that when You returned to the Father, You would send Your Spirit. These readings following Your ascension show the power of the Spirit. Your Spirit is alive and active in the world. Show me, Lord, how to see the action of the Spirit in the world. Help me to see Your hand at work!

➤ *Catechism of the Catholic Church* 691

Seventh Tuesday in Easter
Discipleship

Acts 20:17-27; John 17:1-11a
R: Sing to God, O kingdoms of the earth.

Risen Lord, St. Paul in his speech to the people at Ephesus tells them that he knows his time on earth is coming to an end. He knows that he has made many enemies because he has preached about You. Your Spirit tells him that he will soon be thrown into prison and die. But Paul is at peace. He knows he has done all he could to save as many people as he could by telling them about You. May I be able to say that at the end of my life, too, Lord. May I never let people come in and out of my life without allowing them to see my faith in You and my love for You.

➤ *Catechism of the Catholic Church* 1816

Seventh Wednesday in Easter
St. Paul

Acts 20:28-38; John 17:11b-19
R: Sing to God, O kingdoms of the earth.

Risen Lord, when St. Paul told the people that they wouldn't see him again, they knelt down with him and prayed. St. Paul knew that he would die soon. The people he preached to loved him but knew he did not belong to them. Paul belonged to You. Give me strength like Paul's, Lord, that I may follow You through thick and thin. May others love me because I reflect Your love. May I always seek to do Your will.

➤ *Catechism of the Catholic Church* 1011

Seventh Thursday in Easter
Grace

Acts 22:30; 23:6-11; John 17:20-26
R: Keep me safe, O God; you are my hope.

Risen Lord, when St. Paul was arrested, You stood by him and strengthened him. Eventually, Paul would be taken to Rome where he would be killed. You didn't stop the evil that was happening to him, but You were with him and he knew it. Your grace filled him and gave him peace and even joy till the end. Some of my hurts don't go away either, Lord, even when I ask You to take them away. But You stay with me and give me strength to make it through the hurts. Let me trust Your will, Lord. Sometimes those hurts are forming me and teaching me things I wouldn't otherwise know or understand. Help me to see Your presence with me through it all.

➤ *Catechism of the Catholic Church* 1999

Seventh Friday in Easter
Talents

Acts 25:13b-21; John 21:15-19
R: The Lord has established his throne in heaven.

Risen Savior, St. Paul believed in You. Even when the leaders were yelling at him and asking for his death from the Roman authorities, still Paul kept telling them that You had risen from the dead and established Your throne in heaven. You gave Paul strength and wisdom, and he used your gifts well. May I use the gifts that You have given me, Lord, as well as did St. Paul. St. Paul, pray for me.

➤ *Catechism of the Catholic Church* 2429

Seventh Saturday in Easter
Seeing God

Acts 28:16-20, 30-31; John 21:20-25
R: The just will gaze on your face, O Lord.

Risen Lord, what is it like to see You? Today's responsorial psalm says that the just will gaze on Your face. Moses' face shone when he saw You. Some people I know seem to shine when they talk about You. What is it about You, Lord, that makes people seem to glow? Give me the wisdom to know this, Lord. Give me the desire to see Your face.

➤ *Catechism of the Catholic Church* 208

Pentecost Vigil Mass
Renewal

Cycle A, B, C: Genesis 11:1-9, or Exodus 19:3-8a, 16-20b, or Ezekiel 37:1-14, or Joel 3:15; Romans 8:22-27; John 7:37-39
R: Lord, send out your Spirit, and renew the face of the earth.

Lord Jesus, sometimes I just want to start over again. Sometimes I feel so tired and so depressed that I just want something to make me feel renewed, re-energized. Teach me to ask Your Spirit to breathe new life into me. Lord, send out Your Spirit, and renew the face of the earth.

➤ *Catechism of the Catholic Church* 1989

Pentecost
Holy Spirit

Acts 2:1-11 **(Cycles A, B, C)**; 1 Corinthians 12:3b-7, 12-13 **(Cycle A)**; 1 Corinthians 12:3b-7, 12-13, or Galatians 5:16-25 **(Cycle B)**; 1 Corinthians 12:3b-7, 12-13, or Romans 8:8-17 **(Cycle C)**; John 20:19-23 **(Cycle A)**; John 20:19-23, or John 15:26-27, 16:12-15 **(Cycle B)**; John 20:19-23, or John 14:15-16, 23b-26 **(Cycle C)**
R: Lord, send out your Spirit, and renew the face of the earth.

Dear Holy Spirit, You inspired St. Thomas Aquinas to write one of the Church's most beautiful hymns about You. It is called the *Veni, Sancte Spiritus*. It is also a prayer, and we hear it on Pentecost. May I study its words and make it part of my daily prayer: "Heal our wounds, our strength renew; On our dryness pour your dew; Wash the stains of guilt away: Bend the stubborn heart and will; Melt the frozen, warm the chill; Guide the steps that go astray."

➤ *Catechism of the Catholic Church* 700

Ordinary Time

Tenth Sunday in Ordinary Time
Knowledge of God

Cycle A: Hosea 6:3-6; Romans 4:18-25; Matthew 9:9-13
R: To the upright I will show the saving power of God.

Dear Lord, Your prophet Hosea tells us that You want us to know all we can about You. Give me this desire, Lord. Let me find out all I can about You. Let me make You my lifetime research project! I can find out about You through prayer, through the Sacraments, through the Bible. No matter where You call me in life; no matter what I choose to do, may I commit myself to knowing You!

Cycle B: Genesis 3:9-15; 2 Corinthians 4:13 - 5:1; Mark 3:20-35
R: With the Lord there is mercy, and fullness of redemption.

Lord God, what did Adam and Eve lose when they had to leave the garden? They lost being able to see You. They lost being able to know You. Now, we can only know You by searching hard, by having and nurturing our faith, and by the gift of grace. Grant me the grace to know You, Lord. May I be willing to search for You.

Cycle C: 1 Kings 17:17-24; Galatians 1:11-19; Luke 7:11-17
R: I will praise you, Lord, for you have rescued me.

Dear Lord, today's responsorial psalm calls me to praise You for rescuing me. What have You rescued me from? You rescue me from ignorance about You — You have given me a great faith to build upon. You rescue me from dangers I may not even be aware of. You rescue me from my sins. I thank You, Lord, for the knowledge I have of You!

➤ *Catechism of the Catholic Church 35*

Tenth Monday in Ordinary Time
Encouragement

Year 1: 2 Corinthians 1:1-7; Matthew 5:1-12
R: Taste and see the goodness of the Lord.

Dear Lord Jesus, St. Paul calls You the God of all encouragement. When I need encouraging, Lord, help me to remember to look to You for the help, the strength, and the courage I need. Help me to know how to encourage others so that I may be like You.

Year 2: 1 Kings 17:1-6; Matthew 5:1-12
R: Our help is from the Lord, who made heaven and earth.

Lord Jesus, by giving the Beatitudes to the poor, You encouraged them — and us — when we are mourning, when we are persecuted, when we are hungry for justice. Your words also make us want to be humble, merciful, and meek. And always, Lord, may we strive to be makers of peace.

➤ *Catechism of the Catholic Church* 1946

Tenth Tuesday in Ordinary Time
Approval

Year 1: 2 Corinthians 1:18-22; Matthew 5:13-16
R: Lord, let your face shine on me.

Dear Lord, I want You to be proud of me. You see my every action, my every thought, my every feeling. You see what I do with each day. I want You to approve of how I respond to others, fulfill my duties, and treat my family, friends, and community members. Lord, I want Your face to shine on me.

Year 2: 1 Kings 17:7-16; Matthew 5:13-16
R: Lord, let your face shine on us.

Dear Lord, help me to show approval of others. May I never look down upon another or do something or say something to make another feel ashamed or less than me. Give me the strength to treat all with kindness, even if they are not my friends. Make me like You, Lord.

➤ *Catechism of the Catholic Church* 219

Tenth Wednesday in Ordinary Time
Obedience

Year 1: 2 Corinthians 3:4-11; Matthew 5:17-19
R: Holy is the Lord our God.

Dear Lord, You tell me to obey the commandments. I know that this means to be nice to everyone, to do what I am asked at school and at home, to pray to You, to practice listening to You, and to care for others as best as I can. This is hard sometimes, especially when my emotions get in the way. Be with me, Jesus. Give me strength. Help me to be aware that the Spirit is within me; all I have to do is call on the Spirit and keep trying.

Year 2: 1 Kings 18:20-39; Matthew 5:17-19
R: Keep me safe, O God; you are my hope.

Dear Lord, show me that what I do, what I say, and even how I say it, has an impact on others. Other kids see and hear how I act and speak. Others feel the attitude in my words: Am I impatient? Am I ridiculing? Am I playful? Show me that my example either builds others up or it brings them down. May I be obedient to You, Jesus, by giving an example that builds others up.

➤ *Catechism of the Catholic Church* 564

Tenth Thursday in Ordinary Time
Sincerity

Year 1: 2 Corinthians 3:15 - 4:1, 3-6; Matthew 5:20-26
R: The glory of the Lord will dwell in our land.

Dear Lord, today's responsorial psalm states that the glory of the Lord will dwell in our land. How can I see Your glory, Lord? Through people who dedicate themselves to obeying You: They feed the poor, they protest unjust policies, they don't waste what they have, they take care of the Earth. Through people like this, Your glory shows. Help me to be like these people, Lord. May Your glory show through me.

Year 2: 1 Kings 18:41-46; Matthew 5:20-26
R: It is right to praise you in Zion, O God.

Dear Lord, in Your day there were people who acted religious but really weren't. They came to the temple to be seen, but their hearts were not with You. I know there are people like that today, too. May I be real, Lord. When I am at church, let my heart be with You: Let me search hard for You — in the words being read and sung, in the Eucharist being lifted up for me. It's easy to sit there and be bored. How insulting to You! Help me to search hard for You and hear You.

➤ *Catechism of the Catholic Church* 1437

Tenth Friday in Ordinary Time
Sin

Year 1: 2 Corinthians 4:7-15; Matthew 5:27-32
R: To you, Lord, I will offer a sacrifice of praise.

Dear Jesus, You said that if my right hand causes me to sin, I should cut it off! I know You didn't mean this. You are telling me to be horrified by sin. Sometimes I don't think small sins are that bad — calling people names, being mean to another kid, taking something small that isn't mine. What You tell me is that small sins lead to big ones; small sins hurt me and hurt others. Increase my sensitivity to sin, Lord. May I be horrified by even the small ones.

Year 2: 1 Kings 19:9a, 11-16; Matthew 5:27-32
R: I long to see your face, O Lord.

Dear Lord, Elijah got to see You. Why don't I get to see You, Lord? If I keep myself pure, receive the sacraments often, and pray every day, might I get to see You? Give me this desire, Lord, to see You in the world, to see Your hand in my life working to draw me close to You, working in the lives of others. May I long to see You like Elijah did in the calm of that whispering sound.

➤ *Catechism of the Catholic Church* 1850

Tenth Saturday in Ordinary Time
Commitment

Year 1: 2 Corinthians 5:14-21; Matthew 5:33-37
R: The Lord is kind and merciful.

Dear Lord, sometimes in the gospel readings You are correcting bad habits the people around you have fallen into. What habits of mine, Lord, would You be pointing out to me if You were to physically walk into my world? Help me to change the habits that come to mind, Lord. You are in my life, and You will not hesitate to point things out to me that I can improve upon, because the more I improve, the closer to You I can come.

Year 2: 1 Kings 19:19-21; Matthew 5:33-37
R: You are my inheritance, O Lord.

Dear Lord, You tell us to say yes when we mean yes and no when we mean no. I know what You mean. I'll ask someone to do something with me, and he will say, "Well, maybe." Or my mother asks me to do something for her, and I answer, "Later." Neither answer is a commitment. Help us not to be so afraid of committing ourselves. May I have the courage to say yes, and then follow through with my commitment. Or, give me the courage to say no when I need to.

➤ *Catechism of the Catholic Church* 2464

TRINITY SUNDAY

Sunday after Pentecost
Trinity

Cycle A: Exodus 34:4b-6, 8; 2 Corinthians 13:11-13; John 3:16-18
R: Glory and praise for ever!

Dear Lord, I have always known You as Father, Son, and Holy Spirit. And I have always known that there is only one God. Somehow, You are three Persons in one God. I don't understand this, Lord, but I know there are many things that I do not understand and yet accept as true. Thank You for my faith, Lord. Thank You for the mystery of my faith.

Cycle B: Deuteronomy 4:32-34, 39-40; Romans 8:14-17; Matthew 28:16-20
R: Blessed the people the Lord has chosen to be his own.

Dear Lord, there are lots of people who do not know You. I know You as Father, Son, and Holy Spirit. I know You are one God in three Persons. I can't explain this, but I know it. I thank You for my faith, Lord. I don't understand why some people don't know You as I do, and I am grateful that I am one You chose to know You. May my actions make You proud of me, Lord. May I never lose my faith in You.

Cycle C: Proverbs 8:22-31; Romans 5:1-5; John 16:12-15
R: O Lord, our God, how wonderful your name in all the earth!

Dear Lord, I like this first reading from Proverbs. Its words talk about the existence of different Persons in You from the beginning. It says, "Then was I beside him as his craftsman, and I was his delight day by day, playing before him all the while, playing on the surface of his earth; and I found delight in the human race." Within the Trinity there is love and delight in one another. Move us to be like You, God, loving and delighting and playing with one another.

➤ *Catechism of the Catholic Church* 261

CORPUS CHRISTI (THE BODY AND BLOOD OF CHRIST)

Sunday after Trinity Sunday
Eucharist

Cycle A: Deuteronomy 8:2-3, 14b-16a; 1 Corinthians 10:16-17; John 6:51-58
R: Praise the Lord, Jerusalem.

Dear Lord, how can I thank You for the gift of Your Body and Blood? By committing myself to realizing more and more just Who the Eucharist is. St. Paul tells me receiving the Eucharist is a *participation* in Your Body and Blood. "Participation," Lord. That means I am *doing* something when I receive Your Body and Blood. What am I doing? I'm not meant to just sit back and receive; I am meant to do!

Cycle B: Exodus 24:3-8; Hebrews 9:11-15; Mark 14: 12-16, 22-26
R: I will take the cup of salvation and call on the name of the Lord.

Dear Lord Jesus, when I celebrate Mass, I am doing just what You did in the upper room, just what You did at the Last Supper. There, You gave us Your Body and Blood for the first time, and You said, "Do this in remembrance of me." When I am at Mass, I am doing what You asked Lord. May I refuse to ever let my participation in this event be boring. There are worlds of meaning going on during Mass. May I focus on the words, the actions, and find this meaning — find You — every time!

Cycle C: Genesis 14:18-20; 1 Corinthians 11:23-26; Luke 9:11b-17
R: You are a priest for ever, in the line of Melchisedek.

Dear Lord Jesus, You were preaching outside of a town. Thousands were there listening to You for hours. They were hungry; they were in need. And You showed them and us that You answer our needs. Your apostles brought bread to You. You blessed it, broke it, and there was enough for everyone's need. Your Body and Blood fulfills our every need. May I have great devotion to the Eucharist.

➤ *Catechism of the Catholic Church* 1333

Eleventh Sunday in Ordinary Time
Leading and Following

Cycle A: Exodus 19:2-6a; Romans 5:6-11; Matthew 9:36-10:8
R: We are his people: the sheep of his flock.

Dear Jesus, I know I am one of the sheep of Your flock. Like a sheep, I will follow You wherever You lead me. But, I know You want me to be like You, too. You want me to become the shepherd when others are in need. You want me to be the shepherd when someone else is afraid or lost or hungry or hurt. Help me, Jesus, be a good sheep and give me extra strength when I need to be a shepherd.

Cycle B: Ezekiel 17:22-24; 2 Corinthians 5:6-10; Mark 4:26-34
R: Lord, it is good to give thanks to you.

Dear Lord, You speak often about seeds planted and growing. I know I have the seed of Your ways planted in me. It's growing, too, Lord. I'm realizing right from wrong. I care what You think of things I do and thoughts I have. I realize You want me to be a leader and stand up for what You stand up for. Show me how to keep on growing, Lord. I want to know the strength and the joy that comes from You.

Cycle C: 2 Samuel 12:7-10, 13; Galatians 2:16, 19-21; Luke 7:36 - 8:3 or 7:36-50
R: Lord, forgive the wrong I have done.

Dear Lord, part of being a Christian is following, and part of being a Christian is leading. It takes strength to follow You, Jesus. I know that. It takes even greater strength to lead. Let me come to You often and ask for grace and wisdom, to know right from wrong, to stand up for what is right, to be willing to give of myself.

➤ *Catechism of the Catholic Church* 1694

Eleventh Monday in Ordinary Time
Revenge

Year 1: 2 Corinthians 6:1-10; Matthew 5:38-42
R: The Lord has made known his salvation.

Dear Lord, "an eye for an eye and a tooth for a tooth" is the world's logic. If someone does something mean to me, then I should be able to do something mean to that person. This is not how You want us to be. You want us to be good. I can defend myself, and I don't have to be kind to those who hurt me, but I cannot do any harm in return. Doing harm makes me just like them rather than just like You.

Year 2: 1 Kings 21:1-16; Matthew 5:38-42
R: Lord, listen to my groaning.

Dear Lord, there are some kids who just like to start trouble. They call names; they make fun; they tease way too much. Sometimes I feel like I want to hit these kids or hurt them in some way. Give me wisdom, Lord, to know the best way to handle these situations. Let me know what You would do. You would respond with wisdom and You would have me confide in a trusted adult. May I do what You would want me to, Lord.

➤ *Catechism of the Catholic Church* 2302

Eleventh Tuesday in Ordinary Time
Happiness

Year 1: 2 Corinthians 8:1-9; Matthew 5:43-48
R: Praise the Lord, my soul!

Dear Lord, You want me to have a big heart. I can understand why. People with big hearts smile a lot. They don't have trouble with anyone. They can get along with most people. They seem to be able to be nice to everyone, even people who aren't their friends. They must feel happy a lot. Let me be like them, Lord. Give me a big heart.

Year 2: 1 Kings 21:17-29; Matthew 5:43-48
R: Be merciful, O Lord, for we have sinned.

Dear Lord, loving my enemies is very hard. Loving them doesn't mean going out of my way to be nice to them. It means not returning their anger with anger. It means not returning their cruelty with cruelty. And, it means praying for them. That I can do. I pray for my enemies, Lord, that You will change their hearts and help them to be kind.

➤ *Catechism of the Catholic Church* 2608

Eleventh Wednesday in Ordinary Time
Giving

Year 1: 2 Corinthians 9:6-11; Matthew 6:1-6, 16-18
R: Blessed the man who fears the Lord.

Dear Lord, some people make a big deal about what they give to the poor or about how much they pray. Sometimes it's good to know these things because it reminds others to give and to pray. But, most of the time, Lord, You want us to keep our giving and our praying just between You and us. That way we can be sure that we are giving and praying just for love of You, and not for the praise or attention it might bring us.

Year 2: 2 Kings 2:1, 6-14; Matthew 6:1-6, 16-18
R: Let your hearts take comfort, all who hope in the Lord.

Dear Lord, You want me to fast, to pray, to give to others. Let me see the value in each of these things, Lord. Let me see the value in offering small fasts, small prayers, small gifts to You often and just keeping it between You and me. I can skip a dessert just for You and mention it to You in my heart but tell no one else. I can give something to another without that one knowing who it's from just for love of You. I can offer prayers, just between You and me. The more I do these things, the more I will realize how much they benefit me, as You reward me with Your grace!

➤ *Catechism of the Catholic Church* 2101

Eleventh Thursday in Ordinary Time
Our Father

Year 1: 2 Corinthians 11:1-11; Matthew 6:7-15
R: Your works, O Lord, are justice and truth.

Dear Lord Jesus, You gave us the words of the Our Father to show us how to pray. First, we acknowledge that You are greater than we are and able to bring about goodness and peace. Then we ask that Your will be done now, here on earth, as we know it is in heaven. Then, we are to ask for the day's needs and for the strength and wisdom to provide for those needs for others. And we ask You to forgive us for the things we do wrong, but only if we forgive the things that others do wrong against us. Last, we ask to be delivered from all evil. This is the perfect prayer, Lord. May I pray its words with great respect.

Year 2: Sirach 48:1-14; Matthew 6:7-15
R: Rejoice in the Lord, you just!

Lord Jesus, when I pray the Our Father, I am praying for great things! I am asking that Your kingdom come now, to this world in the midst of all this war and evil that I see. I am asking for the wisdom to know how to supply the daily bread — the daily needs — of those around me. I am asking for forgiveness of sins of all men and women. This is a powerful prayer, Lord. May I realize its power when I pray!

➤ *Catechism of the Catholic Church* 2781

Eleventh Friday in Ordinary Time
Treasure

Year 1: 2 Corinthians 11:18, 21-30; Matthew 6:19-23
R: From all their distress God rescues the just.

Dear Lord, with all that St. Paul went through, how did he keep his faith in You? He was almost killed by his enemies on five different occasions. He was beaten and shipwrecked. You did not make things easy on him. What did You share with him that made him want to keep getting back up and talking about You? Tell me, Lord. I want to know You like St. Paul knew You.

Year 2: 2 Kings 11:1-4, 9-18, 20; Matthew 6:19-23
R: The Lord has chosen Zion for his dwelling.

Dear Lord Jesus, You tell me that where my treasure is, there will my heart be. What does this mean? If I'm thinking all the time about music, then my heart is with my music. If I'm thinking all the time about how much I hate school, then my heart is in a place that is not good for me. I need to make sure that my treasure is good — friends, You, family, good music. My heart is worth a great deal. Don't let me leave my heart with something not worthy of it.

➤ *Catechism of the Catholic Church* 2848

Eleventh Saturday in Ordinary Time
Worry

Year 1: 2 Corinthians 12:1-10; Matthew 6:24-34
R: Taste and see the goodness of the Lord.

Dear Lord, You tell us not to worry. Worrying is not healthy for us. If we trust in You, You will provide for our needs. You help us find jobs to feed our families. You enable us to work. You enable us to think, to study, to learn. Teach me, Lord, to see all that You provide for me, and teach me not to worry about anything but to bring my cares to You in prayer. You know best.

Year 2: 2 Chronicles 24:17-25; Matthew 6:24-34
R: For ever I will maintain my love for my servant.

Dear Lord Jesus, I worry about my mom or dad. I worry about the wars in the world. Sometimes I worry about my grades and my ability to understand my school work. Remind me, Lord, to bring my concerns to You in prayer and ask You to calm my worries and my fears. May I trust in You!

➤ *Catechism of the Catholic Church* 2830

Twelfth Sunday in Ordinary Time
Being God-Centered

Cycle A: Jeremiah 20:10-13; Romans 5:12-15; Matthew 10:26-33
R: Lord, in your great love, answer me.

Dear Lord, help me to know that You are central. You are the center of my life; You need to be the center of all people's lives. May people know that I am Yours by the way I act and by the words I use. May my joy and goodness attract them to You so that they can know You, too.

Cycle B: Job 38:1, 8-11; 2 Corinthians 5:14-17; Mark 4:35-41
R: Give thanks to the Lord, his love is everlasting.

Dear Lord, help me to not forget who You are. You are more than a friend I can come to once in a while for help. You are God. You mean for me to be with You. You mean for me to know You. I not only *can* come to You, I *need* to come to You. I cannot find my true self until I find myself in You. This is hard to understand, but I know it is true. Here I am, Lord; keep me with You.

Cycle C: Zechariah 12:10-11;13:1; Galatians 3:26-29; Luke 9:18-24
R: My soul is thirsting for you, O Lord my God.

Dear Lord, You matter to me. I pray to You. I think of You a lot. It is important to me to have a relationship with You. Thank You for this. This is my faith. Help me to know You more, Lord. May I read the Bible, pray a little more, and pay closer attention at Mass. Pull me closer to You, Lord.

➤ *Catechism of the Catholic Church 27*

Twelfth Monday in Ordinary Time
Picking on Others

Year 1: Genesis 12:1-9; Matthew 7:1-5
R: Blessed the people the Lord has chosen to be his own.

Dear Lord, You know how we pick on one another. You call it judging, and You tell us to stop it. All we are doing is hurting people's feelings. We judge them for their looks; we judge them for how smart or dumb we think they are; we judge them for where they are from. You tell us to straighten up and make ourselves perfect before we pick on someone else. Give me the courage to stop judging others, Lord, and give me the courage to tell others to stop judging too.

Year 2: 2 Kings 17:5-8, 13-15a, 18; Matthew 7:1-5
R: Help us with your right hand, O Lord, and answer us.

Dear Lord, I don't want someone else to look at me and see all my faults. I want them to see how hard I try. I want them to see the good things in me, not the bad. Help me to realize that others want me to see them this way, too. May I not see the bad things, the faults, first. May I look for the good in others and respond to their goodness, not their faults.

➤ *Catechism of the Catholic Church* 1807

Twelfth Tuesday in Ordinary Time
Practice

Year 1: Genesis 13:5-18; Matthew 7:6, 12-14
R: He who does justice will live in the presence of the Lord.

Lord, when You say to enter through the narrow gate, You mean that being good is harder than being mean. I know this. When someone asks me to do something for them, it is much easier to ignore them or say no. But help me to remember, Jesus, that practice makes perfect: Each time I do something good, it makes doing good even easier the next time. Give me grace, Lord, to practice doing good and making that gate wider and wider!

Year 2: 2 Kings 19:9b-11, 14-21, 31-35a, 36; Matthew 7:6, 12-14
R: God upholds his city for ever.

Dear Lord, You tell me not to give what is holy to dogs. Help me to realize that I am holy and I should not be sharing myself with anyone who does not treat me well. My faith, too, Lord, is holy, and anyone who makes fun of my faith is not worthy of my friendship either. Give me courage and wisdom to find good friends.

➤ *Catechism of the Catholic Church* 1733

Twelfth Wednesday in Ordinary Time
Listening

Year 1: Genesis 15:1-12, 17-18; Matthew 7:15-20
R: The Lord remembers his covenant for ever.

Dear Lord, these readings about animals being cut up, burned, and offered to You are weird. I don't understand them. But I do know that these things were understandable to the ancient peoples who did them. You spoke to them in ways that were normal in their culture. You speak to us today through our culture, too. Help me to hear Your messages, Lord, spoken through my culture.

Year 2: 2 Kings 22:8-13; 23:1-3; Matthew 7:15-20
R: Teach me the way of your decrees, O Lord.

Lord Jesus, there are false prophets today, people who say one thing and yet do another. There are people who talk nicely but really are mean. They "talk the talk but do not walk the walk." They are hypocrites. Lord, help me to not be a hypocrite. May I talk nice and be nice. I cannot be everyone's friend, but I can talk and act respectfully to everyone. Give me grace, Lord, to not be hypocritical.

➤ *Catechism of the Catholic Church* 1147

Twelfth Thursday in Ordinary Time
Prayer

Year 1: Genesis 16:1-12, 15-16 or 16:6b-12, 15-16; Matthew 7:21-19
R: Give thanks to the Lord, for he is good.

Dear Lord, it is not enough for us to just listen to Your words. We have to act on Your words. I can't just listen to You talk about the kingdom of heaven here on Earth; I must do all I can to *bring* that kingdom here! Give me courage and wisdom, Lord, to know how to bring your kingdom here and now.

Year 2: 2 Kings 24:8-17; Matthew 7:21-29
R: For the glory of your name, O Lord, deliver us.

Dear Jesus, I wouldn't call a friend and just start saying words I'd memorized to her! I would speak to my friend, thinking about the words I say and listening to her. This is how I should be with You, too. I shouldn't just rattle off prayers, expecting this to please You. That's disrespectful. I will think about the words I say to You, and I will take the time to listen to You, too. Give me the grace to do this, Lord. May I give time and effort to our relationship.

➤ *Catechism of the Catholic Church* 2725

Twelfth Friday in Ordinary Time
Fearing God

Year 1: Genesis 17:1, 9-10, 15-22; Matthew 8:1-4
R: See how the Lord blesses those who fear him.

Dear Lord, the responsorial psalm in today's Mass is "See how the Lord blesses those who fear him." Lord, You don't want me to be afraid of You like I might be afraid of the dark or spooky movies. You want me to have great respect for You — You bless those who have great respect for You. You are the center of all life; may I always keep You the center of my life.

Year 2: 2 Kings 25:1-12; Matthew 8:1-4
R: Let my tongue be silenced, if I ever forget you!

Dear Lord, may I never forget You. People who forget You or never pay any attention to You are not happy people. They have no One to depend on; I have You to depend on. They have no One to hear their prayers, their hopes, their dreams. I have You to hear my prayers, my hopes, and my dreams. Thank You, Lord, for my faith. I pray for those who do not have faith.

➤ *Catechism of the Catholic Church* 29

Twelfth Saturday in Ordinary Time
Caring

Year 1: Genesis 18:1-15; Matthew 8:5-17
R: The Lord has remembered his mercy.

Dear Lord, the promises You made to Your people in Bible times are still the promises You make to me. I receive Your mercy. I receive Your grace, just like Abraham and Sarah did. Just like the centurion did. Just like Peter's mother-in-law did. Let me respond to You just like they did, Lord, with great faith and thanksgiving.

Year 2: Lamentations 2:2, 10-14, 18-19; Matthew 8:5-17
R: Lord, forget not the souls of your poor ones.

Lord, the prophet Isaiah wrote about You: "He took away our infirmities and bore our diseases." You healed many of the sick people who came to You, Jesus. You were hurt when You saw others hurting. You call us to be like this, too, to have love so great that we hurt when we see others hurting. Though we may not be able to heal others as You did, Lord, move us to help them in every way we can: through prayer, through action, through being with them.

➤ *Catechism of the Catholic Church* 207

Thirteenth Sunday in Ordinary Time
Happiness

Cycle A: 2 Kings 4:8-11, 14-16a; Romans 6:3-4, 8-11; Matthew 10:37-42
R: Forever I will sing the goodness of the Lord.

Lord Jesus, the responsorial psalm from today's Mass is "Forever I will sing the goodness of the Lord." Someone who is sad does not sing about Your goodness. Those who follow You, Lord, seem to be happy a lot. What is it about being close to You that makes people happy? Grant me the grace, Lord, to discover this happiness.

Cycle B: Wisdom 1:13-15; 2:23-24; 2 Corinthians 8:7,9,13-15; Matthew 5:21-43 or 5:21-24, 35-43
R: I will praise you, Lord, for you have rescued me.

Dear Lord, Jairus came to You begging for the life of his daughter. Before You could get to his house, others came and told Jairus she was dead, but You told him, "Do not be afraid; just have faith." Did Jairus believe You could give life? Would I have trusted in You had I been there? I would have loved to have been there Lord! Give me eyes to see Your miracles!

Cycle C: 1 Kings 19:16b, 19-21; Galatians 5:1, 13-18; Luke 9:51-62
R: You are my inheritance, O Lord.

Dear Jesus, sometimes I hear things from the gospels that I just don't understand. Give me wisdom, Lord, to discover the meaning of Your words and persistence to keep trying to figure out Your message. I know that my trying hard to understand pleases You.

➤ *Catechism of the Catholic Church* 1718

Thirteenth Monday in Ordinary Time
Ignoring God

Year 1: Genesis 18:16-33; Matthew 8:18-22
R: The Lord is kind and merciful.

Dear Lord, You were trying to shock us when You told the man who wanted to bury his dad before he followed You, "Let the dead bury their dead." You wanted to show how important it is to be a follower of Yours. After all, who else could we follow? It will be Your face we see when we die; it will be You we have to answer to. Better now to get to know You and serve You than to die and try to come up with a good excuse as to why we ignored You!

Year 2: Amos 2:6-10, 13-16; Matthew 8:18-22
R: Remember this, you who never think of God.

Dear Lord, the prophet Amos describes what it will be like for those who choose to ignore You. Ignoring You leaves us weak and ignorant. Ignoring You leaves us open to addiction, pain, bad relationships, and all kinds of evil. I pray for those who choose to ignore You, Lord. Turn their hearts back to You. May I offer You a sacrifice every once in a while for them.

➤ *Catechism of the Catholic Church* 2629

Thirteenth Tuesday in Ordinary Time
Punishment

Year 1: Genesis 19:15-29; Matthew 8:23-27
R: O Lord, your mercy is before my eyes.

Dear Lord, the destruction of Sodom and Gomorrah is a scary story. It is a story that teaches an awful truth: Life without You brings on evil things. We are made to be with You, and when we turn away from You, bad things will occur. It is the way you made the world. Help us to have deep respect for how You made the world, Lord. Help us to abide by this natural order You gave it. Being with You and living how You teach us are part of the natural order.

Year 2: Amos 3:1-8, 11-12; Matthew 8:23-27
R: Lead me in your justice, Lord.

Dear God, I pray for those who do not know You. Give them the grace to see You and know You like I do, Lord. May they see that life doesn't have to be so scary and without foundation. Let them see how much You love them and want goodness and peace for them. And thank You for my faith, Jesus. May I never turn away from You.

➤ *Catechism of the Catholic Church* 2090

Thirteenth Wednesday in Ordinary Time
Suffering

Year 1: Genesis 21:5, 8-20a; Matthew 8:28-34
R: The Lord hears the cry of the poor.

Dear Lord, bad things happened to Hagar. She had to take her child and leave Abraham's household and wander in the wilderness all by herself. You were with her, however, Lord, and You promised her that her son, Ishmael, would grow up to be the head of a great nation, the Arab peoples. Even though bad things do happen to us, may I remember, Lord, that You remain with us to help us.

Year 2: Amos 5:14-15, 21-24; Matthew 8:28-34
R: To the upright I will show the saving power of God.

Lord God, write the words of Amos upon my heart. Amos said, "Seek good and not evil, that you may live." I want to live well, Lord. I want to develop eyes to see Your actions in the world. I want to love good and hate evil. I want to be one whom You call to do great things in the world.

➤ *Catechism of the Catholic Church* 2648

Thirteenth Thursday in Ordinary Time
Pride

Year 1: Genesis 22:1b-19; Matthew 9:1-8
R: I will walk in the presence of the Lord, in the land of the living.

Dear Lord, did you really ask Abraham to sacrifice his son? People-sacrifice was part of many cultures back in ancient times. Abraham may have thought You were asking him to sacrifice what was most precious to him, just like he saw peoples around him doing. Your Angel stopped him just before he did it. You showed all the Israelites by this story that You did not approve of people-sacrifice. Show us, Lord, what You don't like about our cultures, such as abortion and genocide, and give us wisdom to know how to change these practices.

Year 2: Amos 7:10-17; Matthew 9:1-8
R: The judgments of the Lord are true, and all of them are just.

Dear Lord, you forgave the sins of a paralyzed man and healed him. There were men there who got mad at You for doing this. They couldn't be happy for the healed man. They couldn't be happy that God was this close to them. May I never be so full of pride, Lord, that I can't be happy when good things happen to those around me!

➤ *Catechism of the Catholic Church* 2540

Thirteenth Friday in Ordinary Time
Mercy

Year 1: Genesis 23:1-4, 19; 24:1-8, 62-67; Matthew 9:9-13
R: Give thanks to the Lord, for he is good.

Dear Lord, You would much rather have us show mercy to others than make big sacrifices to You. Some people give up many things for You but ignore the needs of the poor. You would prefer that they give to the poor and help the poor, thus showing mercy. May I be merciful, Lord.

Year 2: Amos 8:4-6, 9-12; Matthew 9:9-13
R: One does not live by bread alone, but by every word that comes from the mouth of God.

Dear Lord, listening to Your word is as important as eating! I couldn't go much more than a day without eating; if I did, I would get sick. So, too, if I go too long without listening to Your words and paying attention to You, I will get spiritually sick. May I realize how important You are, dear Lord.

➤ *Catechism of the Catholic Church* 2447

Thirteenth Saturday in Ordinary Time
Favoritism

Year 1: Genesis 27:1-5, 15-29; Matthew 9:14-17
R: Praise the Lord for the Lord is good!

Dear Lord, this story of new wine and old wineskins is an ancient way of saying that we cannot put rules around You and Your ways. You will constantly surprise us, be with us in ways that are beyond our understanding, and pull blessings for us out of both good and bad events. You are greater than we are, O Lord, and for this we give You thanks.

Year 2: Amos 9:11-15; Matthew 9:14-17
R: The Lord speaks of peace to his people.

Dear Jesus, it wasn't fair what Jacob and his mother did to steal Esau's blessing. Do You play favorites, Lord? Do You favor some of us over others? You love all of us, Lord. May I be a delight to You by praying as often as I can, by reading Your Word, by caring just to make You happy. May I be a favored one!

➤ *Catechism of the Catholic Church* 1168

Fourteenth Sunday in Ordinary Time
Peace

Cycle A: Zechariah 9:9-10; Romans 8:9, 11-13; Matthew 11:25-30
R: I will praise your name for ever, my king and my God.

Dear Lord, what could be more peaceful than a donkey? Horses were used for war in ancient times. They symbolized war. But a donkey? They were animals used for labor, domestic things, peaceful things. And You, our King, rode into Jerusalem on a donkey. Zechariah wrote about this entrance hundreds of years before it actually happened. "Shout for joy, O daughter Jerusalem! See, your king shall come to you; a just savior is he, Meek, and riding on [a donkey]." Who would have thought this would be Your way, O God?! Give me eyes to see Your ways, Lord; You are never predictable!

Cycle B: Ezekiel 2:2-5; 2 Corinthians 12:7-10; Mark 6:1-6
R: Our eyes are fixed on the Lord, pleading for his mercy.

Dear Jesus, it must have hurt You when the people of Your own hometown took offense at You. Instead of being proud of You and so grateful for this opportunity to experience such intimacy with You, they were angry with You for "acting" like You were someone special. You are special to me, Lord. When You come to me in Holy Communion, I will show You great respect and reverence. I will never take offense at You.

Cycle C: Isaiah 66:10-14c; Galatians 6:14-18; Luke 10:1-12, 17-20 or 10:1-9
R: Let all the earth cry out to God with joy.

Dear Jesus, when You sent out Your disciples, You told them You were sending them out like lambs among wolves. Lambs are peaceful animals; wolves are not. You want us to be peaceful, Lord. You know that there are lots of people who are violent. Protect us, Lord. May their violence not cause us to abandon our commitment to peace. Prince of peace, hear our prayer for peace!

➤ *Catechism of the Catholic Church* 2305

Fourteenth Monday in Ordinary Time
Prayer

Year 1: Genesis 28:10-22a; Matthew 9:18-26
R: In you, my God, I place my trust.

Dear Lord, in Jacob's dream, he saw a ladder going up to heaven. On the ladder he saw angels going up and coming down. This dream tells us that heaven is open, our angels watch over us and constantly take our prayers up and bring answers down. Thank You, Lord, for the message of Jacob's dream. You hear our prayers, and You answer us.

Year 2: Hosea 2:16, 17c-18, 21-22; Matthew 9:18-26
R: The Lord is gracious and merciful.

Dear Jesus, when You were on this earth, You heard every prayer of those who came to You — even those who did not voice their prayers, like the woman who just wanted to touch Your clothes to be healed. Let me realize, Lord, that it is no different now: You hear every prayer, and You answer every prayer.

➤ *Catechism of the Catholic Church* 2621

Fourteenth Tuesday in Ordinary Time
God's Presence

Year 1: Genesis 32:23-33; Matthew 9:32-38
R: In justice, I shall behold your face, O Lord.

Dear Jesus, so many people need to hear Your message. They need to know how much You love them and how much You care about their lives. I pray for those who most need You right now, Lord. Be with them. Show them a part of You. Let them feel Your mighty love right now.

Year 2: Hosea 8:4-7, 11-13; Matthew 9:32-38
R: The house of Israel trusts in the Lord.

Lord God, there was so much disease and illness in the world when You were here. There is still a lot of disease and illness, Lord. Show us that You are still here with us, healing, forgiving, loving, through the hands and hearts of others, and through my hands and heart, Lord. Remind me that I am a Christian. I have the power to bring You to people who are ill in any way.

➤ *Catechism of the Catholic Church* 788

Fourteenth Wednesday in Ordinary Time
Heaven

Year 1: Genesis 41:55-57; 42:5-7a, 17-24a; Matthew 10:1-7
R: Lord, let your mercy be on us, as we place our trust in you.

Dear Lord, when Joseph's brothers sold him into slavery, You had a plan. You knew Joseph would end up being in charge in Egypt when famine came. You knew You could work through Joseph to feed Your people Israel. You take the bad things that happen to us and bring good from them. Thank You, Lord.

Year 2: Hosea 10:1-3, 7-8, 12; Matthew 10:1-7
R: Seek always the face of the Lord.

Dear Lord, the kingdom of heaven is coming. Every time someone does a good thing, Your kingdom comes even more, but every time an evil thing is done, it hurts Your kingdom. Inspire me, Lord, to do lots of good things so that Your kingdom can come even faster!

➤ *Catechism of the Catholic Church* 567

Fourteenth Thursday in Ordinary Time
Trust

Year 1: Genesis 44:18-21, 23b-29; 45:1-5; Matthew 10:7-15
R: Remember the marvels the Lord has done.

Dear Lord, the responsorial psalm for today's Mass is "Remember the marvels the Lord has done." Why do we need to remember the great things You've done, Lord? Why do I need to remember You walking on water, healing the blind man, or parting the Red Sea? Remembering Your power gives me peace, especially when I am afraid. Remembering Your power makes me want to make sure our relationship is good; after all, You made me!

Year 2: Hosea 11:1-4, 8e-9; Matthew 10:7-15
R: Let us see your face, Lord, and we shall be saved.

Lord God, the prophet Hosea reminds us that You called Your people out of slavery in Egypt. But they didn't stay faithful to You even after You freed them. They got mad when things got hard, and they started to complain and even wanted to go back into slavery! Forgive me, Lord, when I'm like they were. Just because things get hard for me, I complain and want to give up. Give me courage, Lord, to trust in You and try even harder.

➤ *Catechism of the Catholic Church* 2797

Fourteenth Friday in Ordinary Time
Fear

Year 1: Genesis 46:1-7, 28-30; Matthew 10:16-23
R: The salvation of the just comes from the Lord.

Dear Lord, You told Your disciples what to expect when they began to preach about You. You encouraged them and told them not to be afraid. You told them that the Spirit would be with them. May I turn to You when I am afraid, dear Lord. Help me to know that Your Spirit is with me, too.

Year 2: Hosea 14:2-10; Matthew 10:16-23
R: My mouth will declare your praise.

Dear Lord, You sent Your disciples out to preach about You. You still are sending men and women out to preach about You. I pray for these men and women, Lord. For those who suffer because they talk about You, hear my prayer. For those whose lives are threatened because of their faith in You, hear my prayer. I pray, too, for those who threaten Your missionaries: Open their hearts, Lord, to receive You and welcome Your people.

➤ *Catechism of the Catholic Church* 2145

Fourteenth Saturday in Ordinary Time
Disciples

Year 1: Genesis 49:29-32; 50:15-26a; Matthew 10:24-33
R: Be glad you lowly ones; may your hearts be glad!

Dear Lord Jesus, thank You for the work of the apostles and disciples. Were it not for them, I would not know You. You left it to them to spread knowledge of You. Your Spirit guided them, and their word spread. And now, 2000 years later, I, too, know You. These were courageous men and women, Lord. I give thanks for their example and for their love for You!

Year 2: Isaiah 6:1-8; Matthew 10:24-33
R: The Lord is king; he is robed in majesty.

Dear Lord, You have called many people through the years. Some have been prophets, others have been teachers, others have been healers. Where would my faith be if all these men and women said no to Your call? May I be grateful for the faith that I have. Many people have paid for my faith, some with their very lives. May I make these saints proud of me by holding on to my faith and doing everything I can to nurture my faith.

➤ *Catechism of the Catholic Church* 562

Fifteenth Sunday in Ordinary Time
Spiritual Growth

Cycle A: Isaiah 55:10-11; Romans 8:18-23; Matthew 13:1-23 or 13:1-9
R: The seed that falls on good ground will yield a fruitful harvest.

Dear Lord, what kind of path am I? Am I hard so that Your seed gets eaten right away and is gone? Am I rocky ground where Your seed will grow in me a little bit but be forgotten? Or, am I good ground where Your seed will take root and grow and grow inside me? Make me good ground, Lord!

Cycle B: Amos 7:12-15; Ephesians 1:3-14 or 1:3-10; Mark 6:7-13
R: Lord, let us see your kindness, and grant us your salvation.

Lord Jesus, Your disciples went out and preached repentance. To repent means to be sorry and turn away from sin. Do I repent, Lord? Am I sorry when I sin? Do I turn away from sin by trying my hardest to not sin again? Just like the people who listened to Your disciples back then, Lord, may I listen now and repent!

Cycle C: Deuteronomy 30:10-14; Colossians 1:15-20; Luke 10:25-37
R: Turn to the Lord in your need, and you will live.

Dear Lord, the Good Samaritan is one of the best stories You ever told. All those who heard You tell it thought Samaritans were not capable of doing good. But when everyone else was too afraid to help the beaten man, a Samaritan overcame his fear to do what was right and help. Help me, Lord, to not think badly of anyone; may I grow to see You in all people.

➤ *Catechism of the Catholic Church* 543

Fifteenth Monday in Ordinary Time
Evil

Year 1: Exodus 1:8-14, 22; Matthew 10:34 - 11:1
R: Our help is in the name of the Lord.

Dear Lord, just because Israel was growing, the leader in Egypt grew afraid of them, worrying that if they outnumbered the Egyptians, they might try to take over. So the leader made the Israelites slaves. Dear Lord, there are nations today who act terribly toward other nations and even toward their own people. Show us how to have peace, Lord. Show us how to defeat evil. Have mercy on us, Lord.

Year 2: Isaiah 1:10-17; Matthew 10:34 - 11:1
R: To the upright I will show the saving power of God.

Dear Lord, Isaiah voiced Your anger with Your people. He told the people that it didn't matter how many good things they were doing if they were doing evil things as well. They may have been giving money to the Temple, but they were cheating one another in business! They may have been attending prayer services every day, but they were refusing to help the orphans and widows. You want us to care about one another and be good to one another. May I always be mindful of the poor — giving money when I can, praying for them, and looking for ways to help them.

➤ *Catechism of the Catholic Church 324*

Fifteenth Tuesday in Ordinary Time
Faith

Year 1: Exodus 2:1-15a; Matthew 11:20-24
R: Turn to the Lord in your need, and you will live.

Dear Jesus, it wasn't okay with You when people did not listen to You. You worked miracles to get their attention; You spoke words that should have moved their hearts to listen. But some chose to ignore You. Ignoring You is something people have to answer for when they die. Thank You for my faith, Lord. I'm glad I choose to listen.

Year 2: Isaiah 7:1-9; Matthew 11:20-24
R: God upholds his city for ever.

Dear Lord, Isaiah tells us, "Unless your faith is firm, you shall not be firm." When I choose to have faith, I am strong. I am confident. I am joyful. When I turn my back on my faith, I feel weak. I get mad easily, and I am aggravated. When I am feeling badly, Lord, let me look at my faith — am I being faith-filled or do I need to turn back to You and find my strength?

➤ *Catechism of the Catholic Church 166*

Fifteenth Wednesday in Ordinary Time
Faith

Year 1: Exodus 3:1-6, 9-12; Matthew 11:25-27
R: The Lord is kind and merciful.

Dear Lord, Moses knew how strong the Egyptians were. He was raised by their leader. He saw their chariots and their weapons. He knew there were thousands upon thousands of soldiers. And yet You were telling him that You would free the Israelites simply by sending him, one man. Sometimes You ask great things of us, Lord, and if we listen and obey, we can see wonderful things accomplished by You.

Year 2: Isaiah 10:5-7, 13b-16; Matthew 11:25-27
R: The Lord will not abandon his people.

Dear Jesus, sometimes we have to go through bad things for good things to happen. This is the way it was in the Bible, and I can see that this is the way it is often in my world too. Keep our faith strong during the bad times, Lord, and increase our hope for the good times. I pray especially for those who are going through bad times right now, Lord. Strengthen them. Show them Your grace and Your love.

➤ *Catechism of the Catholic Church* 162

Fifteenth Thursday in Ordinary Time
Trust

Year 1: Exodus 3:13-20; Matthew 11:28-30
R: The Lord remembers his covenant for ever.

Dear Lord, I bet Moses was afraid when he started to go back to Egypt to tell Pharoah to let the Israelites go. Following You doesn't mean we won't be afraid, but it does mean that You will be with us at every moment. Moses succeeded because You never left his side. Increase my trust in You, Lord. May I know that You will never leave me.

Year 2: Isaiah 26:7-9, 12, 16-19; Matthew 11:28-30
R: From heaven the Lord looks down on the earth.

Dear Lord, You tell everyone who is tired to come to You and You will give them rest. We can rest in You. You will give us strength. I pray for those who are most in need of strength right now, Lord. Some people are worrying a lot. Others are afraid. Some are really sick. Be with all of them, Lord. Give them rest and strength.

➤ *Catechism of the Catholic Church* 322

Fifteenth Friday in Ordinary Time
Pharisee

Year 1: Exodus 11:10 - 12:4; Matthew 12:1-8
R: I will take the cup of salvation, and call on the name of the Lord.

Dear Lord, both Pharoah and the Pharisees are not willing to recognize that the hand of God is at work right in front of them. What keeps people from wanting to recognize that You are present and that You care enough about us to be right here? May I never doubt Your presence, Lord, nor Your care for me; the evidence of Your love is all around me!

Year 2: Isaiah 38:1-6, 21-22, 7-8; Matthew 12:1-8
R: You saved my life, O Lord; I shall not die.

Dear Lord, the Pharisees were not merciful. They did not have mercy on people. Their judgments were quick and harsh, and they were not forgiving of one who broke the law. You came telling them that mercy was the way of God; our hearts should forgive one another; our hands should give to those who need; our eyes should always look for ways to have mercy on one another.

➤ *Catechism of the Catholic Church 596*

Fifteenth Saturday in Ordinary Time
Mercy

Year 1: Exodus 12:37-42; Matthew 12:14-21
R: His mercy endures forever.

Dear Jesus, You knew that the Pharisees were going to try to kill You. You knew that they did not have power to kill anyone but had to get that power from Rome. Rome crucified people. You probably knew You were going to be crucified. And yet You continued to speak of forgiveness and love and mercy. What strength You must have been drawing from God the Father. Show me how to depend on You, Jesus, for my strength. I want to be able to remain good even when I am afraid, worried, or overwhelmed.

Year 2: Micah 2:1-5; Matthew 12:14-21
R: Do not forget the poor, O Lord!

Dear Lord, the prophet Micah has one of the shortest books in the Bible. He also has one of the neatest. Micah is mad! He is mad that God's ways are not getting attention. The poor are being trampled. There is no one who has mercy on another. God's people are being hurt. And Micah means to announce that God is mad! I want You to be mad, Lord; be mad at the people who let others starve. Be mad at the people who do nothing about the famines, the genocides, the atrocities that happen around the world. I pray for those who suffer, Lord. Hear their prayer!

➤ *Catechism of the Catholic Church* 2447

Sixteenth Sunday in Ordinary Time
Imitating Jesus

Cycle A: Wisdom 12:13, 16-19; Romans 8:26-27; Matthew 13:24-43 or 13:24-30
R: Lord, you are good and forgiving.

Dear Lord, what would we do without forgiveness? What would it be like if we never forgave one another? Everyone would be mad at everyone! It would be terrible. It would be a world I wouldn't want to live in. Help me to forgive others when they hurt me, Lord, and may others forgive me, too.

Cycle B: Jeremiah 23:1-6; Ephesians 2:13-18; Mark 6:30-34
R: The Lord is my shepherd; there is nothing I shall want.

Dear Jesus, the disciples were tired when they got back from the journeys You had sent them on. They were anxious to tell You all about it. You put them in a boat to go off by yourselves for a bit, but when You got to the shore, lots of people were there waiting for You. You didn't get mad or complain that Your plans were interrupted. You felt compassion for the people. You loved them. Make my heart like Yours, Lord.

Cycle C: Genesis 18:1-10a; Colossians 1:24-28; Luke 10:38-42
R: He who does justice will live in the presence of the Lord.

Dear Jesus, sometimes people do stuff to avoid getting to know someone. How often do I just sit with You, trying my best to focus on You? How often do I sit with the Bible, reading a bit about You and then thinking about what I read? It is easier to go off and do something than it is to sit with You. Give me patience and wisdom, Lord, so that I can sit with You and learn more about You.

➤ *Catechism of the Catholic Church* 1694

Sixteenth Monday in Ordinary Time
Choice

Year 1: Exodus 14:5-18; Matthew 12:38-42
R: Let us sing to the Lord; he has covered himself in glory.

Dear Lord, You gave enough signs and taught with wisdom in order to show that You had the authority of God. People who saw but did not believe chose not to believe. My faith is a gift, but whether I build upon it or not is my choice. I choose to nurture my faith, Lord Jesus. Show me how to make it grow. By my words and by my actions, may I always choose You.

Year 2: Micah 6:1-4, 6-8; Matthew 12:38-42
R: To the upright I will show the saving power of God.

Dear Lord, these words of Micah the prophet teach us how we must be in community: "You have been told, O man, what is good, and what the LORD requires of you: Only to do the right and to love goodness, and to walk humbly with your God." Give me wisdom, Lord, that I may remember Micah's words and write them on my heart.

➤ *Catechism of the Catholic Church* 1970

Sixteenth Tuesday in Ordinary Time
God's Will

Year 1: Exodus 14:21 - 15:1; Matthew 12:46-50
R: Let us sing to the Lord; he has covered himself in glory.

Dear Lord, You have no family boundaries. I get to be part of Your family. I get to be Your brother, Your sister, if only I choose to follow You. When Your Mom and family stood outside a place where You were preaching and called for You, You pointed out that everyone who does the will of God is mother, brother, and sister to You. Thank You for this privilege, Lord.

Year 2: Micah 7:14-15, 18-20; Matthew 12:46-50
R: Lord, show us your mercy and love.

Lord Jesus, if I show mercy and love by helping my mother with my younger brother or by straightening up the house, how much greater a deed must You do when You show mercy and love! You are God! Move the hearts of those who have power to feed starving people, Lord. Move the hearts of those who would put guns in the hands of men and children, Lord. Move the hearts of those who choose to commit crimes against Your people. Have mercy, Lord. Show us Your love.

➤ *Catechism of the Catholic Church* 381

Sixteenth Wednesday in Ordinary Time
Patience

Year 1: Exodus 16:1-5, 9-15; Matthew 13:1-9
R: The Lord gave them bread from heaven.

Dear Lord, even though the people were grumbling against You — even after You led them out of Egypt, still You had patience with them and fed them with bread from heaven. Let me think of Your patience and love, Lord, especially when I partake of the "bread from heaven" — Your precious Body and Blood. May I be patient, like You, and may I always have great reverence for the Eucharist.

Year 2: Jeremiah 1:1, 4-10; Matthew 13:1-9
R: I will sing of your salvation.

Dear Lord, when Jeremiah told You he couldn't be a prophet because he was too young, You told him, "Say not, 'I am too young.' To whomever I send you, you shall go; whatever I command you, you shall speak." I pray for those whom You call to be Your prophets. Give them courage and wisdom, Lord, to sow Your seeds on good ground.

➤ *Catechism of the Catholic Church* 1832

Sixteenth Thursday in Ordinary Time
Eucharist

Year 1: Exodus 19:1-2, 9-11, 16-20b; Matthew 13:10-17
R: Glory and praise for ever!

Dear Lord, You told Your disciples that they were especially blessed because they got to see You and hear You. I don't get to see You, Lord, but I do get to take Your Body and Blood into my body. This means that I am especially blessed, too. Grant me a great devotion to the Eucharist, Lord. May I long to receive You.

Year 2: Jeremiah 2:1-3, 7-8, 12-13; Matthew 13:10-17
R: With you is the fountain of life, O Lord.

Dear Lord, people have always had the choice of following You or not. You called the prophet Jeremiah to warn the people about the bad things that happen when they don't follow You. We have our prophets today who warn those who are not following Your way. I pray for those who choose to not listen to You, Lord. Their lives are full of violence and unrest. May they listen to today's prophets and turn their lives over to You.

➤ *Catechism of the Catholic Church* 1324

Sixteenth Friday in Ordinary Time
Commandments

Year 1: Exodus 20:1-17; Matthew 13:18-23
R: Lord, you have the words of everlasting life.

Dear God, You gave Moses the Ten Commandments for Your people. Because I am part of Your people, these Commandments are for me, too. Give me wisdom, Lord, to know how to keep these commandments. If we all kept these laws, we would have peace in the world. May I do my part to keep peace in our world.

Year 2: Jeremiah 3:14-17; Matthew 13:18-23
R: The Lord will guard us as a shepherd guards his flock.

Dear Lord, You told Your people not to walk with hard hearts. If my heart is hard, it means that I am closed to any love or kindness or forgiveness. If my heart is closed, it means I am mad and hurt. I refuse to listen when I have a hard heart. Soften my heart when I'm like this, Lord. Soften the hearts of people who are not open to You.

➤ *Catechism of the Catholic Church* 2067

Sixteenth Saturday in Ordinary Time
Covenant

Year 1: Exodus 24:3-8; Matthew 13:24-30
R: Offer to God a sacrifice of praise.

Dear Lord, blood was very important to the people of Bible times. It represented life, and when they used it in a ritual with You, its use was very serious. It was a covenant, an agreement, that was not to be broken: They would obey Your law. When You died, Lord Jesus, Your Blood was spilled out. This Blood was the sign of a new agreement between Christians and You. I am a Christian. I will honor this agreement. I will honor Your Blood and follow Your law.

Year 2: Jeremiah 7:1-11; Matthew 13:24-30
R: How lovely is your dwelling place, Lord, mighty God!

Dear Lord, You talked about the kingdom of heaven a lot. You wanted us to think about it and wonder what it is like. It is beyond our imagination. By obeying Your covenant — the agreement we made with You at our Baptisms and which we renew every time we bless ourselves with holy water — we are counting on You to lead us to this kingdom. Keep us faithful to You, Lord, that we may all one day be in heaven.

➤ *Catechism of the Catholic Church* 72

Seventeenth Sunday in Ordinary Time
Kingdom of Heaven

Cycle A: 1 Kings 3:5, 7-12; Romans 8:28-30; Matthew 13:44-52 or 13:44-46
R: Lord, I love your commands.

Dear God, there are some things that I would sell all I have to be able to have. That's what You said we would want to do if we just knew what heaven was like: We'd want to give away all we have just to have heaven. Is it really that good, Lord? I pray for those who will die today; may they be with You in heaven.

Cycle B: 2 Kings 4:42-44; Ephesians 4:1-6; John 6:1-15
R: The hand of the Lord feeds us; he answers all our needs.

Dear Lord, I didn't know that the prophet Elisha multiplied loaves of bread, too, to feed a hundred people. Elisha had faith in You, and You fed your people. Your generosity, Lord, is not to be outdone. What must heaven be like, Lord, if it is a place prepared by You in Your generosity? I pray that all my loved ones who have died may be experiencing this great gift of heaven.

Cycle C: Genesis 18:20-32; Colossians 2:12-14; Luke 11:1-13
R: Lord, on the day I called for help, you answered me.

Dear Lord, You promised us that all who seek will find. Many people, Lord, seek hard to find a place where peace dwells all the time, a place where violence doesn't enter, a place where they can relax and be happy. This is heaven, Lord. May I look for heaven, do all I can to bring the ways of heaven here to earth, and one day and enter into heaven with You.

➤ *Catechism of the Catholic Church* 1821

Seventeenth Monday in Ordinary Time
Heaven

Year 1: Exodus 32:15-24, 30-34; Matthew 13:31-35
R: Give thanks to the Lord, for he is good.

Dear Lord, You told us that heaven is like a mustard seed. Mustard seeds are tiny, Jesus. But they grow up into really big bushes. If heaven is like this, then the tiniest seed You plant into my heart can grow very large. May my prayers, my sacrifices, and my actions feed this seed that You have given me and, with Your help, guide me right into heaven!

Year 2: Jeremiah 13:1-11; Matthew 13:31-35
R: You have forgotten God who gave you birth.

Dear Lord, we can lose heaven. Loving You and trying our best to get to heaven is a choice we must make. We can't ignore You and Your ways and make it to heaven. I pray for those, Lord, who do not have You in their lives. May Your grace find a way to turn them to You. I pray especially for those I love who do not know You.

➤ *Catechism of the Catholic Church* 1025

Seventeenth Tuesday in Ordinary Time
Evil

Year 1: Exodus 33:7-11; 34:5b-9, 28; Matthew 13:36-43
R: The Lord is kind and merciful.

Dear Lord, in today's gospel, You teach that evil people are like weeds. They grow up with Your people and try to make them evil, just like weeds grow up and try to choke off the good plants. Give me strength to resist the temptations of evil people: May I be good to my body; may I keep my mind clean; may I never do anything against the law. Give me Your grace, Lord, to be good.

Year 2: Jeremiah 14:17-22; Matthew 13:36-43
R: For the glory of your name, O Lord, deliver me.

Dear God, Jeremiah cried over the people who had turned their backs on You. He saw how they were suffering. He knew if they would turn back to You, things would get better. Doing evil things only ends in suffering. Doing evil things makes innocent others suffer too. Guide us, Lord, to avoid evil. Heal us from the devastation that evil brings upon us.

➤ *Catechism of the Catholic Church* 324

Seventeenth Wednesday in Ordinary Time
Holiness

Year 1: Exodus 34:29-35; Matthew 13:44-46
R: Holy is the Lord our God.

Dear Lord, what does it mean to be holy? You are holy, I know. Can I be holy? Am I expected to be holy? To be holy means to be God or to belong to God. I belong to You. Therefore, I, too, am holy. This is amazing, Lord. This makes me question my behavior, my speech, my perceptions, and my attitude. If I am holy, I can work harder to look the part!

Year 2: Jeremiah 15:10, 16-21; Matthew 13:44-46
R: God is my refuge on the day of distress.

Dear Lord, to be holy means to be whole —You are not divided in any way. You support us, even when we fall into sin. You promise our rescue, even when we have caused our captivity. You are true to Your word, even when we are caught in lies. Thank You for Your holiness, Lord. Help us to see our high calling, that we can and should be holy, too.

➤ *Catechism of the Catholic Church* 2809

Seventeenth Thursday in Ordinary Time
Growth

Year 1: Exodus 40:16-21, 34-38; Matthew 13:47-53
R: How lovely is your dwelling place, O Lord, mighty God!

Dear God, Your presence like a cloud surrounded the Ark in which Moses had placed the Ten Commandments. Your people could see the cloud in the day time and at night they saw fire surrounding the Ark. It would have been so neat to see this, Lord. May I learn more about You by reading more and more of the Bible, God. Give my mind understanding.

Year 2: Jeremiah 18:1-6; Matthew 13:47-53
R: Blessed is he whose help is the God of Jacob.

Lord God, You told Jeremiah to go to the potter's house and watch the potter work with the clay. You told Jeremiah we are like the clay and You, God, are the potter. You mold us and shape us by the events that You permit to happen in our lives. Mold me, Lord, into someone in whom You delight.

➤ *Catechism of the Catholic Church* 794

Seventeenth Friday in Ordinary Time
Sundays

Year 1: Leviticus 23:1, 4-11, 15-16, 27, 34b-37; Matthew 13:54-58
R: Sing with joy to God our help.

Dear Lord, You know us very well. You know we love to celebrate. You know we need rituals to remind us how important You are. This is why we have Sundays. Sundays should be days of celebration, times when we get to focus on You and all you have given us. May we take advantage of Sundays, Lord, and use them well to keep us close to You.

Year 2: Jeremiah 26:1-9; Matthew 13:54-58
R: Sing with joy to God our help.

Dear Lord, sometimes, despite the celebrations and rituals we have to remind us of You, sometimes we still forget. The people Jeremiah was trying to get to turn from their evil ways forgot You. May we recognize it immediately when we forget You, Lord. May we run to get back to You, ask forgiveness, and follow You again.

➤ *Catechism of the Catholic Church* 2187

Seventeenth Saturday in Ordinary Time
Admitting Sin

Year 1: Leviticus 25:1, 8-12; Matthew 14:1-12
R: O God, let all the nations praise you!

Dear Lord, what would our world look like if all the nations praised You? There might still be some misunderstandings now and then, but for the most part, wouldn't we have peace? If all peoples were praising You, then they couldn't be plotting against one another. They couldn't be seeing the bad in other people. They couldn't be nursing fear of one another. O God, let all the nations praise You!

Year 2: Jeremiah 26:11-16, 24; Matthew 14:1-12
R: Lord, in your great love, answer me.

Dear Lord, sometimes when we do bad things, we don't want anyone to point it out to us. St. John the Baptist pointed out to Herod something Herod had done wrong. Herod got so mad, he had John arrested and eventually killed. Help us to see, Lord, that it is best to face our failures, admit them, and say we're sorry. Then it's over, and no one gets hurt any more by our sins.

➤ *Catechism of the Catholic Church* 1490

Eighteenth Sunday in Ordinary Time
Being God-Centered

Cycle A: Isaiah 55:1-3; Romans 8:35, 37-39; Matthew 14:13-21
R: The hand of the Lord feeds us; he answers all our needs.

Dear Lord, when I am thirsty, I can't think of anything else except getting a drink. This is how You want us to be about You — wanting You so badly that we can't think of anything else until we have You. Give me this desire, Lord. Let me think of You, search for You, and find You every day of my life.

Cycle B: Exodus 16:2-4, 12-15; Ephesians 4:17, 20-24; John 6:24-35
R: The Lord gave them bread from heaven.

Dear God, the Israelites were hungry and You gave them bread from heaven in the desert. When You spoke of the bread of heaven to the people, they asked You for this bread and You told them You are the bread. Help us to hunger for Your Body and Blood, Lord, in the Eucharist. May You satisfy our hunger and our thirst.

Cycle C: Ecclesiastes 1:2; 2:21-23; Colossians 3:1-5, 9-11; Luke 12:13-21
R: If today you hear his voice, harden not your hearts!

Lord God, You tell us not to focus so much on things of the earth as on things of heaven. Help me to worry more about my relationship with You than I do about what I'll wear, or what my friends think, or what I'll do this weekend. May I make You number one, Lord.

➤ *Catechism of the Catholic Church* 1618

Eighteenth Monday in Ordinary Time
Wisdom

Year 1: Numbers 11:4b-15; Matthew 14:13-21
R: Sing with joy to God our help.

Dear Lord, Moses was getting tired with all the complaining the people of Israel were doing in the desert, even though You were feeding them miraculously each day. Give me eyes to see and the understanding to appreciate the miracles You surround me with, Lord. Help me not to complain but to grow in patience.

Year 2: Jeremiah 28:1-17; Matthew 14:13-21
R: Lord, teach me your statutes.

Dear God, Hananiah and Jeremiah were preaching to the people at the same time. Their messages were not the same. Jeremiah was sent by You; Hananiah was giving the people a false message. There are lots of messages in my world today, Lord. May I know which messages are from You; may I trust that You will guide me both in my everyday decisions and in my lifetime decisions.

➤ *Catechism of the Catholic Church* 1954

Eighteenth Tuesday in Ordinary Time
Admitting Sin

Year 1: Numbers 12:1-13; Matthew 14:22-36 or Matthew 15:1-2, 10-14
R: Be merciful, O Lord, for we have sinned.

Dear God, the first reading shows that there are consequences to our sins. When we ask You to, You forgive us and give us grace to not sin so much. But we are left with the results of our sins. If I cheat on a test and get caught, You will forgive me if I ask; but I still will have to face my teacher and principal and my parents. Like Aaron and Miriam, let me take responsibility for my sins, admit them, and ask forgiveness. In this way, the consequences are not so hard to bear.

Year 2: Jeremiah 30:1-2, 12-15, 18-22; Matthew 14:22-36 or Matthew 15:1-2, 10-14
R: The Lord will build up Zion again, and appear in all his glory.

Dear Lord, when I am willing to admit I've done wrong, things get so much easier. When I won't admit it and get mad, then things just get harder. Give me grace, Lord, to admit it when I mess up. Even though it feels like I'm losing something to admit wrongdoing, I'm actually making myself stronger and gaining character. I'm also making You proud of me.

➤ *Catechism of the Catholic Church* 1781

Eighteenth Wednesday in Ordinary Time
Trust

Year 1: Numbers 13:1-2, 25 - 14:1, 26a-29a, 34-35; Matthew 15:21-28
R: Remember us, O Lord, as you favor your people.

Dear Lord, I see the difference between the people in the first reading and the woman in the gospel. The people in the first reading complained and were frightened; they did not turn to You in trust even after all the miracles they had seen You perform for them — the parting of the sea, the manna in the desert, Miriam's leprosy and her healing. But the woman in the gospel turns to You and refuses to go away, trusting that You will grant her her prayer. Gift me, Lord, with great trust in You. May I think of turning to You with all my concerns.

Year 2: Jeremiah 31:1-7; Matthew 15:21-28
R: The Lord will guard us as a shepherd guards his flock.

Dear Lord, the woman in the gospel kept calling after You. You decided to not respond to her at first. Your disciples got embarrassed and asked You to send her away. But You knew better. You were very aware of the woman and of her need. Perhaps You were teaching Your disciples that they must keep asking, just like this woman was doing. I'll learn from her example, too, Lord; I will trust and keep asking.

➤ *Catechism of the Catholic Church* 2828

Eighteenth Thursday in Ordinary Time
Church

Year 1: Numbers 20:1-13; Matthew 16:13-23
R: If today you hear his voice, harden not your hearts.

Dear Lord, today's first reading shows Moses striking a rock and water pouring forth to quench the thirst of the people in the desert. The gospel shows You calling Peter "rock" and telling him that You will build Your Church with him as its first leader. The Church will quench the thirst of people in every land and in every age — even me. Show me, Lord, how the Church can quench my thirst — my thirst for You, my thirst for peace in the world, my thirst for understanding.

Year 2: Jeremiah 31:31-34; Matthew 16:13-23
R: Create a clean heart in me, O God.

Dear Lord, You asked the disciples who they thought You were. They knew You were special, but did they know You were God? When Peter spoke up, You knew he had been chosen to guide Your new Church. You knew the Holy Spirit had spoken through Peter and would do so as Your Church began and continued through all ages. The Holy Spirit speaks through the Church even today.

➤ *Catechism of the Catholic Church* 688

Eighteenth Friday in Ordinary Time
Life

Year 1: Deuteronomy 4:32-40; Matthew 16:24-28
R: I remember the deeds of the Lord.

Dear Lord, the responsorial psalm in today's Mass calls on us to "remember the deeds of the Lord." The reason we need to remember Your deeds — the miracles that brought the people out of slavery in Egypt, the parting of the sea, the manna in the desert, the water from the rock and now, Lord, Your coming as man, Your miracles, Your death and resurrection — is so that we can realize how precious we are to You. We remember these deeds so we know that we can trust You in all circumstances, whether things are easy for us or difficult. I will remember, Lord!

Year 2: Nahum 2:1, 3; 3:1-3, 6-7; Matthew 16:24-28
R: It is I who deal death and give life.

Lord God, today's responsorial psalm is a verse from Deuteronomy: "It is I who deal death and give life." We need to remember that life belongs to You, Lord. I pray for all those who are working in the medical fields, especially those who are working with genetics and stem cells. May we realize, Lord, that we cannot play with life itself. May those in this research show proper reverence for life and for You, the giver of life.

➤ *Catechism of the Catholic Church* 2280

Eighteenth Saturday in Ordinary Time
Friendship

Year 1: Deuteronomy 6:4-13; Matthew 17:14-20
R: I love you, Lord, my strength.

Lord Jesus, You call us to a great faith. Fear can sap the strength of our faith. Remind us to pray always so that our faith is not weak. May we realize that our true strength is in You and from You. As in today's responsorial, may we sing the words from Psalm 18: "I love you, Lord, my strength."

Year 2: Habakkuk 1:12 - 2:4; Matthew 17:14-20
R: You forsake not those who seek you, O Lord.

Lord, I do not have to be perfect in order to get Your attention. I just have to come to You. I don't have to earn Your attention or love. You meet me with open arms when I come to You. Teach me to honor our relationship. My friendship with You is sacred. May I guard it well.

➤ *Catechism of the Catholic Church* 374

Nineteenth Sunday in Ordinary Time
Conscience

Cycle A: 1 Kings 19:9a, 11-13a; Romans 9:1-5; Matthew 14:22-33
R: Lord, let us see your kindness, and grant us your salvation.

Dear God, St. Paul writes to the Romans that his conscience joins with the Holy Spirit. Is my conscience joined with the Holy Spirit? I am called, dear Lord, to form my conscience. I do this through praying a lot, through listening to the Church, through reading the Bible, and listening to the people of authority that You have put in my life. Bless my efforts, Lord. May my conscience always be joined with the Holy Spirit so that I will always know right from wrong.

Cycle B: 1 Kings 19:4-8; Ephesians 4:30 - 5:2; John 6:41-51
R: Taste and see the goodness of the Lord.

Dear Lord, St. Paul urges the Ephesians not to grieve the Holy Spirit. How do we grieve Your Spirit, Lord? When we don't listen to Your Spirit speaking within our hearts? When we turn away from what we know the Spirit is urging us to do or to speak or to believe? May I listen, Lord! May I hear what the Spirit is guiding me to do, to think, to speak and may I act accordingly. May I never grieve Your Spirit!

Cycle C: Wisdom 18:6-9; Hebrews 11:1-2, 8-19 or 11:1-2, 8-12; Luke 12:32-48 or 12:35-40
R: Blessed the people the Lord has chosen to be his own.

Dear Lord, today's responsorial psalm tells us that we are blessed to be chosen by You to belong to You. What can I give You in return, Almighty God, for choosing me to be Your own? I can give You my heart, my mind, my soul. I can listen to Your word and give You my life to do with what You will. Today, Lord, I give You my mind, my heart, my soul. Thank You for calling me to be Your own.

➤ *Catechism of the Catholic Church* 1784

Nineteenth Monday in Ordinary Time
Loving God

Year 1: Deuteronomy 10:12-22; Matthew 17:22-27
R: Praise the Lord, Jerusalem.

Dear Lord, the people in the Bible circumcised all little boys. This was a ritual they did to show that each boy belonged to You. Moses tells the people in the first reading, though, to circumcise their hearts also. Moses meant for the people to make their hearts open to You, loving of You, ready to do Your will. And this was for all people, not just boys. I open my heart to You, Lord.

Year 2: Ezekiel 1:2-5, 24-28c; Matthew 17:22-27
R: Heaven and earth are filled with your glory.

Dear Lord, in today's gospel You are asked to pay a temple tax. This tax is for the upkeep of God's temple. You question the tax because You are God, but You do not push the point, instead telling Peter to pay the tax. I wonder who around You, Jesus, realized what You were saying. They had God in their midst and did not recognize You! Give me eyes to see You, Lord. Give me a heart to love You deeply.

➤ *Catechism of the Catholic Church* 222

Nineteenth Tuesday in Ordinary Time
Children

Year 1: Deuteronomy 31:1-8; Matthew 18:1-5, 10, 12-14
R: The portion of the Lord is his people.

Dear Lord, in Your gospel reading today, the people ask You who is most important in the kingdom of heaven and You place a child beside You. Children are open, accepting, and believing. They do not doubt. They love freely, and they depend entirely on others for their well-being. This is how You want us to be with You, Lord: open, accepting of Your word, believing, and realizing that we depend on You for our very lives.

Year 2: Ezekiel 2:8 - 3:4; Matthew 18:1-5, 10, 12-14
R: How sweet to my taste is your promise!

Dear Jesus, I would have liked to see You with little kids. I bet You played with them, and I bet they felt very comfortable around You. Pull me close to You, Jesus. Let me know You as they did. When I would like You to slip Your arm around me, let me know that I can ask for Your presence in this way. How You were with those children, You are with me. Thank You for Your presence and Your love, Jesus.

➤ *Catechism of the Catholic Church* 2785

Nineteenth Wednesday in Ordinary Time
God's Presence

Year 1: Deuteronomy 34:1-12; Matthew 18:15-20
R: Blessed be God who filled my soul with fire!

Dear Lord, the responsorial psalm for today comes from Psalm 66: "Blessed be God who filled my soul with fire!" What does it feel like to have your soul filled with fire? Is that how Moses felt when he spoke with You, Lord? Will I ever feel this way? Will Your presence ever fill me so much that I feel like I'm on fire? This must be a wonderful feeling, Lord — like I feel when I'm the happiest, but multiplied by hundreds! May I experience this fire, Lord.

Year 2: Ezekiel 9:1-7; 10:18-22; Matthew 18:15-20
R: The glory of the Lord is higher than the skies.

Dear Lord, You told us that wherever two or three of us are gathered in Your name, You will be right there with us. There are two or three in my family, Lord. May we pray to You together so that Your presence will be with us. There are many more than two or three at school and at church. I know, then, that You are with us there. Give me eyes to see You with us, Lord. Give me ears to hear Your word.

➤ *Catechism of the Catholic Church* 2594

Nineteenth Thursday in Ordinary Time
Leaders

Year 1: Joshua 3:7-10a, 11, 13-17; Matthew 18:21 - 19:1
R: Alleluia!

Dear Lord, I didn't know that You parted the waters of the Jordan for Joshua and the Israelites. You did this to show the Israelites that Your power was now with Joshua, since Moses had died. Thank You, Lord, for appointing people to care for us; people who have Your power and Your authority to lead us. I pray for these people, Lord, every day. May they continue to find favor with You as they listen to You in prayer.

Year 2: Ezekiel 12:1-12; Matthew 18:21-19:1
R: Do not forget the works of the Lord!

Lord Jesus, the stories You told let Peter and the other disciples know Your will. You wanted them to teach like You taught, to see how You see, and to love as You love. Thank You for these teachers, Lord. Thank You for the teachers I have who lead me in our faith. May I listen to them, Lord. By listening to them, I am listening to You.

➤ *Catechism of the Catholic Church* 1269

Nineteenth Friday in Ordinary Time
Faith

Year 1: Joshua 24:1-13; Matthew 19:3-12
R: His mercy endures forever.

Dear God, in today's first reading, You tell the people through the words of Joshua that they are entering a land that they did not earn. They will eat of food they did not grow or plant, and they will live in buildings they did not build. You told them this because You wanted them to realize that they have things only because You have given them these things. You want me to know that my faith is a gift from You, a gift I must treasure and not take for granted, a gift I must nurture so that I never lose it.

Year 2: Ezekiel 16:1-15, 60, 63 or 16:59-63; Matthew 19:3-12
R: You have turned from your anger.

Dear God, the Old Testament shows You getting angry because the people disobey You and bring hard times upon themselves. You are always promising to forgive them and gift them with faith in You once again. Thank You for my faith, Lord. May my actions not anger You. When I do sin, may I come to You for forgiveness; but may I never take advantage of Your promise to forgive!

➤ *Catechism of the Catholic Church* 1815

Nineteenth Saturday in Ordinary Time
Choice

Year 1: Joshua 24:14-29; Matthew 19:13-15
R: You are my inheritance, O Lord.

Dear Lord, after Moses died, Joshua told the people that they had to choose whether they were going to follow You as God or turn away from You. He wanted them to make a decision and stick by that decision. They chose You. I choose You, too, Lord, not just at my Baptism, not just at my Confirmation but for now, for every day, for today. I choose You.

Year 2: Ezekiel 18:1-10, 13b, 30-32; Matthew 19:13-15
R: Create a clean heart in me, O God.

Dear Lord, You show us that choosing You is much more than just words. We must do as You do: show mercy, walk humbly, pray often, forgive others. We must be like little children, too, and we must do nothing to hinder someone else from getting to know You. Remind me, Lord, that my actions need to match my choice of You!

➤ *Catechism of the Catholic Church* 1033

Twentieth Sunday in Ordinary Time
Missionaries

Cycle A: Isaiah 56:1, 6-7; Romans 11:13-15, 29-32; Matthew 15:21-28
R: O God, let all the nations praise you!

Dear Jesus, a Canaanite woman asked You to heal her daughter. You ignored her at first, probably to get Your disciples' attention. Then, when Your disciples were getting impatient with her as she kept asking, You turned to the woman and gave her what she asked. You showed Your disciples that You are for all peoples, not just for the Jews. I pray for those who have not yet heard Your message, Lord. Send missionaries to all Your people so that all can come to know just how much You love us.

Cycle B: Proverbs 9:1-6; Ephesians 5:15-20; John 6:51-58
R: Taste and see the goodness of the Lord.

Dear God, the writer of Proverbs writes of Your wisdom: "She calls from the heights out over the city." Your Spirit, Lord, calls to everyone. There are some people, Lord, who have not heard Your invitation. Use me and others to make Your message known. No one should miss hearing how much You love us. No one should miss out on knowing what You have done for us through Jesus.

Cycle C: Jeremiah 38:4-6; Hebrews 12:1-4; Luke 12:49-53
R: Lord, come to my aid.

Dear Lord, the world does not want to accept You. The prophet Jeremiah was thrown into a cistern where he almost died. St. Paul urged us to keep our eyes fixed on You because he knew we would face difficulties from the world. And You, Lord, You knew Your message would cause division. May we be faithful to You in times of difficulty. I pray for Your missionaries, Lord. Give them courage and hope, especially when they are suffering.

➤ *Catechism of the Catholic Church* 849

Twentieth Monday in Ordinary Time
Faithfulness

Year 1: Judges 2:11-19; Matthew 19:16-22
R: Remember us, O Lord, as you favor your people.

Dear Lord, as I hear more and more of the Old Testament stories, I see that Your people sinned a lot. I sin a lot, too, Lord as I try to follow You. But I have something greater than they ever had: I have Jesus. I have the Body and Blood of Jesus in the Eucharist to help me stay faithful. Thank You for this great gift, Lord. Keep me faithful to You.

Year 2: Ezekiel 24:15-23; Matthew 19:16-22
R: You have forgotten God who gave you birth.

Dear Jesus, the young rich man was addicted to his wealth. His wealth was more important to him than anything, or anyone, else. And You knew it. So, when You looked at him, You told him that God has to be first in his life. That's all there is to it. God must be first. Help me to make You first, Lord. Always.

➤ *Catechism of the Catholic Church* 2545

Twentieth Tuesday in Ordinary Time
War

Year 1: Judges 6:11-24a; Matthew 19:23-30
R: The Lord speaks of peace to his people.

Dear God, the people of the Old Testament were surrounded by wars. They were attacking or being attacked. They saw You as with them when they were winning and against them if they were losing. But this wasn't always true. Show us, Lord, how to know Your will in our time. There are lots of wars surrounding us, too. Help us to know how to follow You in this confusing and violent world.

Year 2: Ezekiel 28:1-10; Matthew 19:23-30
R: It is I who deal death and give life.

Dear God, You know how difficult and confusing life can be. It is hard to know what is right and what is wrong. But You tell us that if we give ourselves to You, You will show us the way. You told us what seemed impossible for us is easy for You. Show us how to have peace, to be at peace, in this world that is not at peace.

➤ *Catechism of the Catholic Church* 2304

Twentieth Wednesday in Ordinary Time
God's Ways

Year 1: Judges 9:6-15; Matthew 20:1-16
R: Lord, in your strength the king is glad.

Dear Lord, our ways are just not Your ways. Teach me to respect and believe in Your ways even if I don't understand them. Your heart is bigger than mine. Your mind is bigger than mine. Let me not hold so tightly to my own thinking, but realize that You are God.

Year 2: Ezkiel 34:1-11; Matthew 20:1-16
R: The Lord is my shepherd; there is nothing I shall want.

Dear Lord, as my heart grows, I will come to understand Your ways better than I do now. For now, let me trust in You. Let me trust that You know what You are doing with my life. Let me trust that You have our world under control even when it seems it is in the control of evil people. I pray for those who suffer because of evil people, Lord. Save them soon. Help us all to trust in You.

➤ *Catechism of the Catholic Church* 273

Twentieth Thursday in Ordinary Time
New Hearts

Year 1: Judges 11:29-39a; Matthew 22:1-14
R: Here I am, Lord; I come to do your will.

Dear Lord, You have told us that many are invited but few are chosen. What does this mean? You invite everyone to know You and to follow You. But only those who respond in word and in deed will be among the chosen. Give me the grace, Lord, to follow You not only in my words but also in how I act.

Year 2: Ezekiel 36:23-28; Matthew 22:1-14
R: I will pour clean water on you and wash away all your sins.

Dear God, through Ezekiel Your prophet You have promised us to create new hearts within us and place new spirits within us. I pray that You continue to do this, Lord. Each day renew my heart and my spirit that I may follow You with a fresh start each day and be faithful to You. May I do something to delight You each day, Lord.

➤ *Catechism of the Catholic Church* 1432

Twentieth Friday in Ordinary Time
Example

Year 1: Ruth 1:1, 3-6, 14b-16, 22; Matthew 22:34-40
R: Praise the Lord, my soul!

Dear Lord, Ruth sees something in Naomi that makes her want to follow her back to her people, back to her God —You. Ruth was attracted to You, Lord, through Your follower Naomi. Thank You, Lord, for calling people to You in so many ways. May my example and way of life attract others to You.

Year 2: Ezekiel 37:1-14; Matthew 22:34-40
R: Give thanks to the Lord; his love is everlasting.

Dear Lord, Your prophet Ezekiel walks among bones. You raise the bones, put flesh on them, and bring them back to life. You are the giver of life. I want to know You, O Lord. I want to know You as Ezekiel knew You. Place Your words in my heart. Draw me to You. Reveal to me Your ways. I want to know You, Lord!

➤ *Catechism of the Catholic Church* 1709

Twentieth Saturday in Ordinary Time
Loving God

Year 1: Ruth 2:1-3, 8-11; 4:13-17; Matthew 23:1-12
R: See how the Lord blesses those who fear him.

Dear Lord, when You ask that I fear You, I know You don't mean for me to be afraid of You, as I would be afraid of ghosts. You want me to respect You, to listen to Your every word, so that I will come to know You as best as I can. May I see that this is not only best for me but it is also what will bring me the greatest peace and joy. Bless me, Lord, as I fear You.

Year 2: Ezekiel 43:1-7ab; Matthew 23:1-12
R: The glory of the Lord will dwell in our land.

Dear Lord, You do not like it when people show off by letting other people know how much they pray and how much they give to the church or charities. You want people to pray and to give to others because they love You, not so they can show off. Help me to love You, Lord, to pray quietly, to give to others without drawing attention to myself. May I do something for You every day and keep it just between You and me.

➤ *Catechism of the Catholic Church* 222

Twenty-First Sunday in Ordinary Time
Belief

Cycle A: Isaiah 22:19-23; Romans 11:33-36; Matthew 16:13-20
R: Lord, your love is eternal; do not forsake the work of your hands.

Dear Jesus, You asked Your disciples who the people said You were. Then You asked them who *they* thought You were. Today, through this gospel reading, You are asking *me* who I think You are. I can say You are God, but do I act like that's what I believe? Do I dare speak to You without kneeling, without really thinking about it? Do I just say words at Mass, or do I really mean what I am saying? Help me to realize, Lord, just Who You are!

Cycle B: Joshua 24:1-2a, 15-17, 18b; Ephesians 5:21-32 or 5:2a, 25-32; John 6:60-69
R: Taste and see the goodness of the Lord.

Dear Lord, when You performed miracles, many in your company loved it. They were happy to be around You. When You spoke words that shamed the evil leaders of the people, these disciples loved that too. But, then, You spoke about giving us Your Body and Blood to eat and to drink. "This saying is hard," they said, and they walked away from You. You turned to the twelve and asked if they would leave You too. Peter said, "Master, to whom shall we go? You have the words of everlasting life." Peter didn't understand Your words about Your Body and Blood, but what he had seen and heard from You convinced him to believe anything that You said. May I be like Peter, Lord. I may not understand, but I believe.

Cycle C: Isaiah 66:18-21; Hebrews 12:5-7, 11-13; Luke 13:22-30
R: Go out to all the world and tell the good news.

Dear Lord, the people of Your day were like the people of my day: We want to be first in all things. We like being first. To be last is to be weak or not special. Not so in Your way of thinking, Lord. You tell those who push others aside to be first that they will end up last. And You tell those who allow others in front of them that they will be first. Even though I don't understand Your ways, dear Jesus, help me to believe.

➤ *Catechism of the Catholic Church 548*

Twenty-First Monday in Ordinary Time
Leaders

Year 1: 1 Thessalonians 1-5, 8b-10; Matthew 23:13-22
R: The Lord takes delight in his people.

Dear Jesus, Your words are beginning to get tough now as You defend Your people and call others to a true following of You. You yelled at some of the Pharisees who make up rules that don't make any sense. These are the leaders of the people, and so they bear a greater responsibility than others to lead a holy life and lead others to You. Instead, these leaders were making it harder for the people to know and follow You. I pray for all leaders in the Church. Grant them grace and wisdom. Grant them great love for You and for all people in the Church.

Year 2: 2 Thessalonians 1:1-5, 11-12; Matthew 23:13-22
R: Proclaim God's marvelous deeds to all the nations.

Dear God, every one of us gives an example. We either lead others toward You or away from You. Remind us, Lord, that we are providing an example to others, whether we mean to do so or not. May we be concerned that our example cause others to want to know You, to love You, and to serve You.

➤ *Catechism of the Catholic Church* 2287

Twenty-First Tuesday in Ordinary Time
Pride

Year 1: 1 Thessalonians 2:1-8; Matthew 23:23-26
R: You have searched me and you know me, Lord.

Dear Lord, when You yelled at the Pharisees, You were hoping that they would see their sins and ask forgiveness. Some of them did. Others just got mad at You and began to hate You. They would not let go of their own pride in order to see what You were saying was true. I let my pride blind me sometimes, too, Lord. I don't want to admit it when I'm wrong. But, if I don't, then I become just like some of the Pharisees that You got so mad at. I don't want You to be mad at me, Lord. Help me to admit it when I am wrong.

Year 2: 2 Thessalonians 2:1-3a, 14-17; Matthew 23:23-26
R: The Lord comes to judge the earth.

Dear Lord, some of the Pharisees were full of false pride. When we are full of false pride, we don't see anything wrong with what we are doing. This kind of pride only lets us see what others are doing wrong. Good pride helps us to feel good about ourselves, and it connects us with others. False pride separates us from others and makes us feel better than others. Help me, Lord, to get rid of false pride. I don't want to feel better than anyone.

➤ *Catechism of the Catholic Church* 2540

Twenty-First Wednesday in Ordinary Time
Others

Year 1: 1 Thessalonians 2:9-13; Matthew 23:27-32
R: You have searched me and you know me, Lord.

Dear Lord, St. Paul insisted that the people of Thessalonica live in a manner worthy of You who called them. Am I living in a manner worthy of You, Lord? How do I treat my friends? How do I treat those who are not my friends? How do I speak to my parents? How do I treat my spiritual life? Do I pray often? Do I take advantage of the sacraments You have given me? Give me the courage to evaluate myself and change what needs changing.

Year 2: 2 Thessalonians 3:6-10, 16-18
R: Blessed are those who fear the Lord.

Dear Lord, sometimes Your words are confusing to me. On one hand I hear that I should accept everyone. But then I hear that I should stay away from someone who behaves in any way against You. May I see, Lord, that accepting others doesn't mean I have to be their friend. I need to protect my spiritual life from anything or anyone I fear can cause me to do something wrong.

➤ *Catechism of the Catholic Church* 425

Twenty-First Thursday in Ordinary Time
Choice

Year 1: 1 Thessalonians 3:7-13; Matthew 24:42-51
R: Fill us with your love, O Lord, and we will sing for joy!

Dear Lord, do for me what the responsorial psalm proclaims in today's Mass: "Fill us with your love, O Lord, and we will sing for joy!" I would like to be filled with Your love, God. Help to remember, though, that love is a choice, not just a feeling. I can choose to show love for You any time I want, not just when I feel it.

Year 2: 1 Corinthians 1:1-9; Matthew 24:42-51
R: I will praise your name forever, Lord.

Dear Jesus, You told us to stay awake, to be on guard for our spiritual lives because we don't know when You will come. Help me, Lord, to be very serious about my spiritual life: May I get to know You well by praying a lot, by reading the Bible, by listening to You, and by talking about You with others who love You, too. May my relationship with You be precious to me, as I know it is precious to You.

➤ *Catechism of the Catholic Church 2786*

Twenty-First Friday in Ordinary Time
Purity

Year 1: 1 Thessalonians 4:1-8; Matthew 25:1-13
R: Rejoice in the Lord, you just!

Lord God, You call us not to impurity but to holiness; so, if we ignore this call, we are ignoring not only St. Paul, who wrote these words in his letter to the Thessalonians, but we are ignoring You, too. We have to make ourselves clean and keep ourselves clean. May I watch over what I allow my eyes to see, my ears to hear, and my mouth to say. Keep me clean and pure, O Lord.

Year 2: 1 Corinthians 1:17-25; Matthew 25:1-13
R: The earth is full of the goodness of the Lord.

Dear Lord, as much as I think there is evil in the world, there is even more goodness. But, the world does not teach me to see goodness. The world wants me to think that goodness is boring and dumb. Give me eyes to see like You see, Lord. Keep me pure and show me the goodness that is all around me.

➤ *Catechism of the Catholic Church 2525*

Twenty-First Saturday in Ordinary Time
Talents

Year 1: 1 Thessalonians 4:9-11; Matthew 25:14-30
R: The Lord comes to rule the earth with justice.

Dear Lord, if I have a talent, I can make that talent grow if I practice and practice. But if I don't pay any attention to that talent, then I may lose it! My faith is just like this: If I nurture it, it will grow, with Your blessing. If I ignore it, I may lose it altogether. This is what You mean in today's gospel. Let me take heed, Lord. Let me nurture my faith so that I don't lose it!

Year 2: 1 Corinthians 1:26-31; Matthew 25:14-30
R: Blessed the people the Lord has chosen to be his own.

Dear Lord, You have given me talents to use for Your glory. How am I to do this? Help me, Lord, as I grow, to discover what gifts, what talents, You have given to me. Help me to nurture these talents and make them grow. Then, Lord, teach me how to use them for Your glory. You have given them to me; You will show me how best to put them to use.

➤ *Catechism of the Catholic Church* 546

Twenty-Second Sunday in Ordinary Time
Doers

Cycle A: Jeremiah 20:7-9; Romans 12:1-2; Matthew 16:21-27
R: My soul is thirsting for you, O Lord my God.

Dear God, Your love requires sacrifice. To sacrifice means to give up something for what we see as something better. You gave up Your life to gain our entrance into eternal life, and You saw that as better than living. May I give up things for You, Lord, and for others. Teach me what sacrifice means.

Cycle B: Deuteronomy 4:1-2, 6-8; James 1:17-18, 21b-22, 27; Mark 7:1-8, 14-15, 21-23
R: The one who does justice will live in the presence of the Lord.

Dear Lord, St. James tells us to be doers of the word and not hearers only. People who hear it only and don't put it into practice are fooling themselves if they think they are saved. We must show that we are Christians by how well we treat one another, by how well we treat our own bodies and souls, by how well we use what has been given to us. May I be a doer and not just a hearer.

Cycle C: Sirach 3:17-18, 20, 28-29; Hebrews 12:18-19, 22-24a; Luke 14:1, 7-14
R: God, in your goodness, you have made a home for the poor.

Dear Lord, following You isn't easy. We must be very honest with ourselves when we follow You. You will call us to be better, love more, try harder. You accept us for who we are and call us to be who we can be. May I have the courage and the grace to answer Your call.

➤ *Catechism of the Catholic Church* 1039

Twenty-Second Monday in Ordinary Time
Openness to God

Year 1: 1 Thessalonians 4:13-18; Luke 4:16-30
R: The Lord comes to judge the earth.

Dear Lord, the people of Nazareth were expectant; they invited You to read in the synagogue, which You did, telling them that You were fulfilling the very Scriptures that You had read. They turned against You in only the fourth chapter of Luke's gospel. It didn't take long for Your words to cause division. May I welcome Your words, Lord Jesus. May I never take offense at You. May You always find my heart open and ready for Your word.

Year 2: 1 Corinthians 2:1-5; Luke 4:16-30
R: Lord, I love your commands.

Lord Jesus, I come to You expectant. I sit before You in prayer, waiting for Your word. Speak to my heart, Lord. Help me to hear Your message. Help me to be open to Your word and to act on it. You are my Lord; I wait on You.

➤ *Catechism of the Catholic Church* 1101

Twenty-Second Tuesday in Ordinary Time
Evil

Year 1: 1 Thessalonians 5:1-6, 9-11; Luke 4:31-37
R: I believe that I shall see the good things of the Lord in the land of the living.

Dear Lord, You call us children of the light because we have You. Your words show us how to live. Your presence with us can make all darkness go away if we but turn to You and ask. Though there is evil in the world, Your love for us protects us from the dangers of evil. Thank You, Lord, for Your Light!

Year 2: 1 Corinthians 2:10b-16; Luke 4:31-37
R: The Lord is just in all his ways.

Lord Jesus, there is evil in our world. There was evil in the world when You came as a man, too. You cast demons out from people and freed them from the power of the devil. Continue to free us, Lord, from the power of the devil. Sometimes evil can look really good, but help us to see it for what it really is — ugly and deadly. May we cling to You, O Lord!

➤ *Catechism of the Catholic Church* 2854

Twenty-Second Wednesday in Ordinary Time
Example

Year 1: Colossians 1:1-8; Luke 4:38-44
R: I trust in the mercy of God for ever.

Dear Lord, St. Paul said he had heard of the faith of the people of Colossae. What would someone say of the faith of my community? Would they be amazed by our faith? Would they be inspired by our love for You, Lord? Would they remark about how we care for the poor? May I be a good example for You, Lord. For love of You, may I do good works.

Year 2: 1 Corinthians 3:1-9; Luke 4:38-44
R: Blessed the people the Lord has chosen to be his own.

Dear Lord, remind us that we are chosen by You. May people not hear us complaining or arguing with one another. May we not bicker and show envy of one another. Make our hearts big and our love great. Grant us patience with one another for love of You. May our example draw others to Your name.

➤ *Catechism of the Catholic Church* 932

Twenty-Second Thursday in Ordinary Time
Obedience

Year 1: Colossians 1:9-14; Luke 5:1-11
R: The Lord has made known his salvation.

Dear Jesus, Peter had fished all night and came up with nothing. You told him to put out into deep water. Peter told You how he had tried all night, but still he did as You told him. I know the story, Lord. He caught so many fish, his nets were about to break. You showed Peter, Lord, that You were not only a great teacher, but You are God. What Peter could not do with his own strength, You could do through him. Peter would not forget this lesson. Let me not forget it either: You can accomplish great things through me, if I listen well.

Year 2: 1 Corinthians 3:18-23; Luke 5:1-11
R: To the Lord belongs the earth and all that fills it.

Lord, make my faith in You great. Peter tried and tried to catch fish on this one evening. You told him to cast his net one more time. Peter assured You he would not catch anything, but he did! He caught so much! If he hadn't done what You asked, Peter would have missed such a miracle. Peter would have missed a sign that You are God. Like Peter, Lord, even when I doubt, may I do as You ask — come to Mass, read the Bible, do my work as best I can, obey my parents. May I never miss an opportunity to see Your glory.

➤ *Catechism of the Catholic Church* 1831

Twenty-Second Friday in Ordinary Time
Peace

Year 1: Colossians 1:15-20; Luke 5:33-39
R: Come with joy into the presence of the Lord.

Dear Jesus, the word "peace" is used so many times in the New Testament. The people You lived with needed peace; we need peace also. Your ways were new to the people of Your time; they are still new to my culture. Why is this so, Lord? Why has it taken so long for Your ways to become our ways? We do not have peace because we don't live by Your ways. Give us eyes to see, minds to understand, and wills to live by Your way, the way of peace.

Year 2: 1 Corinthians 4:1-5; Luke 5:33-39
R: The salvation of the just comes from the Lord.

Dear Lord, when You came, You wanted to shake people from the old way of doing things. Your ideas and teachings were new, full of life and truth. You wanted them to stand up and recognize the gift that was being offered to them. You want me to stand up and recognize the gift that is being offered to me — You, Lord. Your ways are now accessible to us, even through the fog of sin that we create. Help me to take hold of Your ways, Lord.

➤ *Catechism of the Catholic Church* 2305

Twenty-Second Saturday in Ordinary Time
Value

Year 1: Colossians 1:21-23; Luke 6:1-6
R: God himself is my help.

Dear Lord, You have shown that You are God in many ways in Luke's gospel. You showed Your power over the fish of the sea. Now You show Your power over the Sabbath as well. You are telling the people of Your time as well as us that You are God and we should look to You for our salvation. Help me to pray more, Lord, that I may know You better. Grant that I may be close to You, my God.

Year 2: 1 Corinthians 4:6b-15; Luke 6:1-6
R: The Lord is near to all who call upon him.

Dear Lord, let me see Your wisdom. The world I live in does not respect You or Your ways. My culture calls Your ways boring and binding. Help me to see that Your ways are the ways of freedom, and following You has no match for adventure. Your ways challenge my culture. Use me to challenge what my culture values. May I always find my true value in You.

➤ *Catechism of the Catholic Church* 1368

Twenty-Third Sunday in Ordinary Time
Love

Cycle A: Ezekiel 33:7-9; Romans 13:8-10; Matthew 18:15-20
R: If today you hear his voice, harden not your hearts.

Dear Lord, St. Paul tells us that we will fulfill the law by loving one another. But what exactly does St. Paul mean by loving one another? You give us a clue by Your words, Lord, to the prophet Ezekiel. You tell Ezekiel that if he knows another is doing wrong and does not tell that person to stop, You will hold him responsible. Therefore, our love for others must extend to helping one another act justly and obey Your will.

Cycle B: Isaiah 35:4-7a; James 2:1-5; Mark 7:31-37
R: Praise the Lord, my soul!

Dear Lord, You took the deaf man off to a private place and healed him. Please heal us of all the ways we are deaf: deaf to the cries of the poor, deaf to the rules of my family or school, deaf to Your commands. Give us hearing, O Lord, that we may heed Your word and speak Your truths.

Cycle C: Wisdom 9:13-18b; Philemon 9-10, 12-17; Luke 14:25-33
R: In every age, O Lord, you have been our refuge.

Dear Lord, sometimes the words of Your gospels confuse me. As I hear them, open my heart to understand Your meaning, Jesus. I know You call me to love with a love that comes from You. Help me to realize just what this calls me to do as I grow. I want to do Your will, Lord, and grow into the person You call me to become.

➤ *Catechism of the Catholic Church* 2196

Twenty-Third Monday in Ordinary Time
Pride

Year 1: Colossians 1:24-2:3; Luke 6:6-11
R: In God is my safety and my glory.

Dear Lord, some people try to get others in trouble. Some of the Pharisees were trying to get You in trouble. It was against the law to do work on the Sabbath. A man with a withered hand was there. He wanted to be healed. You weren't going to tell him, "No, wait until tomorrow." Besides, You are God, and God trumps the Sabbath. But, even though You healed someone, giving the gift of health, still the Pharisees were enraged against You, calling what You did work. Lord, let me never be like those Pharisees, so blinded by pride that they couldn't see the truth. They missed seeing God Himself! What an opportunity lost!

Year 2: 1 Corinthians 5:1-8; Luke 6:6-11
R: Lead me in your justice, Lord.

Dear Lord, just as some of the Pharisees were blinded by their own pride, so in this first reading Paul accuses a man of being so full of pride that he cannot see his own sin. Lord, any time I get angry with another who calls me to account for something I did wrong, help me to admit my sin instead of nursing my anger. By growing angry and refusing to admit sin, I become like those who cannot see You. I want to see You, Lord. Have mercy on me.

➤ *Catechism of the Catholic Church* 2540

Twenty-Third Tuesday in Ordinary Time
Prayer

Year 1: Colossians 2:6-15; Luke 6:12-19
R: The Lord is compassionate toward all his works.

Dear Lord, even though You are God's Son, you spent the night in prayer before choosing the twelve apostles. If You who are God spent the night in prayer when You were with us as man, all the more reason for me to spend a great deal of time in prayer before I make big decisions. Teach me how to pray, O Lord.

Year 2: 1 Corinthians 6:1-11; Luke 6:12-19
R: The Lord takes delight in his people.

Dear Lord Jesus, each of the gospels takes the time to name the twelve You chose after spending the night in prayer. These twelve were special. These twelve were charged with great responsibility; and, they were given an immense gift — being the closest to the very Son of God. Sometimes I think they had it easy because they were so close to You. But I know their temptations must have been great because I know what happened to Judas. Thank You, Lord, for the apostles, for their example, and for their love and commitment to You after Your resurrection. I ask them to pray for me, and I ask You to inspire me to follow You the way they did.

➤ *Catechism of the Catholic Church* 2725

Twenty-Third Wednesday in Ordinary Time
Growth

Year 1: Colossians 3:1-11; Luke 6:20-26
R: The Lord is compassionate toward all his works.

Dear Lord, You call me to put to death in me all things that displease You: greed, envy, cruelty, laziness, hatred, prejudice. Show me how to do this, Lord. I pray for a bigger heart that I may love more. I pray for wisdom that I may see others like You see them. And I pray for patience, with others and with myself, as we grow in Your presence.

Year 2: 1 Corinthians 7:25-31; Luke 6:20-26
R: Listen to me, daughter; see and bend your ear.

Lord God, You blessed those who are poor; may I see how poor I am without You. You blessed those who are hungry; may I hunger for You. You blessed those who are weeping; may I weep for them and lift them up to You. In all ways, Lord, may I be pleasing to You. May I receive Your blessing as well.

➤ *Catechism of the Catholic Church* 794

Twenty-Third Thursday in Ordinary Time
Imitating Jesus

Year 1: Colossians 3:12-17; Luke 6:27-38
R: Let everything that breathes praise the Lord!

Dear Lord, St. Paul tells us to put on love. We should wear love, just as visibly as we wear our clothes. Just as people see our clothes; so, too, they should be able to see our love. St. Paul tells us to put on heartfelt compassion, kindness, humility, gentleness, and patience. All these would make me like You, Jesus, and that is what You call me to, to become like You.

Year 2: 1 Corinthians 8:1b-7, 11-13; Luke 6:27-38
R: Guide me, Lord, along the everlasting way.

Lord Jesus, my culture tells me to love those who love me, to hate those who hate me, to get back at those who hurt me. But this is not Your way. I have to love those who hate me. This means I have to pray for them, wish the best for them, and resist taking revenge. Give me courage to live Your way, Lord. It is a hard way, but I want to be like You, Lord.

➤ *Catechism of the Catholic Church* 2825

Twenty-Third Friday in Ordinary Time
Heaven

Year 1: 1 Timothy 1:1-2, 12-14; Luke 6:39-42
R: You are my inheritance, O Lord.

Lord Jesus, many people receive gifts of money from loved ones when those loved ones die. This is called an inheritance. The responsorial psalm from today's Mass reminds me that You are my inheritance. I will receive You, Lord, not only in my life now, little by little, as I am able to receive You, but wholly in heaven.

Year 2: 1 Corinthians 9:16-19, 22b-27; Luke 6:39-42
R: How lovely is your dwelling place, Lord, mighty God!

Lord Jesus, I know I cannot begin to imagine how good heaven is. I know I should want to be in heaven; and I do, but You know I like my life right now, Lord. And this is okay with You. I thank You for my life right now, and I pray for those whose lives are not as nice as my own. You mean for me to be right where I am right now. May I learn more about Your will for me, and in this way, I will learn more about heaven.

➤ *Catechism of the Catholic Church* 1026

Twenty-Third Saturday in Ordinary Time
Commitment

Year 1: 1 Timothy 1:15-17; Luke 6:43-49
R: Blessed be the name of the Lord for ever.

Dear God, You taught us that a good tree bears good fruit. This was Your way of saying that if we want to be good, we must do good things. If we want to be good, then others should be better off for having come into our presence. Are others better off for having known me, Lord? Am I a blessing to those around me? If I am not a blessing, then help me to start being one!

Year 2: 1 Corinthians 10:14-22; Luke 6:43-49
R: To you, Lord, I will offer a sacrifice of praise.

Dear Lord, if I trust in You and act upon Your words, then You will make me firm and my faith won't fail me at the slightest fearful thing. But if I just say I know You but don't behave as if I know You, then my faith will be weak and it will fail me when the slightest difficulty comes along. I must not only say that I know You; I must behave like I know You. In other words, Lord, I must be totally committed to You.

➤ *Catechism of the Catholic Church* 2609

Twenty-Fourth Sunday in Ordinary Time
Forgiveness

Cycle A: Sirach 27:30 - 28:9; Romans 14:7-9; Matthew 18:21-35
R: The Lord is kind and merciful, slow to anger, and rich in compassion.

Lord God, in the first reading Sirach tells us that sinners hug their anger tight. I don't want to hug my anger, Lord. When I am angry, I feel mean. I probably am mean. Show me how to deal with my anger right away, forgiving another or myself if I need to. Forgiving isn't an option if I am to follow You, Lord; it is a have-to. May I always forgive and release my anger properly.

Cycle B: Isaiah 50:5-9a; James 2:14-18; Mark 8:27-35
R: I will walk before the Lord, in the land of the living.

Dear Lord, this Sunday is a reminder of the cross. Isaiah writes about the suffering Messiah: "I gave my back to those who beat me." And You begin to prepare Your disciples for what will happen to You, letting them know that every follower of Yours will bear a cross of some kind. I, too, have a cross, Lord. Show me how to carry it well, for love of You.

Cycle C: Exodus 32:7-11, 13-14; 1 Timothy 1:12-17; Luke 15:1-32 or 15:1-10
R: I will rise and go to my Father.

Lord Jesus, the need for forgiveness is in every reading for Mass today. Moses asks You to forgive the people who have turned away from You yet again. St. Paul considers his sins — hunting down and killing Christians — before You called him to stop. And You tell of Your delight in having just one sinner return to You and ask forgiveness. Forgiveness is hard work, Lord. Help me to forgive.

➤ *Catechism of the Catholic Church* 2844

Twenty-Fourth Monday in Ordinary Time
Pray!

Year 1: 1 Timothy 2:1-8; Luke 7:1-10
R: Blessed be the Lord, for he has heard my prayer.

Lord Jesus, St. Paul urges us to pray for others so that we may all live in peace. St. Paul believes, then, that by praying we will have peace. There is no question about it. And You, Lord, hold up the centurion's example for us — the centurion asked for healing and knew You could give it with just a word. Asking in such confidence — this is prayer. Teach us to pray, Lord. May we pray without ceasing.

Year 2: 1 Corinthians 11:17-26, 33; Luke 7:1-10
R: Proclaim the death of the Lord until he comes again.

Dear Lord, it is easy for us to become distracted from You in our lives. We can argue easily, forget one another's needs, focus only on ourselves. But we are not to be like this. We are Christians. We are to be about caring for one another. Every time we look at a crucifix, Lord, let us remember what we are supposed to be about.

➤ *Catechism of the Catholic Church* 2742

Twenty-Fourth Tuesday in Ordinary Time
Think!

Year 1: 1 Timothy 3:1-13; Luke 7:11-17
R: I will walk with blameless heart.

Dear Jesus, the responsorial psalm for today's Mass is "I will walk with blameless heart." Is my heart blameless, Lord? Am I not a good example for You? Can someone say that I am mean to others? Can anyone say that I do not forgive others? Can anyone accuse me of gossiping, lying, cheating, or not including others? Teach me to examine myself, Lord, and do better to walk with a blameless heart.

Year 2: 1 Corinthians 12:12-14, 27-31a; Luke 7:11-17
R: We are his people: the sheep of his flock.

Dear Lord, if You appeared with me now, would I not change my life because I had seen You, heard You, and spoken with You? Help me to see, Jesus, that You have appeared with me. I can hear You. I do speak with You. It is my job to realize this more and more, living in Spirit with You as well as I do in the flesh with others. Teach me, Lord, to know that You visit Your people.

➤ *Catechism of the Catholic Church* 1785

Twenty-Fourth Wednesday in Ordinary Time
Imitating Christ

Year 1: 1 Timothy 3:14-16; Luke 7:31-35
R: How great are the works of the Lord.

Lord Jesus, some people just won't admit that something is wonderful. They will find something negative to say. Help me not to be like that. Give me the freedom to love Your creation, to follow You without full understanding, to be happy without seeing something wrong in everything. Let me not point out the bad in all things, but focus on the good. This will make me strong and make others around me strong, too.

Year 2: 1 Corinthians 12:31 - 13:13; Luke 7:31-35
R: Blessed the people the Lord has chosen to be his own.

Lord Jesus, if there was one passage in the Bible that You would want me to read over and over, it would be today's first reading of St. Paul's letter to the Corinthians. St. Paul tells me what love is:

> Love is patient and kind; love is not jealous or boastful; it is not arrogant or rude. Love does not insist on its own way; it is not irritable or resentful; it does not rejoice at wrong, but rejoices in the right. Love bears all things, believes all things, hopes all things, endures all things. Love never ends. (1 Corinthians 13:4-8a, RSV)

Let me write this verse and put it above my bed and read it every day.

➤ *Catechism of the Catholic Church* 932

Twenty-Fourth Thursday in Ordinary Time
Snobs

Year 1: 1 Timothy 4:12-16; Luke 7:36-50
R: How great are the works of the Lord.

Dear Jesus, I look down my nose at some people. Those who I think are weird or smelly or messy or dumb or even those who think they are just so cool — I look down on all of them. This is exactly how the Pharisee and his guests felt about the woman who dared come into their dinner and kneel at Jesus' feet and cry. She was evil, they thought, and they looked down their noses at her. But You, Jesus, You saw right through to her heart. You looked right past what she did, how she looked, how she smelled, how she acted, right into her heart. And You loved her. Make me like You, Jesus. May I look down my nose at no one. May I see their hearts, not the things that make them different.

Year 2: 1 Corinthians 15:1-11; Luke 7:36-50
R: Give thanks to he Lord, for he is good.

Dear Lord, the Pharisee expected You to recoil and not allow the woman crying at Your feet to touch You. She was a great sinner, and some Jews believed that it was unclean to be touched by someone who was a sinner. I would not like to live in their society, Lord. You not only allowed her to touch You, but You touched her in return and forgave her. Thank You, Lord, for showing us how to have mercy on one another and be accepting of one another.

➤ *Catechism of the Catholic Church* 1825

Twenty-Fourth Friday in Ordinary Time
Poor in Spirit

Year 1: 1 Timothy 6:2c-12; Luke 8:1-3
R: Blessed the poor in spirit; the kingdom of heaven is theirs!

Dear Lord, what do You mean by poor in spirit? Can I be poor in spirit? I want to be so that I can receive Your blessing. Teach me, Lord, that poor in spirit means that I know I must depend on You for all good things. To be poor in spirit means that I know I need You and want You. To be poor in spirit means that I do not put myself above any other human being. Help me, Lord, to understand how to be poor in spirit.

Year 2: 1 Corinthians 15:12-20; Luke 8:1-3
R: Lord, when your glory appears, my joy will be full.

Dear Jesus, there were some in Your day who said You did not rise from the dead. There are some in my day, too, who say You were a good man but You were not God; You didn't really rise from the dead. Dear Jesus, may none of this shake my faith in You. I see evidence of Your resurrection all around me — in my own heart, in the faith of those I love and who love me, in the words of Your Holy Bible. There is enough evidence, Lord. I pray for those who do not believe.

➤ *Catechism of the Catholic Church* 2546

Twenty-Fourth Saturday in Ordinary Time
God's Presence

Year 1: 1 Timothy 6:13-16; Luke 8:4-15
R: Come with joy into the presence of the Lord.

Dear Lord, how strong I am when I am joyful. Today's responsorial psalm is "Come with joy into the presence of the Lord." I am in Your presence at all times, Lord. May I discover the strength that comes from joy. May I bless myself and others around me by being joyful.

Year 2: 1 Corinthians 15:35-37, 42-49; Luke 8:4-15
R: I will walk in the presence of God, in the light of the living.

Lord Jesus, not only can I be joyful in Your presence, but I can also see! Being in Your presence, being aware of You, connecting my heart with Your heart, allows me to see and understand things that I could not see and understand if I did not open myself to You. May I desire to walk in Your presence, Lord, all the time.

➤ *Catechism of the Catholic Church* 736

Twenty-Fifth Sunday in Ordinary Time
Choosing God

Cycle A: Isaiah 55:6-9; Philippians 1:20c-24, 27a; Matthew 20:1-16
R: The Lord is near to all who call upon him.

Dear Lord, You are near, but You will not show Yourself to us until we call upon You. You show us that it is dumb not to choose You, but still we have to do the choosing; we have to do the seeking, as the prophet Isaiah says, seek the Lord while he may be found. I choose You, Lord; show Yourself to me. I seek You, Lord. May I find You.

Cycle B: Wisdom 2:12, 17-20; James 3:16 - 4:3; Mark 9:30-37
R: The Lord upholds my life.

Dear Lord, in these readings I see how our sins can result in evil things. I am sometimes the one who commits the sins; at other times, I am the one who suffers because of another's sins. Help me, Lord, to depend on You to show me when I need to ask forgiveness, and to strengthen me when I am suffering. Thank You for Your constant help.

Cycle C: Amos 8:4-7; 1 Timothy 2:1-8; Luke 16:1-13 or 16:10-13
R: Praise the Lord who lifts up the poor.

Dear Lord, the prophet Amos tells about people who can't wait to cheat others out of their money. In the gospel You tell us, Lord Jesus, that we cannot separate how we act with You and how we act with people. If we are stingy with people, then we will be stingy with You. If we look for ways to cheat others, we will also look for ways to cheat You. May I be the same, Lord, with You as I am with others. May I try my hardest to love others and try my hardest to love You, too.

➤ *Catechism of the Catholic Church* 1718

Twenty-Fifth Monday in Ordinary Time
Light

Year 1: Ezra 1:1-6; Luke 8:16-18
R: The Lord has done marvels for us.

Lord, what You have given me You want me to share with others. You did not give me talents so that I could ignore them and refuse to nurture and develop them. You mean for me to work and practice so that I can use my talents as You expect me to, for the good of many others, and for my own good. I bear Your light within me, Lord Jesus. May I let my light shine bright.

Year 2: Proverbs 3:27-34; Luke 8:16-18
R: The just one shall live on your holy mountain, O Lord.

Dear Lord, I have Your light within me. If I do not nurture this light by praying, by reading the Bible, by being kind to others, then I am being like the person who lit a lamp and put it under the table. I must pay attention to the light within me and nurture it; otherwise I might lose the light that I have. Don't let me lose this light, Lord. May I act to make the light grow brighter and brighter!

➤ *Catechism of the Catholic Church* 1704

Twenty-Fifth Tuesday in Ordinary Time
Pleasing God

Year 1: Ezra 6:7-8, 12b, 14-20; Luke 8:19-21
R: Let us go rejoicing to the house of the Lord.

Dear Lord, the first reading tells us that Your people completed their work on the Temple. Then they celebrated. They had great reverence for the Temple because they knew Your presence was in the Temple in a special way. Your presence is in my church in a special way, too, Lord. That is where people pray and call to You. That is where Your Supper is celebrated. That is where the Eucharist is. Give me great respect for my church. May I love to enter it and meet You inside its walls.

Year 2: Proverbs 21:1-6, 10-13; Luke 8:19-21
R: Guide me, Lord, in the way of your commands.

Dear Lord, the book of Proverbs tells me a lot about how You see things. You look at each person's heart. May You look at my heart and be pleased. Show me how to make my heart more pleasing to You. Inspire me to read Proverbs and other books in Your Bible.

➤ *Catechism of the Catholic Church* 1996

Twenty-Fifth Wednesday in Ordinary Time
God's Presence

Year 1: Ezra 9:5-9; Luke 9:1-6
R: Blessed be God, who lives for ever.

Dear God, the prophet Ezra continues to talk about the Temple in the first reading for today's Mass. Building Your Temple showed the people that You were pleased with them and You were dwelling among them. When You came, Lord Jesus, You taught them that the Temple building would be destroyed in future wars but Your presence would never leave Your people. Thank You, Lord, for Your presence, with us always.

Year 2: Proverbs 30:5-9; Luke 9:1-6
R: Your word, O Lord, is a lamp for my feet.

Dear Lord, Your disciples went out proclaiming the kingdom of God and heal-ing the sick. Your presence was with them. Your presence is with us, too, Lord Jesus. Your presence is in our church, in the Eucharist, in your people who come together to pray, in Your word that is read aloud, and within me. May we carry Your presence in ways worthy of You.

➤ *Catechism of the Catholic Church* 2802

Twenty-Fifth Thursday in Ordinary Time
Priorities

Year 1: Haggai 1:1-8; Luke 9:7-9
R: The Lord takes delight in his people.

Dear Lord, the people the prophet Haggai was preaching to did not have their priorities straight. They had their own houses built but did not have a house for You. Are my priorities straight, Lord? Do I put You first? In all the time I have each day, do I make talking with You a priority? Of all the topics I give my mind to during each day, do I set aside time to read about You either from the Bible or a book about You? Challenge me, Lord, to begin giving You more of my time.

Year 2: Ecclesiastes 1:2-11; Luke 9:7-9
R: In every age, O Lord, you have been our refuge.

Dear Jesus, Herod must have been afraid. He had John the Baptist killed because John pointed out Herod's sins. Now You were here and people were saying even greater things about You. Herod had a choice. He could get his life in order and ask forgiveness, or he could continue to try to kill all reminders of his sin. When I am faced with choices, Lord, give me the courage and wis-dom to take responsibility for myself, for what I've done or didn't do, and for where I want my spiritual life to go. Lord, let me choose You.

➤ *Catechism of the Catholic Church* 2732

Twenty-Fifth Friday in Ordinary Time
Rising Above

Year 1: Haggai 2:1-9; Luke 9:18-22
R: Hope in God; I will praise him, my savior and my God.

Dear Lord, You asked the disciples who people were saying You were. When Peter said You were the Christ, You told them not to tell anyone. You want each of us to see You for ourselves and choose to believe in You. Each day, Lord, I choose to believe in You. Each day, may my actions, my words, and my thoughts show my belief in You and my love for You.

Year 2: Ecclesiastes 3:1-11; Luke 9:18-22
R: Blessed be the Lord, my Rock!

Dear Lord Jesus, this reading from Ecclesiastes is one of the best in the Bible. There are times for all things — our loves, our hate, our war, our peace, our building up, our tearing down — but You rise above all these times. And we can rise above them with You. This is why we can have peace and joy in our hearts even when times are difficult. Thank You, Lord, for Your power, for Your love, for Your invitation to me to rise above.

➤ *Catechism of the Catholic Church* 202

Twenty-Fifth Saturday in Ordinary Time
Choosing God

Year 1: Zechariah 2:5-9, 14-15a; Luke 9:43b-45
R: The Lord will guard us as a shepherd guards his flock.

Dear Lord, any time there is measuring in the Bible, it means You are staking out Your territory. This is meant to give us security because if You draw a measuring line around us, then nothing on Earth can harm us, not even death itself. We need this assurance from You, Lord, especially when things are difficult in our world, in our families, in our friendships, or at school. May I be sure that I am within Your measuring lines, not on the outside of them!

Year 2: Ecclesiastes 11:9 - 12:8; Luke 9:43b-45
R: In every age, O Lord, you have been our refuge.

Lord Jesus, help me to get in the habit of choosing You every day now while I am young. I choose You by giving time to You and to my spiritual life every day. I choose You by treating others with respect. I choose You by attending to things I know I must do well. If I choose You now, choosing You when I get older and busier will be much easier. Bless me, Lord, and keep me close to You.

➤ *Catechism of the Catholic Church* 218

Twenty-Sixth Sunday in Ordinary Time
Try!

Cycle A: Ezekiel 18:25-28; Philippians 2:1-11 or 2:1-5; Matthew 21:28-32
R: Remember your mercies, O Lord.

Dear Lord, I can make it look like I am being a good Christian. I can go to Mass and say all the words. I can even say my rosary. I can even take food to the poor. But, Lord, if I keep my heart from doing all these things, if I say all the words without meaning or trying to mean them, then I am not a good Christian. Let me try, Lord. Even when the words don't make sense to me, let me try. Even when I'd rather be playing than sorting food for the poor, let me try to put my heart into it. Trying to put my heart into things is like trying to give my heart to You, Lord. I want my heart to belong to You.

Cycle B: Numbers 11:25-29; James 5:1-6; Mark 9:38-43, 45, 47-48
R: The precepts of the Lord give joy to the heart.

Lord Jesus, in the first reading it says that some of the spirit that was on Moses came to rest on others. When we are touched with Your Spirit, Lord, we can't help but have a good influence on those around us. May I have Your Spirit, Lord, and may it touch all those around me. Then we won't have so much fighting, so much arguing, so much jealousy, so much complaining. May we all focus on sharing Your Spirit.

Cycle C: Amos 6:1, 4-7; 1 Timothy 6:11-16; Luke 16:19-31
R: Praise the Lord, my soul!

Dear Lord, St. Paul tells us to run after faith, love, patience, and gentleness. It is easier to not have faith, easier to not love, easier to be impatient, easier to not be gentle. Let me not settle for what's easy, Lord. May You be proud of me for choosing to have faith, to love all I can, to be patient with myself and others, and to be gentle in all I do. Motivate me, Lord. Teach me Your ways.

➤ *Catechism of the Catholic Church* 821

Twenty-Sixth Monday in Ordinary Time
Peace

Year 1: Zechariah 8:1-8; Luke 9:46-50
R: The Lord will build up Zion again, and appear in all his glory.

Dear God, I see lots of war around the world. I see lots of suffering around me. This wouldn't be so if we all would just be faithful to You. We could help one another instead of hate one another. But You promise to restore peace to us, Lord. May I help You restore peace. May I be a peaceful person. May I do all I can to teach peace and to bring peace about in my family, my school, my church, my community. Inspire me, Lord, to work for peace.

Year 2: Job 1:6-22; Luke 9:46-50
R: Incline your ear to me and hear my word.

Dear Jesus, I don't understand what happened to Job. That book scares me. I know bad things happen sometimes. Job had a lot of bad things happen to him. I look around the world, and it seems like a lot of people's lives are bad. How do you want me to understand all this, Lord? What do You want me to do? May I keep lifting all this suffering up to You, Lord, and may You keep teaching me how I am to understand it all.

➤ *Catechism of the Catholic Church* 2305

Twenty-Sixth Tuesday in Ordinary Time
Revenge

Year 1: Zechariah 8:20-23; Luke 9:51-56
R: God is with us.

Dear Lord, others could see the example of the Jews: They knew that You were with this people, and they saw the miraculous things that You did for them. Others around me see my church community. May I do my part to make sure that others see a good example. May they not see bickering or jealousy or gossiping. May they see a group of friendly people willing to help others and willing to welcome others to join.

Year 2: Job 3:1-3, 11-17, 20-23; Luke 9:51-56
R: Let my prayer come before you, Lord.

Dear Lord, You were not welcome in a Samaritan town, and James and John wanted You to use Your power to destroy the city. You rebuked them. Your way, which You came to teach us, was new: Your way is one of love, of understanding, of forgiveness. It is so hard for us to learn that revenge, get-backs, are just not Your way. Help us, Lord, to not seek revenge when someone does something wrong to us.

➤ *Catechism of the Catholic Church* 2302

Twenty-Sixth Wednesday in Ordinary Time
Yes, Lord

Year 1: Nehemiah 2:1-8; Luke 9:57-62
R: Let my tongue be silenced if I ever forget you!

Dear Lord, You ask for a commitment from each of us that is very firm. You don't want "maybe" for an answer. You insist on a firm "yes." I can give You that, Lord. I can say "yes" to You in my heart. I know that following You isn't going to be boring. You will challenge me to do great things. I say "yes," Lord.

Year 2: Job 9:1-12, 14-16; Luke 9:57-62
R: Let my prayer come before you, Lord.

Dear Lord, I can't wait until I am grown up to answer Your call. You call now. Your call is always now. What will happen when I say yes, Lord? What will Your next move be? Do I have the courage to find out? Let me take some quiet time to tell You "Yes, I choose You, Lord; yes I will follow You" and follow it up with a firm decision to pay more attention to You, to watch for You, to listen for You.

➤ *Catechism of the Catholic Church* 429

Twenty-Sixth Thursday in Ordinary Time
Strength

Year 1: Nehemiah 8:1-4a, 5-6, 7b-12; Luke 10:1-12
R: The precepts of the Lord give joy to the heart.

Dear Lord, the prophet Nehemiah tells us that rejoicing in You can be our strength. I do feel strong when I am full of joy. When I rejoice in You, Lord, I will feel strong and You will give me grace, too. When I am down and need strength, help me to remember this truth, Lord Jesus: Rejoicing in You brings strength.

Year 2: Job 19:21-27; Luke 10:1-12
R: I believe that I shall see the good things of the Lord in the land of the living.

Dear Lord, Job has lost everything: his family, his property, his health. His friends come and blame something that he has done for all that has happened to him. He tells them that he has done nothing wrong. And yet with all this, he still longs for You, Lord. May I have such faith! May those who lose everything in natural disasters have the faith of Job and still long for You, O Lord! You will be their strength.

➤ *Catechism of the Catholic Church* 2133

Twenty-Sixth Friday in Ordinary Time
Unbelievers

Year 1: Baruch 1:15-22; Luke 10:13-16
R: For the glory of your name, O Lord, deliver us.

Dear Lord, there are some people who just refuse to believe in You. They hear Your words as I do. They see the example of so many others who love You, as I do. But, for some reason, they refuse to give themselves to You. I pray for them, Lord. May their hearts somehow open up to You. I pray especially for those in my family who don't think about You at all. Move their hearts, Lord.

Year 2: Job 38:1, 12-21; 43:3-5; Luke 10:13-16
R: Guide me, Lord, along the everlasting way.

Dear God, Job dares to question You for what has happened to him. You ask him if he has ever "commanded the morning and shown the dawn its place." You who make the sun rise in the morning are so much greater than we are, we cannot begin to understand why You allow some things to happen and others not. We just must trust in You. Increase my trust in You, Lord.

➤ *Catechism of the Catholic Church* 185

Twenty-Sixth Saturday in Ordinary Time
Bad Things

Year 1: Baruch 4:5-12, 27-29; Luke 10:17-24
R: The Lord listens to the poor.

Dear Lord, sometimes You allow bad things to happen to people to get them to see that they need You in their lives. I pray for those who have bad things happen to them. May they reach out to You and ask You for faith and strength. Thank You, Lord, that You bring good out of bad things.

Year 2: Job 42:1-3, 5-6, 12-17; Luke 10:17-24
R: Lord, let your face shine on me.

Dear Lord, sometimes we just can't figure things out. We have to be okay with that. Just like Job said to You, "I have dealt with great things that I do not understand; things too wonderful for me, which I cannot know," so, for us there are things that just are beyond our understanding, too. We should not expect to understand things before we believe in them. I cannot understand You, Lord, but I do believe in You. And that's okay.

➤ *Catechism of the Catholic Church* 312

Twenty-Seventh Sunday in Ordinary Time
Holy Spirit

Cycle A: Isaiah 5:1-7; Philippians 4:6-9; Matthew 21:33-43
R: The vineyard of the Lord is the house of Israel.

Dear Lord, St. Paul told the people of Philippi: What you have learned and received and heard and seen in me keep on doing. St. Paul's example must have been very, very good. Let me be able to say that to someone, Lord, with Your grace. May my example be so good that I can come to someone who is looking for You and say: Just do what you see me do.

Cycle B: Genesis 2:18-24; Hebrews 2:9-11; Mark 10:2-16 or 10:2-12
R: May the Lord bless us all the days of our lives.

Dear Lord, in this reading from Genesis, You show us that it is not good for us to be alone. We are meant to be with one another, to have families, to have friends. We grow from having relationships. We discover more about You from having relationships. Bless the relationships I have, Lord. May they help me to grow and may I have a good influence on those around me.

Cycle C: Habakkuk 1:2-3; 2:2-4; 2 Timothy 1:6-8, 13-14; Luke 17:5-10
R: If today you hear his voice, harden not your hearts.

Dear God, St. Paul tells people to stir into flame the gift of God within them. What happens when something gets stirred? It moves faster, it mixes in well, sometimes it can even fly out of its container! May I stir into flame your Spirit within me, Lord, that You fly out of this container of myself onto those around me!

➤ *Catechism of the Catholic Church* 1091

Twenty-Seventh Monday in Ordinary Time
God Is Persistent

Year 1: Jonah 1:1 - 2:1-2, 11; Luke 10:25-37
R: You will rescue my life from the pit, O Lord.

Dear Jesus, You may never have me swallowed by a big fish to get my attention, but You will keep telling me what I need to do, just like You told Jonah. Give me courage, Lord, to do what You ask of me not just when I grow older, but now. What are You asking of me right now?

Year 2: Galatians 1:6-12; Luke 10:25-37
R: The Lord will remember his covenant for ever.

Dear Lord, promises You make You don't forget. You set up an agreement between me and You at my baptism, and You won't forget it. You will always be with me; help me, Jesus, to always be with You. Help my understanding of just what this means in my everyday life.

➤ *Catechism of the Catholic Church* 2567

Twenty-Seventh Tuesday in Ordinary Time
Listening

Year 1: Jonah 3:1-10; Luke 10:38-42
R: If you, O Lord, mark iniquities, who can stand?

Dear Lord, the people of Nineveh had lost sight of You and were sinning big-time. You told Jonah to go and tell them they were doing wrong. Jonah had to walk through the city and tell these people that You would destroy the city if they didn't shape up. I bet that was hard for Jonah to do. But what if Jonah hadn't told the people? Their sins would have resulted in their city being destroyed. It's good Jonah obeyed You, Lord. My place in Your kingdom is just as important as Jonah's. May I listen to You and obey You.

Year 2: Galatians 1:13-24; Luke 10:38-42
R: Guide me, Lord, along the everlasting way.

Dear God, Martha got mad that Mary wasn't helping her with dinner for You. You told Martha that Mary had chosen to sit and listen to You and that was better for right now. Teach me, Lord, that sometimes I have to do things, helping, cleaning, studying, playing, but always, always, I must give time to sit at Your feet and listen to You, look to You, and just be with You.

➤ *Catechism of the Catholic Church* 151

Twenty-Seventh Wednesday in Ordinary Time
Saved

Year 1: Jonah 4:1-11; Luke 11:1-4
R: Lord, you are merciful and gracious.

Dear Jesus, Jonah was mad. He was mad because You did not destroy the city You threatened to destroy if they didn't shape up. Jonah had gone up to a hill to see the city's destruction, but it did not come. Perhaps the people had been mean to him as he walked through it and told them to turn from their sins. Enough of them must have done so. Jonah should have been happy that his preaching had worked. I'd like to see bad things happen to some people, Lord: leaders who don't feed their citizens; people who torture others; people who are just plain mean. But You ask me to pray for them instead. Your grace can do much more to turn these people away from their sins than can my anger against them.

Year 2: Galatians 2:1-2, 7-14; Luke 11:1-4
R: Go out to all the world, and tell the Good News.

Dear God, everybody gets to hear Your word. You appeared on earth as a man for everyone, not just for those who happen to hear about You. Is God appearing on Earth as a man not important enough for all the world to hear? Let me see how important this is, Lord, especially in my society that thinks people can believe in whatever they want to believe in. If we don't believe in You, what truths about God are we missing out on?

➤ *Catechism of the Catholic Church* 74

Twenty-Seventh Thursday in Ordinary Time
Gas

Year 1: Malachi 3:13-20b; Luke 11:5-13
R: Blessed are they who hope in the Lord.

Dear Lord, if I bug You a lot when asking for something, will You give it to me? In this gospel reading, You say You will. Why did You say this, Lord? Is it because You want me to know that if I keep praying hard, You will answer me in one way or another? Prayer does something inside me, Lord. When I am praying, things inside me are changing, changing to make me more like You, changing to help me know Your will better. Teach me, Jesus, to pray to You a lot.

Year 2: Galatians 3:1-5; Luke 11:5-13
R: Blessed be the Lord, the God of Israel: he has come to his people.

Dear Lord, sometimes we can think we're just so good because of the good things we do. The Galatians were feeling this way. They must have been pretty proud of themselves. St. Paul calls them stupid. They had forgotten that the only reason they are capable of doing good things is because of the gift of faith from You. They thought they were all good just because of themselves. That's like a car thinking it can go fast all by itself without gas! You are our gas, Lord. We do good things because You enable us to do good things. We need to say thank You and make sure we feed that gift of faith You gave us. Otherwise, we'll lose that gift. We'll run out of gas!

➤ *Catechism of the Catholic Church* 1997

Twenty-Seventh Friday in Ordinary Time
With God

Year 1: Joel 1:13-15; 2:1-2; Luke 11:15-26
R: The Lord will judge the world with justice.

Dear Jesus, You said that whoever is not with You is against You. Therefore, I cannot just live my life without You and think that will be okay. My example will teach others that it is okay to just go along day by day without paying attention to You. I won't gain happiness this way, Lord, and I sure won't be teaching others to gain happiness either. Let me get my life together right now, Lord, and decide that I'm going to be with You, as close to You as I can possibly get. May Your Spirit within me teach me how.

Year 2: Galatians 3:7-14; Luke 11:15-26
R: The Lord will remember his covenant for ever.

Dear Lord, those Galatians really thought that just obeying the law word for word was going to save them. They had no real relationship with You. They didn't pray to You. They didn't do anything to nurture that gift of faith within them. It was like they were afraid to believe that You — Almighty God — would be there for them in prayer, in conversation. Thank You, Lord, for being this close to me.

➤ *Catechism of the Catholic Church* 2564

Twenty-Seventh Saturday in Ordinary Time
Judgment Day

Year 1: Joel 4:12-21; Luke 11:27-28
R: Rejoice in the Lord, you just!

Dear Lord, judgment day will happen. Lots of people act like it won't. They don't pay much attention to You. They certainly don't let You affect how they live or what they believe. What if we have to know something about You in order to get into heaven, Lord? What will happen to those people then? What if we have to be able to recognize You? What if we never take the time to learn what You look like; what will happen to us then?

Year 2: Galatians 3:22-29; Luke 11:27-28
R: The Lord remembers his covenant for ever.

Lord God, You call blessed anyone who hears the word of God and keeps it. Am I blessed, Lord? I will be blessed if I hear what You say and put it into practice. What do You say, Lord? Put God first. Pray. Care for others. Take care of the poor. Keep myself pure. I want to be blessed, Lord. Help me to hear Your word and keep it.

➤ *Catechism of the Catholic Church* 1040

Twenty-Eighth Sunday in Ordinary Time
Gratitude

Cycle A: Isaiah 25:6-10; Philippians 4:12-14; Matthew 22:1-14 or 22:1-10
R: I shall live in the house of the Lord all the days of my life.

Dear Lord, You repeat over and over that just because we're invited to heaven doesn't mean that we will be among the chosen. We have to respond to You. We have to choose You. We have to put our "money where our mouth is," meaning we have to behave like Christians. In my every action, Lord, may I choose You by doing and saying and thinking what is pleasing to You.

Cycle B: Wisdom 7:7-11; Hebrews 4:12-13; Mark 10:17-30 or 10:17-27
R: Fill us with your love, O Lord, and we will sing for joy!

Dear Lord, may I pray for wisdom so that I can know what is truly important in my life. Wisdom will tell me right from wrong. Wisdom will show me how great You are. Wisdom will help me to be grateful for all that I have. Thank You for this gift of wisdom. May I grow in wisdom in Your sight.

Cycle C: 2 Kings 5:14-17; 2 Timothy 2:8-13; Luke 17:11-19
R: The Lord has revealed to the nations his saving power.

Dear Lord, You healed ten people who had a terrible skin disease. Only one of the ten came back to thank You. Help me to see all that You have given me, God. Your blessings are around me so much, I take them for granted. Give me a heart of gratitude.

➤ *Catechism of the Catholic Church* 2099

Twenty-Eighth Monday in Ordinary Time
Sin

Year 1: Romans 1:1-7; Luke 11:29-32
R: The Lord has made known his salvation.

Dear Lord, some people ask You for a sign that You are with them when they are going through a difficult time. They love You already, so You don't mind this request every once in a while. But, the people who demand a sign before they will even listen to You don't deserve a sign of Your love. Their hearts are closed to even knowing You. How can people not want to know You, Jesus? I pray for them. May at least one of them turn to You today and ask for Your help.

Year 2: Galatians 4:22-24, 26-27, 31 - 5:1; Luke 11:29-32
R: Blessed be the name of the Lord forever.

Lord Jesus, we are slaves to sin. This is not living in freedom. When people say they are free to do what they want, they are not making sense. We are never free to sin. True freedom is doing what is right. Sin causes bad things. Who wants to be free to cause bad things? That is slavery. Free me from the slavery to sin, Lord!

➤ *Catechism of the Catholic Church* 1733

Twenty-Eighth Tuesday in Ordinary Time
Soul

Year 1: Romans 1:16-25; Luke 11:37-41
R: The heavens proclaim the glory of God.

Dear Lord, even though it is important for me to keep my body clean, it is even more important for me to keep my soul clean. I must look at myself every day to see if I am growing more and more like You. I can do this by praying every day, reading the Bible every day, and trying my best to be good. Challenge me, Lord, to keep my soul clean.

Year 2: Galatians 5:1-6; Luke 11:37-41
R: Let your mercy come to me, O Lord.

Dear Jesus, giving alms is very important. You said in Luke's gospel that giving alms can make our souls clean. This is true, we give with great love and thank You for the generosity of heart that motivates us to give. Help me to understand, Lord, that if I have more than I need, then I am obligated to help You take care of those who do not have enough. May I make this my way of life.

➤ *Catechism of the Catholic Church* 363

Twenty-Eighth Wednesday in Ordinary Time
Sin

Year 1: Romans 2:1-11; Luke 11:42-46
R: Lord, you give back to everyone according to his works.

Dear Jesus, You were very angry with some of the Pharisees. They were not teaching Your people the right things. They, as leaders, accepted responsibility to guide people to You, but they were not doing this. They were keeping people from You, and this made You very angry. I pray for the leaders of Your people, Lord. This is a big responsibility You give to them. You also give them the grace to accomplish this responsibility. May they be open to Your grace, open to Your love, open to Your many blessings.

Year 2: Galatians 5:18-25; Luke 11:42-46
R: Those who follow you, Lord, will have the light of life.

Dear Jesus, how did some of the Pharisees go so wrong? What tempted them to focus just on the rules and insist on following the rules without mercy and without exception? How did their hearts go so far away from love of You? I know sin can do this, Lord. Sin can make us not care about loving You. Sin can make us hard-hearted, even mean. Have mercy on us, Lord. Help us to seek forgiveness when we sin.

➤ *Catechism of the Catholic Church* 1850

Twenty-Eighth Thursday in Ordinary Time
Jesus' Death

Year 1: Romans 3:21-30; Luke 11:47-54
R: With the Lord there is mercy and fullness of redemption.

Dear Jesus, You came to save us from our sins. Without You, we would just keep on sinning and fall further and further from You. But because You came, You showed us the way to follow You. Your dying gave us the Holy Spirit to guide us. Your dying broke open heaven's doorway and allowed us to come in, washed clean by Your Body and Blood. Thank You, Lord Jesus. You gave me Your life; I thank You by giving You mine.

Year 2: Ephesians 1:1-10; Luke 11:47-54
R: The Lord has made known his salvation.

Lord Jesus, we can know Your will. You do not keep it secret from us. Let me know Your will when I pray, and help me to follow Your will in my daily life. Let me speak in ways that please You, act in ways that please You, and think in ways that please You. Thank You, Lord, that I can know You so well.

➤ *Catechism of the Catholic Church* 601

Twenty-Eighth Friday in Ordinary Time
People Are Important

Year 1: Romans 4:1-8; Luke 12:1-7
R: I turn to you, Lord, in time of trouble, and you fill me with the joy of salvation.

Dear Jesus, You tell me that every hair on my head is counted. You probably do know how many hairs are on my head, but the real reason You said this is to point out how important I am to You. If I am important to Almighty God, then no one can say I am unimportant and be believed. Even when I feel unimportant, You still love me and uphold me. Thank You, Lord.

Year 2: Ephesians 1:11-14; Luke 12:1-7
R: Blessed the people the Lord has chosen to be his own.

Dear Lord Jesus, if You know how many hairs are on my head, then You know how many hairs are on the heads of those around me, too. I am important to You, and so are the people around me. May I not look down on anyone, Lord, but treat others with respect. You have chosen them, just as You have chosen me.

➤ *Catechism of the Catholic Church* 287

Twenty-Eighth Saturday in Ordinary Time
Heart-Sight

Year 1: Romans 4:13, 16-18; Luke 12: 8-12
R: The Lord remembers his covenant for ever.

Dear Jesus, You don't want me to be ashamed of telling others that You are important to me. When I get the opportunity of telling others what I believe in, may I have the courage and wisdom — and common sense! — to let them know that You are number one in my life.

Year 2: Ephesians 1:15-23; Luke 12:8-12
R: You have given your Son rule over the works of your hands.

Dear Jesus, St. Paul prays: "May the eyes of your hearts be enlightened." If my heart sees, Lord, then I understand and then I love. Let the eyes of my heart see You, Jesus. Let the eyes of my heart see Your ways and follow You anywhere You lead me.

➤ *Catechism of the Catholic Church* 2639

Twenty-Ninth Sunday in Ordinary Time
Jesus Was Once a Kid

Cycle A: Isaiah 45:1, 4-6; 1 Thessalonians 1:1-5b; Matthew 22:15-21
R: Give the Lord glory and honor.

Dear God, St. Paul told us that the gospel comes to us, not in word alone, but in power. This means that the Holy Spirit enters us as we hear Your word and the Spirit gives us the grace to understand and follow Your word. No other word comes to us with power, God — not the words of the books I read, not the words of the newspaper, not the words of the billboards along the highway. But Your word, the words of the Bible, You have promised, come to us with power.

Cycle B: Isaiah 53:10-11; Hebrews 4:14-16; Mark 10:35-45 or 10:42-45
R: Lord, let your mercy be on us, as we place our trust in you.

Lord Jesus, no one can say that You don't know how things are on Earth. No one can say You don't know pain, or heartache, or loss of a loved one, or temptation to sin. You experienced all these things. You struggled in school, got bored in the Temple, forgot to do your chores, and had Your feelings hurt by another kid. You know what it is like to be a kid. I like that, Jesus. Let me know that I can bring my cares, my hurts, my worries to You. You will understand.

Cycle C: Exodus 17:8-13; 2 Timothy 3:14 - 4:2; Luke 18:1-8
R: Our help is from the Lord, who made heaven and earth.

Dear Jesus, You tell us to pray always without ceasing. How can we do this and why should we do this? We can pray always, Lord, just by offering up to You all that we do each day. This will help us to become aware of You all the time, as if we could see Your Spirit beside us always. Why should we do this? It will make us strong; it will bring us joy; it will help others around us. Why would I not want to do this?

➤ *Catechism of the Catholic Church* 540

Twenty-Ninth Monday in Ordinary Time
Power of Faith

Year 1: Romans 4:20-25; Luke 12:13-21
R: Blessed be the Lord, the God of Israel; he has come to his people.

Dear Lord, Abraham was empowered by faith. Does my faith empower me? My faith has the power to allow me to choose what is right; my faith has the power to help me stand up for what I believe in; my faith has the power to help me to understand my schoolwork; my faith has the power to help me to understand others. Thank You, Lord, for the power of my faith.

Year 2: Ephesians 2:1-10; Luke 12:13-21
R: The Lord made us, we belong to him.

Dear Lord, there is no greater reason for our devotion to You than the fact that You made us. We belong to You, Lord. We owe You our very lives. You who created the world millions of years ago, You who made dinosaurs and the tiniest of amoebas, You are interested in me and invite me to get to know You. This is just awesome, Lord. Thank You for making me.

➤ *Catechism of the Catholic Church* 124

Twenty-Ninth Tuesday in Ordinary Time
God's Will

Year 1: Romans 5:12, 15b, 17-19, 20b-21; Luke 12:35-38
R: Here I am, Lord; I come to do your will.

Dear Jesus, can I really say the responsorial psalm honestly? It is "Here I am, Lord; I come to do your will." I want to say this honestly, Lord. Your will is for me to do my schoolwork the best I can, to honor my parents by doing what they ask, to seek You through prayer and the sacraments, to respect myself and those around me, and to help those less fortunate than I am in any way I can. I can do these things, Lord, with Your help. "Here I am, Lord; I come to do your will."

Year 2: Ephesians 2:12-22; Luke 12:35-38
R: The Lord speaks of peace to his people.

Dear Jesus, may I work every day on my soul. May I have my soul ready for You to see any time. Every good thing I do helps my soul. Every prayer I say helps my soul. Every nice word I speak helps my soul. May You be pleased when You look at me, Lord.

➤ *Catechism of the Catholic Church* 2579

Twenty-Ninth Wednesday in Ordinary Time
God's Name

Year 1: Romans 6:12-18; Luke 12:39-48
R: Our help is in the name of the Lord.

Dear Jesus, the responsorial psalm for today's Mass is "Our help is in the name of the Lord." If help can come to us, Lord, simply by saying Your name, what power You have! No wonder I should have great respect for Your name and never use it in a negative way. Grant me, Lord, the grace to have great reverence for Your name.

Year 2: Ephesians 3:2-12; Luke 12:39-48
R: You will draw water joyfully from the springs of salvation.

Dear Jesus, water is a symbol of the Holy Spirit in the Bible. Just as we cannot live without water, so, too, we cannot live without the Holy Spirit. In today's Mass the responsorial psalm is "You will draw water joyfully from the springs of salvation." One of the fruits of the Holy Spirit is joy. Fill me with Your Holy Spirit, Lord. Fill me with joy. May I look forward to the day of my Confirmation (or thank You for the great gifts of my Confirmation).

➤ *Catechism of the Catholic Church* 2162

Twenty-Ninth Thursday in Ordinary Time
Is Sin Fun?

Year 1: Romans 6:19-23; Luke 12:49-53
R: Blessed are they who hope in the Lord.

Dear Lord, You did not intend for Your message to bring peace to everyone. If we are choosing to sin, then we will not gain peace from Your message. Your message will challenge us to start a new way of life, to clean up our acts. Not everyone around us will be happy if we choose to do that. Some people don't want us to be close to You. Some people want to keep on sinning because they think it's easier and more fun. May we see, Lord, that true happiness — and the fun that can come from it — is found in You, and only in You.

Year 2: Ephesians 3:14-21; Luke 12:49-53
R: The earth is full of the goodness of the Lord.

Dear Lord, do I have enough faith that You can answer my prayers? St. Paul said that You are able to accomplish far more than all I can ask or even imagine. I see so much that I want to ask for, Lord — healing for those who are sick, food for the kids who are starving, shelter for those who are cold, a job for those who are out of work, help for those who are addicted to things, and help for me in my schoolwork. I give all these concerns to You, O Lord, and I trust that Your heart is even bigger than mine.

➤ *Catechism of the Catholic Church* 1849

Twenty-Ninth Friday in Ordinary Time
Self-Control

Year 1: Romans 7:18-25a; Luke 12:54-59
R: Lord, teach me your statutes.

Dear Jesus, I fight against myself sometimes. I want to do what is right but sometimes I slip up. Sometimes I lose my temper and yell at someone or even hit someone. I don't mean to. Help me to ask You for help a lot more than I do, Lord. You can help me control my temper. You can help me control the tendencies in me that allow me to sin.

Year 2: Ephesians 4:1-6; Luke 12:54-59
R: Lord, this is the people that longs to see your face.

Dear Lord, give us the courage to admit what we know. Like You said in Luke's gospel, if we see dark clouds, we know it is going to rain. If we feel the wind from the south, we know it is going to be hot. There is so much evidence in the world, Lord, that You exist, that You made us, and that You love us, that no one has any excuse not to believe in You. I pray for those who insist on ignoring all these signs. Shake them, Lord! Give them the grace to get right with You!

➤ *Catechism of the Catholic Church 1832*

Twenty-Ninth Saturday in Ordinary Time
Christ's Body

Year 1: Romans 8:1-11; Luke 13:1-9
R: Lord, this is the people that longs to see your face.

Dear God, St. Paul tells us that the Spirit of the one who raised Jesus from the dead dwells in us. That same Spirit that opened Jesus' eyes after that horrible death dwells in me? Good God, this Spirit can accomplish anything! What will this Spirit do in me? What will this Spirit ask of me? May I remember that this Spirit, the Holy Spirit, is within me, especially when I grow afraid of anything!

Year 2: Ephesians 4:7-16; Luke 13:1-9
R: Let us go rejoicing to the house of the Lord.

Lord Jesus, St. Paul tells us that if we live the truth in love, we should grow more and more like You. St. Paul doesn't just mean me. He means me with those around me. All of us together can be like You. Maybe I will be like You in the way I care for others, and someone else will be like You in the way they understand and teach the Bible. All of us together can be Your Body, the Church, just like You.

➤ *Catechism of the Catholic Church 789*

Thirtieth Sunday in Ordinary Time
Bartimaeus

Cycle A: Exodus 22:20-26; 1 Thessalonians 1:5c-10; Matthew 22:34-40
R: I love you, Lord, my strength.

Dear Lord God, You tell us to turn from our idols. People in your day knew what that meant. I don't know what it means, Lord. If I look at myself and see that I will go along with anything my friends want to do, even if it's something wrong, then I have made these friendships an idol — I've made them more important than following Your rules. Help me to understand this, Jesus, and give me wisdom and courage to do what is right by putting You first.

Cycle B: Jeremiah 31:7-9; Hebrews 5:1-6; Mark 10:46-52
R: The Lord has done great things for us; we are filled with joy.

Dear Lord, the story of Bartimaeus holds so many lessons for me. First of all, Bartimaeus had no shame of You — he called for You loud and strong and kept calling even when the others yelled at him for making so much noise. When You called for him, the disciples said to him, "Take courage; get up, he [Jesus] is calling you." This is a command I need to obey, too. Then, when Bartimaeus came before You, Jesus, You asked him what he wanted, even though it must have been obvious that he was blind. I can make Bartimaeus's request my own — "Master, I want to see." I can be so blind in so many ways. And last, what did Bartimaeus do once he was healed? He followed You. Thank You for this story, Lord. Help me to learn from it all I can.

Cycle C: Sirach 35:12-14, 16-18; 2 Timothy 4:6-8, 16-18; Luke 18:9-14
R: The Lord hears the cry of the poor.

Dear Lord, I like this reading from Sirach: "The prayer of the lowly pierces the clouds; it does not rest till it reaches its goal." If I am lowly, my prayer will reach You, and You will respond to me. Teach me how to be lowly, Lord. It doesn't mean I must be weak. It means that I just know that I am not You; I don't control things, nor should I try to; You are God; I am lowly before You. And that is good. I am glad You are in control. Make me lowly, Lord, and hear my prayers!

➤ *Catechism of the Catholic Church* 544

Thirtieth Monday in Ordinary Time
Ugliness

Year 1: Romans 8:12-17; Luke 13:10-17
R: Our God is the God of salvation.

Dear Jesus, we're ugly when our hearts are hard. In this gospel story a woman had suffered for 18 years. You noticed her and healed her — on the Sabbath. One of the leaders was angry because he considered healing work and Jews were not supposed to work on the Sabbath. I can't believe how hard his heart was! Our hearts can get hard when we're caught doing wrong; our hearts can get hard when we don't want to do what is right or what we're being asked to do; our hearts can get hard when we don't get what we want. Help me to remember how ugly it is when our hearts get hard. Help me to ask You to soften my heart, admit my wrong, do what is right, or say it is okay that I didn't get what I wanted. It's all not worth the pain and ugliness of a hard heart.

Year 2: Ephesians 4:32 - 5:8; Luke 13:10-17
R: Behave like God as his very dear children.

Dear Lord, we are dear to You. When I know that I am dear to someone, it affects how I feel. Being dear to someone can make me feel very good. I feel special; I feel unique; I feel loved; I feel needed; I feel valuable. And I am not dear to just a human being, as important as that fact is. I am dear to Almighty God. The same God who parted the sea and healed the blind man. Thank You, dear God, for choosing me, for allowing me to be dear to Your heart.

➤ *Catechism of the Catholic Church* 2840

Thirtieth Tuesday in Ordinary Time
Fearing God

Year 1: Romans 8:18-25; Luke 13:18-21
R: The Lord has done marvels for us.

Dear Lord, I wonder what the kingdom of heaven is like. You described the kingdom more than You described any other thing. If I looked at all Your descriptions, I can learn that the kingdom grows, that it is power-filled, that it is worth far more than anything I can imagine, and that it is harder to get into than I think. Teach me about the kingdom, Lord Jesus. Show me its gates, and may I bring as many people along with me to the kingdom as I can.

Year 2: Ephesians 5:21-33; Luke 13:18-21
R: Blessed are those who fear the Lord.

Dear Jesus, whom do I fear? The principal? I like the principal, but I fear being sent to the principal when I've done something wrong. The principal represents what is right, what I should have done. The principal represents facing what I've done wrong. This is how I should fear You, Lord. You represent what is right. Just looking at You makes me realize what I should have done, and coming to You makes me face what I've done wrong. Thank You that I fear You in this way, Lord — and the principal too. This type of fear keeps me on the right path. This is a healthy type of fear.

➤ *Catechism of the Catholic Church* 2090

Thirtieth Wednesday in Ordinary Time
Weakness

Year 1: Romans 8:26-30; Luke 13:22-30
R: My hope, O Lord, is in your mercy.

Dear Jesus, the first reading says the Holy Spirit comes to the aid of our weakness. This is good news. I know I get weak in the face of some temptations. The temptation to watch TV instead of study? I'm weak. The temptation to argue with my siblings? I'm weak. The temptation to speak harshly to my mom or dad when I'm mad? I'm weak. Give me the grace, Lord, to ask Your Spirit to flood my soul at these times of weakness. Thank You, Jesus, for Your strength.

Year 2: Ephesians 6:1-9; Luke 13:22-30
R: The Lord is faithful in all his words.

Dear Lord, You know my life's situation right now. You know that my duties are few: learn my school work, obey my parents, do my chores, play within limits, respect the rights of others, honor You in all You ask of me. I can do each of these things for love of You — not to be noticed, not to be number one, not because I am afraid of punishment if I don't, but just for love of You. I can say to You, "Jesus, I'm doing this just for love of You."

➤ *Catechism of the Catholic Church* 741

Thirtieth Thursday in Ordinary Time
God's Side

Year 1: Romans 8:31b-39; Luke 13:31-35
R: Save me, O Lord, in your mercy.

Dear Lord, in the first reading for today's Mass, I read, "If God is for us, who can be against us?" If I do what You ask and love You the best I can, You are for me, Lord. What, then, should I fear? Yes, there are terrible things going on in the world, but You are for us, Lord. You are in control, and You will see us through it. Increase our faith in You.

Year 2: Ephesians 6:10-20; Luke 13:31-35
R: Blessed be the Lord, my Rock!

Dear Jesus, some of the Pharisees came to warn You of the others who wanted to kill You. You were aware of this, and You refused to run away. You would meet their evil head on. I am glad, dear Jesus, that You rose from the dead. You took the worst they could give — killing You — and won out in the end. I am glad I am on Your side, Lord. Keep me close to You. Help me to do all I can to make sure I stay close to You.

➤ *Catechism of the Catholic Church* 654

Thirtieth Friday in Ordinary Time
Jerusalem

Year 1: Romans 9:1-5; Luke 14:1-6
R: Praise the Lord, Jerusalem.

Dear Jesus, the responsorial psalm for today's Mass is "Praise the Lord, Jerusalem." Jerusalem is a sacred city. It is a holy place because so much of the Bible happened there. It was the city You promised to Your people. But, most of all, Lord, the name of Jerusalem represents Your kingdom that is to come and is coming. Jerusalem is heaven. Every time I do something for love of You, I help Jerusalem on earth to grow. Open my eyes, Lord, to understand Your word in the Bible.

Year 2: Philippians 1:1-11; Luke 14:1-6
R: How great are the works of the Lord!

Dear Jesus, You healed again on the Sabbath. Some of the leaders considered healing work and got mad at You, but their anger did not stop You from giving relief to Your people. Some people might get mad at me for doing what is right. Give me strength to do what is right anyway, Lord. People got mad at You; they can get mad at me, too. I'll be all right.

➤ *Catechism of the Catholic Church* 1044

Thirtieth Saturday in Ordinary Time
Belonging

Year 1: Romans 11:1-2a, 11-12, 25-29; Luke 14:1, 7-11
R: The Lord will not abandon his people.

Dear Lord, we care so much about our place: Will we get picked first on a team? Who will we sit by? Where do we stand in line? We worry about how we will look, who will talk to us, and whether we will be left out. You know how much these things can affect us, Lord. Give us strength to do what we can to make sure everyone feels like they belong. If we all were to look out for one another, then we wouldn't have to worry so much.

Year 2: Philippians 1:18b-26; Luke 14:1, 7-11
R: My soul is thirsting for the living God.

Lord Jesus, if I make your concerns my concerns, then maybe I won't worry so much about being first or being noticed or being a part of the accepted crowd. Making You first makes me strong in just being myself, and then those other things just don't seem all that important. I can be okay with others and I can be okay just by myself too. Make me strong, Lord. Let me be concerned more with You than with anything else.

➤ *Catechism of the Catholic Church* 1004

Thirty-First Sunday in Ordinary Time
Worship

Cycle A: Malachi 1:14b - 2:2b, 8-10; 1 Thessalonians 2:7b-9, 13; Matthew 23:1-12

R: In you, Lord, I have found my peace.

Dear Lord God, You do not need us to worship You. You tell us to worship You because doing so is best for us. Worshipping You helps us to know right from wrong, it gives us strength, it gives us joy, it makes us better off with one another. Worshipping You is like putting the right kind of gas in our cars — things just run better.

Cycle B: Deuteronomy 6:2-6; Hebrews 7:23-28; Mark 12:28-34

R: I love you, Lord, my strength.

Lord God, You are my strength. I am weak without You. With You, I see and understand my world better. I get along with others better. I know how to seek forgiveness because You have taught me. I know how best to grow because of Your example. You are everything to me, Lord.

Cycle C: Wisdom 11:22 - 12:2; 2 Thessalonians 1:11 - 2:2; Luke 19:1-10

R: I will praise your name for ever, my king and my God.

Dear Jesus, You didn't intend to stay in Jericho when You were traveling. You were just going to pass through. But You knew that Zacchaeus was trying hard to see You, climbing up into a tree in order to do so. When You saw his desire, You stopped in that town just for that one man. Teach me, Lord, how important each human being is to You. Thank You for loving each of us this much, and help me to never dismiss anyone as unworthy.

➤ *Catechism of the Catholic Church* 2114

Thirty-First Monday in Ordinary Time
Gratitude

Year 1: Romans 11:29-36; Luke 14:12-14
R: Lord, in your great love, answer me.

Dear Lord, I can never say thank You enough for what You have given to me. May I hold tight to You, Lord Jesus, and think about the gift that is You, in coming to earth as a man, in teaching us, in suffering and dying for us, and in Your rising from the dead for us. All this You, God, did for love of us, for love of me. Let me spend my life thinking about You, wondering about You, and spending time with You.

Year 2: Philippians 2:1-4; Luke 14:12-14
R: In you, O Lord, I have found my peace.

Dear Lord Jesus, You are my peace, even when things are difficult for me — my parents arguing, my grades failing, my friends being hard to deal with. Still, I have a deep peace, and I know this comes from You. I will be okay because You love me and You will guide me. May I follow Your commands so that I can better see Your will for me.

➤ *Catechism of the Catholic Church* 448

Thirty-First Tuesday in Ordinary Time
Bugs

Year 1: Romans 12:5-16ab; Luke 14:15-24
R: In you, O Lord, I have found my peace.

Dear Lord Jesus, I have heard it said over and over that we are all one Body. If we are all one Body, then I depend on others to help me move the Body and to help me keep the Body healthy. That, in turn, means that others depend on me to help them do the same thing. We are one Body, the Church. I am an important part of that Body. May I take this part, this participation, very seriously.

Year 2: Philippians 2:5-11; Luke 14:15-24
R: I will praise you, Lord, in the assembly of your people.

Lord Jesus, I need to meditate for a long time on this reading from Philippians. It tells me that even though You are God, You set aside, in a sense, Your Godliness and became a man. If I were watching a group of bugs trying to build a home and failing to do so time after time, would I agree to become a bug and go down to show them how best to build their home? And, if after I did it, they killed me for it, what would I want to do to those bugs when I became a human again? I'd want to squash them! But not You, Lord, Your love is just tremendous. I love You, Lord. Let me remember Your gift in coming here to us, Your gift in dying for us, and Your gift in not wanting to squash us for our many sins.

➤ *Catechism of the Catholic Church* 461

Thirty-First Wednesday in Ordinary Time
It's Up to Me

Year 1: Romans 13:8-10; Luke 14:25-33
R: Blessed the man who is gracious and lends to those in need.

Dear Lord, love is much more than a feeling. St. Paul teaches that love is the fulfillment of all the commandments. We can sum up all the commandments in love. But, we have to know just what love is. Love, St. Paul says, does no evil. Love is a choice. When I love, I choose to do, say, think what is best for another and for myself. Deepen my understanding of love, O Lord.

Year 2: Philippians 2:12-18; Luke 14:25-33
R: The Lord is my light and my salvation.

Dear God, St. Paul tells me that I have to work out my own salvation. I can't just expect You to do it for me. I have to make good choices. I have to put myself in the right places. I have to listen to the right voices. You will show me how, but I must do it.

➤ *Catechism of the Catholic Church* 1970

Thirty-First Thursday in Ordinary Time
Judging One Another

Year 1: Romans 14:7-12; Luke 15:1-10
R: I believe that I shall see the good things of the Lord in the land of the living.

My Lord Jesus, the ninety-nine sheep are safe if they stay together. This is why the shepherd can go off in search of the one sheep who is lost and alone. We are very vulnerable when we are off by ourselves. We are safer when we stick together and take care of one another. Keep us together, Lord. Show us how to get along with one another so that we can stay together. I pray for those who are off by themselves, Lord. Good Shepherd, go and find them and bring them back.

Year 2: Philippians 3:3-8a; Luke 15:1-10
R: Let hearts rejoice who search for the Lord.

My Lord Jesus, we are so quick to judge one another. Some of the Pharisees judged Your every move: He eats with sinners; He didn't follow the rules; He broke the Sabbath. We make rash judgments too: She dresses sloppy; he eats too much; she is really weird. Help us to see that being judgmental just separates and divides us; it weakens us. Forgive us, Lord, and give us the strength and the love to be accepting of one another.

➤ *Catechism of the Catholic Church* 806

Thirty-First Friday in Ordinary Time
Sin

Year 1: Romans 15:14-21; Luke 16:1-8
R: The Lord has revealed to the nations his saving power.

Dear Lord, St. Paul told the Romans that he was convinced that they were full of goodness. We, too, are full of goodness, but this does not mean that we cannot sin. We do sin, and sometimes we sin often. Help us, Lord, to take advantage of the goodness that is within us, to use its strength, and to turn away from sin.

Year 2: Philippians 3:17 - 4:1; Luke 16:1-8
R: Let us go rejoicing to the house of the Lord.

Dear Lord, St. Paul condemns those who are occupied with earthly things. Teach me what this means. Let Your ways be what matters to me. Let me work to bring about Your kingdom here on Earth by watching You, by imitating You, by praying to You. Make my mind like Yours, Lord Jesus, so that I am not occupied with earthly things.

➤ *Catechism of the Catholic Church* 1863

Thirty-First Saturday in Ordinary Time
Change

Year 1: Romans 16:3-9, 16, 22-27; Luke 16:9-15
R: I will praise your name for ever, Lord.

Dear Jesus, St. Paul mentions the names of the disciples in Rome whom he remembers well. If a saint were to visit my community, would I stand out? Would she remember me and my example as following You, Lord, in a deep and committed way? Help me to examine the example I give, Lord, and do some changing if I need to change.

Year 2: Philippians 4:10-19; Luke 16:9-19
R: Blessed the man who fears the Lord.

Dear God, I have to put You first. Deepen my understanding of what this means in my daily life. Show me how to put You first. Show me what in my life is tempting me and show me how to deal with this temptation. May I be willing to change, Lord, if I'm not putting You first.

➤ *Catechism of the Catholic Church* 1431

Thirty-Second Sunday in Ordinary Time
Now

Cycle A: Wisdom 6:12-16; 1 Thessalonians 4:13-18 or 4:13-14; Matthew 25:1-13
R: My soul is thirsting for you, O Lord my God.

Dear Lord, we need to be ready to meet You at any time. This means we can't put off getting to know You; we can't put off opening the Bible; we can't put off going to Church regularly. Let me increase my commitment to You, Lord, to know You better and to love You more, now.

Cycle B: 1 Kings 17:10-16; Hebrews 9:24-28; Mark 12:38-44 or 12:41-44
R: Praise the Lord, my soul!

Dear Lord, it doesn't matter what we give, whether large amounts or small, whether lots of good deeds or just a few. What matters is where our heart is when we give. If we give with great love, then our offering is great. If we give only to be noticed, if we give just with little love, then our offering — no matter how large — is not great. Our hearts must be in what we give to You. Our hearts must belong to You.

Cycle C: 2 Maccabees 7:1-2, 9-14; 2 Thessalonians 2:16-3:5; Luke 20:27-38 or 20:27, 34-38
R: Lord, when your glory appears, my joy will be full.

Dear Lord, it is easy to see the work of evil people in the world. We read the news about people starving, people being tortured, people calling for the deaths of others. I look forward to the time when You will come again, Lord, and stop all this evil. In the meantime, Lord, guide my actions and my thoughts, that I may not add to any evil in the world, but bring love, forgiveness, and Your wisdom.

➤ *Catechism of the Catholic Church* 1041

Thirty-Second Monday in Ordinary Time
Forgiveness

Year 1: Wisdom 1:1-7; Luke 17:1-6
R: Guide me, Lord, along the everlasting way.

Dear Lord Jesus, if I get hurt seven times by the same person in one day, and that person apologizes seven times, you say I should forgive him. I know my parents forgive me for doing the same things wrong over and over. I need their forgiveness; it would be horrible if they were mad at me all the time. I guess I need to forgive like they do, like You do, Lord. Help me to forgive.

Year 2: Titus 1:1-9; Luke 17:1-6
R: Lord, this is the people that longs to see your face.

My Lord Jesus, following You is not easy. My heart has to be big. My mind has to be wise. My actions have to be noble. I can't do this by myself, and You do not expect me to. You offer Your Spirit to me, to empower me. Thank You, Lord. In You I can love, I can forgive, I can be all that You call me to be.

➤ *Catechism of the Catholic Church 2862*

Thirty-Second Tuesday in Ordinary Time
Being Good

Year 1: Wisdom 2:23 - 3:9; Luke 17:7-10
R: I will bless the Lord at all times.

My Lord Jesus, some things the world urges me to do are just plain bad things. But the world tells me that if I do these things, then I will be popular and I will have fun and I will feel good. Give me Your wisdom, Lord, so that I can see the consequences of these things — what can happen after I do them. These consequences will usually let me know whether these things are bad or good. Guide me, Lord. Give me wisdom.

Year 2: Titus 2:1-8, 11-14; Luke 17:7-10
R: The salvation of the just comes from the Lord.

Dear Lord, St. Paul urges us to be a people who are eager to do what is good. Teach me what is good in my day and age, Lord. I see lots of bad around me, but there is good, too. May I join with the good, helping all I can, pleasing You.

➤ *Catechism of the Catholic Church 1766*

Thirty-Second Wednesday in Ordinary Time
Healing

Year 1: Wisdom 6:1-11; Luke 17:11-19
R: Rise up, O Lord, bring judgment to the earth.

My Lord Jesus, just like the lepers, we stand at a distance from You and call to You, asking for healing. Some of us need to be healed from addictions. Some of us need to be healed from prejudices. Some of us need to be healed from just not caring about You. You healed all the lepers. Heal us, too, Lord. May we want to be healed. May we accept Your call to turn away from sin.

Year 2: Titus 3:1-7; Luke 17:11-19
R: The Lord is my shepherd; there is nothing I shall want.

Dear Lord, St. Paul tells us that You poured out Your Holy Spirit on us. How can I tell that You poured Your Spirit out on me, Jesus? Do my actions and my words and my thoughts make the Spirit welcome within me? Or do I fight the Spirit? Help me to listen to Your Spirit within me, Lord, and allow the Spirit to help me to grow.

➤ *Catechism of the Catholic Church* 1421

Thirty-Second Thursday in Ordinary Time
Kingdom of Heaven

Year 1: Wisdom 7:22b - 8:1; Luke 17:20-25
R: Your word is for ever, O Lord.

Dear Lord Jesus, You are setting up Your kingdom on this earth. I can add to Your kingdom or take away from it by my actions, my words, and my thoughts. May I please You, my Lord, by doing what is holy, by speaking what is holy, by thinking what is holy. Make me more and more like You, Lord.

Year 2: Philemon 7-20; Luke 17:20-25
R: Blessed is he whose help is the God of Jacob.

Dear Lord, St. Paul is writing to a friend named Philemon from prison. He will soon be killed in Rome. He is not thinking of himself but another friend whom he is sending to Philemon. He is asking Philemon to accept his friend as an equal even though this man was a slave. How large are the hearts of the people who love You, Lord, that even when they are facing death, they are thinking of others. Bless my heart, O Lord, make it pleasing to You.

➤ *Catechism of the Catholic Church* 567

Thirty-Second Friday in Ordinary Time
God's Law

Year 1: Wisdom 13:1-9; Luke 17:26-37
R: The heavens proclaim the glory of God.

Dear Lord, some of the things You say I just don't understand. Help me to look to You for answers, to trust that You will help me to understand what I need to understand when I need to understand it. May I be patient with myself as You are patient with me. In turn, Lord, may I be patient with others and they with me, as we grow together in our knowledge of You and our love for You.

Year 2: 2 John 4-9; Luke 17:26-37
R: Blessed are they who follow the law of the Lord!

Dear Lord, there is enough of Your law that I do understand to keep me busy; I don't have to worry about the parts of Your law that I don't understand. I know I need to pray; I know I need to honor my parents and do what they ask of me; I know I need to fulfill my duties as a student. These things I know. Let me get busy obeying these laws.

➤ *Catechism of the Catholic Church* 1972

Thirty-Second Saturday in Ordinary Time
Peace

Year 1: Wisdom 18:14-16; 19:6-9; Luke 18:1-8
R: Remember the marvels the Lord has done.

Dear Lord, sometimes we can get tired of praying for the same thing over and over. Like peace in the world — it never seems to come. Give me eyes like Your eyes, Lord. Help me to see the little advances we do make with the help of Your grace in the way of peace. Teach us, Lord, how to make peace.

Year 2: 3 John 5-8; Luke 18:1-8
R: Blessed the man who fears the Lord.

Dear Lord, I pray for those who work for peace in our world. We pray and we pray and we pray for peace. There are lots of people who work nonstop for peace. Bless them, Lord. Bless their efforts. Show them the way. Show the leaders of countries that they cannot persist in their evil ways of war and violence. May I constantly ask you for peace.

➤ *Catechism of the Catholic Church* 2854

Thirty-Third Sunday in Ordinary Time
End of the World

Cycle A: Proverbs 31:10-13, 19-20, 30-31; 1 Thessalonians 5:1-6; Matthew 25:14-30 or 25:14-15, 19-21
R: Blessed are those who fear the Lord.

Dear Lord, St. Paul calls us children of the light. And the writings in the Old Testament tell me that if I love You, then I will be given wisdom. Therefore, I will know how to be a light for others, how to show others Your way, how to be a good disciple of Yours in the world.

Cycle B: Daniel 12:1-3; Hebrews 10:11-14, 18; Mark 13:24-32
R: You are my inheritance, O Lord!

Dear God, we are nearing the end of the Church year. The Church wants us to think about the end of the world and how important it is to be ready. Also, the Church wants to encourage us because it sometimes seems as if evil is winning out. You are King, Lord Jesus, and we celebrate Your kingship next weekend. Thank You for Your power, Lord. I am glad to know that goodness will triumph over evil.

Cycle C: Malachi 3:19-20; 2 Thessalonians 3:7-12; Luke 21:5-19
R: The Lord comes to rule the earth with justice.

Dear Lord, we do not know too much about the end of the world. We just know that You will come to rule with Your justice. There will be no more suffering, no more wars, no more violence. I pray for this day, Lord, when You will be in charge.

➤ *Catechism of the Catholic Church* 681

Thirty-Third Monday in Ordinary Time
The Lord Knocks

Year 1: 1 Maccabees 1:10-15, 41-43, 54-57, 62-63; Luke 18:35-43
R: Give me life, O Lord, and I will do your commands.

Dear Lord, the story of Maccabees is scary. We will be reading from this book all during this next week. A mother's sons are tortured and killed because they will not turn away from You. The whole city is against You, burning the Bible, committing many sins, and forgetting the agreement they had made with You. There are people who live in cities like this today, Lord. I pray for them that their faith may be strong. May the power of Your Spirit soon sweep over the earth, O Lord, and bring Your justice.

Year 2: Revelation 1:1-4; 2:1-5; Luke 18:35-43
R: Those who are victorious I will feed from the tree of life.

Dear Lord, the book of Revelation tells us about the end of the world. Before the world ends, there will be many warnings and many signs. John writes to each of the churches in his day and tells them to be faithful to You, to renew themselves. Bad things will happen in the world, and our faith must be strong. Strengthen me, Lord, so that I may never lose my faith.

➤ *Catechism of the Catholic Church* 681

Thirty-Third Tuesday in Ordinary Time
Martyrdom

Year 1: 2 Maccabees 6:18-31; Luke 19:1-10
R: The Lord upholds me.

Dear Lord, the story of Eleazar is one worthy of remembering. The people who put him to death gave him the chance to pretend that he was doing what they wanted, and so save his life. But Eleazar said no. Eleazar thought of the young people and knew he had to be a good example for them, an example of being faithful to God. Give strength to our present-day martyrs, Lord. May we learn of their stories and increase our own faith because of their courage and love.

Year 2: Revelation 3:1-6, 14-22; Luke 19:1-10
R: I will seat the victor beside me on my throne.

Lord Jesus, the book of Revelation says that You stand at the door and knock. We must open the door and let You in, Lord. You will not force Your way in. We have to do our part. I pray for those who have not yet let You in, Lord. May my example and my prayers give them wisdom to open the door.

➤ *Catechism of the Catholic Church* 2474

Thirty-Third Wednesday in Ordinary Time
Glory

Year 1: 2 Maccabees 7:1, 20-31; Luke 19:11-28
R: Lord, when your glory appears, my joy will be full.

Dear Lord, there are some people who believe that the judgment will go easy. Because You are love, they think they will sneak into heaven without having to do much. This is not so. You give each of us certain talents and skills and You mean for us to use these talents and skills for Your glory. If we do not, we will have to answer to You. May I take Your word seriously, Lord.

Year 2: Revelation 4:1-11; Luke 19:11-28
R: Holy, holy, holy Lord, mighty God!

Dear Lord, the picture of Your glory in the book of Revelation is overwhelming. You flash like lightning. You are seated on a throne with a sea of glass like crystal before You. This vision is meant to remind me of Your majesty, Lord. What You ask of me, You expect me to do. This can be fearful, dear Lord, but it is also exciting. Let me rise to the challenge You are giving me.

➤ *Catechism of the Catholic Church* 2809

Thirty-Third Thursday in Ordinary Time
The Lamb

Year 1: 1 Maccabees 2:15-29; Luke 19:41-44
R: To the upright I will show the saving power of God.

Dear Lord, now we hear the story of Mattathias, who was threatened with death unless he turned his back on You. He refused and ran through the city calling on everyone who wanted to remain faithful to You to run into the desert with him. Many did so. Sometimes, Lord, we need to run away, to take some time away from our culture, to strengthen ourselves so that we do not fall into sin. Strengthen me, Lord, so that I do not fall into sin.

Year 2: Revelation 5:1-10; Luke 19:41-44
R: The Lamb has made us a kingdom of priests to serve our God.

Dear Lord, there is one way to heaven. The book of Revelation shows us the scroll on which this is written down. There was no one worthy enough to open the scroll, and John wept because of this. But then You came, Lord. You are the Lamb with seven horns and seven eyes. All in heaven fell down before You as You opened the scroll. May You find my name written on that scroll, Lord.

➤ *Catechism of the Catholic Church* 1137

Thirty-Third Friday in Ordinary Time
God Wins

Year 1: 1 Maccabees 4:36-37, 52-59; Luke 19:45-48
R: We praise your glorious name, O mighty God.

This is a good time, Lord, in the book of Maccabees. The house of Israel is restored, and the king who was making them turn away from You and killing those who would not turn away from You is dead. In the gospel, You walk in and drive out the people who are not worshipping the Father sincerely. Both readings show us that evil will not last; You will triumph. May my trust be in You, Lord.

Year 2: Revelation 10:8-11; Luke 19:45-48
R: How sweet to my taste is your promise!

Dear Lord, in the book of Revelation, God tells the prophet to eat the scroll — the scroll represents Your word. The scroll makes the prophet sick because Your words are not being followed. Therefore, he must tell each church what they are doing wrong. You, Jesus, in the gospel then walk into the Temple and throw out those who are doing wrong. We can't do bad things and remain in Your presence, Lord. That's what these readings teach me. Help us to do what is right so that we can stay with You.

➤ *Catechism of the Catholic Church* 680

Thirty-Third Saturday in Ordinary Time
Faithfulness

Year 1: 1 Maccabees 6:1-13; Luke 20:27-40
R: I will rejoice in your salvation, O Lord.

Dear Lord, in both readings, those who would try to defeat You are silenced. Your strength wins out. I would have liked to see You answer all those who were trying to trip You up in Your speech, Jesus. I would be very proud to be with You. Motivate me, O Lord, to learn all I can about You, to love You with all my heart, and to offer my life to You.

Year 2: Revelation 11:4-12; Luke 20:27-40
R: Blessed be the Lord, my Rock!

Dear Lord, in the book of Revelation, three of Your people are killed by evil. For three days their bodies lie in front of everyone, and evil people brag about having killed Your three holy ones. But then, the three bodies rise to life again as the evil ones look on and are struck by great fear. You win again, Lord. May these readings encourage us when following You gets hard, Lord. Keep us faithful to You!

➤ *Catechism of the Catholic Church* 2145

Thirty-Fourth Sunday in Ordinary Time: Christ the King
Christ the King

Cycle A: Ezekiel 34:11-12, 15-17; 1 Corinthians 15:20-26, 28; Matthew 25:31-46
R: The Lord is my shepherd; there is nothing I shall want.

Dear Lord, look how important doing good to others is in Your kingdom. You judge us based on how well we loved You in others. If we helped another, You see it as having helped You. If we gave food to another, You see it as having fed You. We are one Body: what we do for others, we do for You.

Cycle B: Daniel 7:13-14; Revelation 1:5-8; John 18:33b-37
R: The Lord is king; he is robed in majesty.

Dear Lord Jesus, on this Christ the King Sunday, I rejoice that You are King. You defeat evil and run Your kingdom with love and justice. No more do we have to fear evil or war or violence or hatred. You are our King, Lord Jesus Christ. You are my King.

Cycle C: 2 Samuel 5:1-3; Colossians 1:12-20; Luke 23:35-43
R: Let us go rejoicing to the house of the Lord.

Dear Lord, You did not throw Your weight around when You were a man here on Earth with us. As You hung there on the cross, You could have made those nails release You, You could have pushed down to the ground all those who were making fun of You, but this is not Your way. Instead, You looked at the good thief and promised him that he would be with You that very day in Paradise. I am proud that You are my King, Lord Jesus.

➤ *Catechism of the Catholic Church* 786

Thirty-Fourth Monday in Ordinary Time
God's Kingdom

Year 1: Daniel 1:1-6, 8-20; Luke 21:1-4
R: Glory and praise for ever!

Dear Lord Jesus, in Your kingdom, things will not go as they do in the world. In the world, the biggest and best get noticed. In Your world, the small and meek gain reward. Teach me the ways of Your kingdom, O Lord.

Year 2: Revelation 14:1-3, 4b-5; Luke 21:1-4
R: Lord, this is the people that longs to see your face.

Lord Jesus, in Your kingdom, we will look upon Your face as much as we want. We have access to You. In the world, important people cannot be called or seen very easily. But, You, Lord God, You are right here, right inside my heart, right in my Church, right here in Your growing kingdom of heaven.

➤ *Catechism of the Catholic Church* 203

Thirty-Fourth Tuesday in Ordinary Time
Judgment

Year 1: Daniel 2:31-45; Luke 21:5-11
R: Give glory and eternal praise to him.

Dear Lord, in the world, we lift up those who are rich and powerful. But in Your kingdom, Lord, the servants are the ones You bless with Your gifts. Daniel was given the gift of interpreting dreams, and this gift brought great blessing on Your people. May we learn to live by Your ways, Lord, so that we may be part of Your kingdom.

Year 2: Revelation 14:14-19; Luke 21:5-11
R: The Lord comes to judge the earth.

Christ the King, the last judgment is not a myth. It will happen. You will come as King to judge each of us according to our deeds. We can only gain Your favor as long as we are on this Earth. So, Lord, move us to learn of Your ways, take joy in You, and try to please You every day of our lives.

➤ *Catechism of the Catholic Church* 729

Thirty-Fourth Wednesday in Ordinary Time
Wisdom

Year 1: Daniel 5:1-6, 13-14, 16-17, 23-28; Luke 21:12-19
R: Give glory and eternal praise to him.

Dear God, the king did not take You seriously. He took the cups from the Temple and drank from them himself. He did not bother paying You any attention. Suddenly he saw a hand writing on the wall in mid-air. Daniel told him You were the true King and soon his kingdom would pass away. And it did. All of the kingdoms on this earth, Lord, will pass away. Your Kingdom is the only one that will last. Make me a part of Your Kingdom, Lord Jesus Christ.

Year 2: Revelation 15:1-4; Luke 21:12-19
R: Great and wonderful are all your works, Lord, mighty God!

Christ our King, it does not make much sense to give praise and honor to human beings but ignore the very One who made human beings. Teach us the wisdom of the Kingdom of heaven, and help us to see how silly the wisdom of this world is.

➤ *Catechism of the Catholic Church* 1954

Thirty-Fourth Thursday in Ordinary Time
Power

Year 1: Daniel 6:12-28; Luke 21:20-28
R: Give glory and eternal praise to him.

Dear Christ the King, Daniel was not eaten in the lion's den. He was thrown into the lion's den by his enemies, but You, Lord, shut the mouths of the lions, and Daniel's life was saved. You have power over life and death, dear Lord; we do not. Forgive us when we think we have this power.

Year 2: Revelation 18:1-2, 21-23; 19:1-3, 9a; Luke 21:20-28
R: Blessed are they who are called to the wedding feast of the Lamb.

Dear Lord, You told everyone that Jerusalem would fall. Some forty years after Your death and resurrection, Lord Jesus, Jerusalem did fall. The great Temple was torn down, and it has never been built again. The reading from Revelation and Your words from Luke's gospel are fearful, Lord. Remind me that I need only look to You for salvation. Have mercy on us, Christ our King.

➤ *Catechism of the Catholic Church* 273

Thirty-Fourth Friday in Ordinary Time
Kingdom of Heaven

Year 1: Daniel 7:2-14; Luke 21:29-33
R: Give glory and eternal praise to him.

Christ our King, Daniel sees a vision in which the Ancient One — this is You, Lord Jesus — takes His throne and His kingship will never be destroyed. Daniel is talking about the end of the world. At the end, Lord, I want to be with You in Your kingdom. I want to see Your glory. I want to see Daniel and all those I read about in the Bible. This will be a time of great celebration. Keep me faithful to You, O Lord.

Year 2: Revelation 20:1-4, 11 - 21:2; Luke 21:29-33
R: Here God lives among his people.

Dear Lord, John sees a new heaven and a new earth. Everything will be made new. All those whose names are in the Book of Life get to live in this new heaven and new earth. I don't know how this will happen, Lord Jesus, but I want to be among those whose names are in that book. Keep me faithful to You, Lord. May I go overboard in my love for You.

➤ *Catechism of the Catholic Church* 2016

Thirty-Fourth Saturday in Ordinary Time
Eternity

Year 1: Daniel 7:15-27; Luke 21:34-36
R: Give glory and eternal praise to him.

Christ our King, sin will bring about horrible things on the earth. These readings at the end of the Church year tell me this fact. But I know, too, from these readings that You are King. You have control. You shall not be defeated by sin, and You shall save all of us who remain faithful to You. Keep me faithful to You, O Lord; I pray for those whose faith is weak.

Year 2: Revelation 22:1-7; Luke 21:34-36
R: Marana tha! Come, Lord Jesus!

Christ our King, on this final day of the Church year, I see in the first reading from the book of Revelation a marvelous picture of heaven. There is the tree from the Garden of Eden! Where we began, now here we end, back in the Garden, back with You in intimacy and love. Christ my King, lead me to this garden where I can be with You for eternity.

➤ *Catechism of the Catholic Church* 1085

Holy Days of Obligation

For the Solemnity of the Nativity of the Lord (Christmas), see page 22.

For the Solemnity of Mary, Mother of God, see page 26.

For the Solemnity of the Ascension of the Lord, see page 126.

SOLEMNITY OF THE IMMACULATE CONCEPTION

December 8: Immaculate Conception of the Blessed Virgin Mary
Immaculate Conception

Genesis 3:9-15, 20; Ephesians 1:3-6, 11-12; Luke 1:26-38

R: Sing to the Lord a new song, for he has done marvelous deeds.

Dear Lord, You set Mary apart from the beginning of her life. She was special and her life was meant to be centered around You. Mary is a gift to all of us. She shows us how to follow You. She brings us to You. She constantly tells us to do whatever You ask of us. Help me to be like Mary, God. Help me to be centered on You.

➤ *Catechism of the Catholic Church* 492

August 15: Assumption of the Blessed Virgin Mary
Assumption

Vigil Mass: 1 Chronicles 15:3-4, 15-16; 16:1-2; 1 Corinthians 15:54b-57; Luke 11:27-28
R: Lord, go up to the place of your rest, you and the ark of your holiness.

Dear Mary, on this feast of your Assumption, we celebrate that your body was taken directly to heaven instead of being buried and decaying. From the beginning, Mary, you were special, not so much because you got to be the mother of Jesus, but because you said yes to God, over and over. Your life was centered on God — doing His will and pleasing Him. Teach me how to center my life on Jesus, Mary. Teach me how to please your Son.

Mass during the day: Revelation 11:19a; 12:1-6a, 10ab; 1 Corinthians 15:20-27; Luke 1:39-56
R: The queen stands at your right hand, arrayed in gold.

Dear Mary, I don't understand how you are portrayed in the book of Revelation, but I do know that you pleased God with your heart, with your actions, with your mind. Touch my heart, my ways, and my mind, O Mother of God, that I may please God and trust Him totally, as you did. Mary, Woman assumed body and soul into heaven, pray for us!

➤ *Catechism of the Catholic Church* 966

November 1: All Saints Day
All Saints

Revelation 7:2-4, 9-14; 1 John 3:1-3; Matthew 5:1-12a

R: Lord, this is the people that longs to see your face.

Dear Lord, Your beatitudes tell me who You will bless: those who mourn for others; those who are meek; those who thirst for justice; those who are merciful; those who know You are most important; those who work for peace; and those who are willing to suffer because they do what is right. Teach me what each of these things mean, Lord. I want Your blessing.

➤ *Catechism of the Catholic Church* 828

Index of Topics

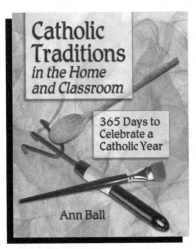